THE

SCIENCE OF KNOWLEDGE.

BY

J. G. FICHTE.

Johann Gottlieb Fichte
Born 1762 died 1814
Roused Germany to patriotism & Education

———

TRANSLATED FROM THE GERMAN BY A. E. KROEGER.

———

PHILADELPHIA:
J. B. LIPPINCOTT & CO.
1868.

INTRODUCTORY.

———

CONCERNING THE CONCEPTION

OF THE

SCIENCE OF KNOWLEDGE.

TRANSLATOR'S PREFACE.

THE object and general conception of the work, herewith
submitted to the American public, is too clearly set forth in
the Introduction which precedes it to require any additional
explanation from me. Suffice it historically to state, that
this its object was not achieved in Germany; and that the
motive which inspired its translation was the hope that it
might be achieved in America. Whether success would come
at once or after many years, I did not choose to speculate
upon ; but the certainty has always been in my mind, that,
sooner or later, the science of knowledge will be taught in
every college and university of the land, as the science of all
sciences, as the science which will, when once recognized, put
a stop to those stale and unprofitable metaphysical specula-
tions, by indulging in which mankind has wasted time and
energies enough to advance true culture beyond the most
daring dreams. Not to encourage metaphysical studies, but
henceforth and forever to silence them, and to lead mankind
back to true life, has this work been written and translated.

A. E. KROEGER.

ST. LOUIS, December 28, 1866.

PART FIRST.

———◆———

*CONCERNING THE CONCEPTION OF THE
SCIENCE OF KNOWLEDGE GENERALLY.*

§ 1.—HYPOTHETICAL CONCEPTION OF THIS SCIENCE.

To unite divided parties it is best to proceed
from the point wherein they agree. Philosophy is
a science; in this all descriptions of philosophy are
as agreed as they are divided in determining the
object of this science. This division, may it not
have arisen, because the conception of that science, which they unanimously asserted philosophy
to be, had not yet been wholly developed? And
may not the determination of this one characteristic, wherein they all agree, suffice to determine
the conception of philosophy itself? A science has
systematic form. All propositions in it are connected in one single fundamental proposition or
principle, and unite with it to form a whole. This
is universally conceded. But does this characteristic exhaust the conception of a science?

Supposing somebody were to build up ever so

systematic a natural history of certain spirits of the air, on the unproven and unprovable assumption, that such creatures exist in the air, with human passions, inclinations, and conceptions, should we call such a system a science, no matter how closely its several parts might be connected with each other into a whole ? On the other hand, supposing somebody were to utter a single proposition—a mechanic, for instance, the proposition that a pillar erected on a horizontal base in a right angle stands perpendicular, and will not incline toward either side, however far you extend it into infinity—a proposition which he may have heard at some time and approved as true in experience : would not all men concede that such a person had a scientific knowledge of the proposition, although he should not be able to evolve the deduction of his proposition from the first fundamental principle of geometry ? Now, why do we call the fixed system, which rests on an unproven and unprovable first principle, no science at all, and why do we assert the knowledge of the mechanic to be science, although it does not connect in his reason with a system ?

Evidently, because the first, in spite of its correct form, does not contain any thing that can be known ; and because the second, although without a correct form, asserts something which is really *known* and *can be known.* The characteristic of science, therefore, seems to consist in the quality of its content and the relation thereof to the consciousness of the person of whom a knowledge is asserted ; and the systematic form appears to be only accidental to the science ; is not the object of science, but merely a means to attain that object.

This may, perhaps, be conceived in the following manner. If we suppose that from some reason or another the human mind can know only very little, and can have of every thing else only opinions, presentiments, or arbitrary meanings ; and if we suppose, moreover, that from some reason or another the human mind can not well rest content with this limited or uncertain knowledge : then the only means of extending and securing that knowledge would be to compare all uncertain knowledge with the certain knowledge, and to draw conclusions from the equality or inequality of both as to the correctness or incorrectness of the former. If an uncertain knowledge were thus discovered to be equal to a certain knowledge, it might be properly assumed to be also certain ; but if it were discovered unequal, it would now be definitely known as false, and could no longer deceive. We should be delivered from an error, although we might not have gained positive truth.

I speak plainer. Science is to be one and a whole. The proposition that a pillar erected in a right angle on a horizontal base occupies a perpendicular position, is doubtless a whole, and in so far a science for a person who has no connected knowledge of geometry.

But we also consider the whole geometry, which contains much more than that one proposition, a

science. How then, and by what means do a multi-
tude of very different propositions unite into *one*
science, into one and the same whole ?

Clearly by this, that the separate propositions
are not science, but form a science only in the
whole, and through their connection in the whole.
But by a composition of parts you can not put
something into the whole which is not to be found
in one of the parts. Hence, if none of the connected propositions had certainty, there would also
be no certainty in the whole formed by them. One
of the propositions, at least, therefore, must be
certain, and this one, perhaps, communicates its
certainty to the others in this manner : that if the
one *is to be* true, then the second *must be* true,
etc. Thus a multiplicity of propositions would attain only one certainty, and result in only one science, for the very reason that they *all* have certainty and *the same certainty*. That one proposition which we have just now spoken of as positively
certain, can not obtain its certainty from its connection with the others, but must have it before-
hand ; for by uniting parts you can not produce
something which is in none of the parts. But all
other propositions receive their truth from the first
one. *The first* one must therefore be certain before all connection with the others ; and *all the
others* must receive their certainty only through
and after the connection. From this it immediately appears that our above assumption is the
only correct one, and that in a science there can

only be one proposition which is certain before the connection with others. For if there were many such propositions, they would either be not at all connected with the former, and then they would not belong with it to the same whole ; or they would be thus connected ; but since they are only to be connected by one and the same certainty— that is, *if* the one theorem is true, then the other *must* be true—they can not have independent certainty ; for in that case one proposition might have independent certainty, although others had no certainty, and hence they would not be connected through common certainty.

[margin note: unless they separately relate to the same world]

Such a proposition, which has certainty before and independent of all connection, is a *fundamental principle.* Every science must have a fundamental principle ; nay, it might consist of simply such one principle, which in that case could not be called fundamental, however, since it would not be the foundation of others. But a science also can *not* have more than one fundamental principle, for else it would result in *many* sciences.

[margin note: demarcation between sciences → demarcation btwn. fundamental principles]

The other propositions which a science may contain get certainty only through their connection with the fundamental principle ; and the connection, as we have shown, is this : If the proposition A is true, then the proposition B is also true ; and if B is true, then must C be true, etc. This connection is called the systematic form of the whole, which results from the several component parts. Wherefore this connection ? Surely not to produce

an artistic combination, but in order to give certainty to propositions, which have not certainty in
themselves. And thus the systematic form is not
the object of science, but an accidence, a means,
and on the condition that the science is to have a
manifold of propositions. It is not the essence of
science, but an accidental quality thereof.

Let science be a building, and let the chief object of this building be firmness. The foundation
is firm, and as soon as it is laid down, the object
would therefore be attained. But since you can
not live on the foundation, nor protect yourself by
its means against the arbitrary attacks of enemies,
or the unarbitrary attacks of the weather, you proceed to erect walls, and over the walls you build a
roof. All the parts of the building you connect
with the foundation and with each other, and thus
the whole gets firmness. But you do not build a
building in order to connect the parts ; rather you
connect the parts in order to make the building
firm ; and it is firm in so far as all its parts rest
upon a firm foundation.

The foundation is firm, for it is not built on another foundation, but rests on the solid earth. But
whereupon shall we erect the foundation of our scientific structure ? The fundamental principles of
our systems must and shall be certain in advance
of the system. Their certainty can not be proven
within the system ; but every possible proof in
the system presupposes already their certainty.
If *they* are certain, then of course all their results

are certain ; *but from what does their own certainty follow ?*

And even after we shall have satisfactorily answered this question, does not a new and quite different one threaten us ? We are going to draw ᐟ our conclusions thus : *If* the fundamental principle is certain, *then* another proposition also is certain. ᐟ How do we get at this *then ?* What is the ground of the necessary connection between the two, whereby the one is to have the same certainty which belongs to the other ? What are the conditions of this connection, and whence do we know that they are the conditions and the *exclusive* conditions and the *only* conditions of this connection ? And how do we get at all to assume a necessary connection between different propositions, and exclusive but exhausted conditions of this connection ?

In short, how shall *the absolute certainty of the fundamental principle,* and how *shall the authority to draw from it conclusions as to the certainty of other propositions,* be demonstrated ? That which the fundamental principle is to have itself and to communicate to all other propositions which occur in the science, I call the *inner content* of the fundamental principle and of science generally ; the manner in which it communicates this certainty to other propositions I call the *form* of science. The question is, therefore, How are form and content of a science possible ? or how is science itself possible ?

That which would give an a⁻swer to this ques-

tion would be itself a science, and would be, moreover, *the science of science generally.*

It is impossible to determine in advance of the
investigation whether such an answer is possible or
not ; that is, whether our whole knowledge has a
cognizable, firm basis, or whether it rests, after all
·—however closely its separate parts may be connected—upon nothing, that is to say, upon nothing ‹
for us. But if our knowledge is to have a basis
for us, then such an answer must be possible, and
there must be a science which gives this answer.
And if there is such a science, then our knowledge
has a cognizable ground.   Hence, in advance of the
investigation, it is impossible to say whether our
knowledge has a basis or has no basis at all ; and
the possibility of the science in question can only
be demonstrated by its actual realization.

The naming of such a science, whereof the very
possibility is as yet problematical, is altogether arbitrary.   Still, if it should appear that all the terri-
tory hitherto considered useful for the cultivation
of sciences has already been appropriated, and that
only one piece of uncultivated land has been left
vacant for the science of all other sciences ; and if,
moreover, it should appear that under a well-known
name—the name of *Philosophy*—the idea of a science exists which pretends to be, or wishes to be,
also a science, and is only in doubt where to settle
down ; then it might not be improper to assign this
science to the empty and uncultivated place.   Whether the word Philosophy has hitherto signified pre-

cisely that very same object is immaterial ; and,
moreover, if this science should really thus turn out
to be a science, it would doubtless very justly dis-
card a name which it has hitherto borne from a
surely not over great modesty, namely, that of a
Dilettanteism. The nation which shall discover this
science is well worthy of giving it a name from its
own language, and might name it simply Science,
or the Science of Knowledge. What has been heretofore called philosophy would thus be *the science of
science generally.*

§ 2.—EXPLANATION OF THE CONCEPTION OF THE SCIENCE OF KNOWLEDGE.

It is not allowable to draw conclusions from defi-
nitions. This rule signifies : from the fact that it
is possible to *think* a certain characteristic in the
description of a thing, which thing exists altogether
independently of such a description, it is not allowable to conclude that this characteristic is therefore
really discoverable in the thing ; or, when we produce
a thing after a conception formed of it, which conception expresses the purposes of the thing, it is
not allowable to conclude from the thinkability of
the purpose that it is actually realized.   On no account, however, can the above rule signify that we
must have no well-defined purpose in our bodily or
mental labors, but must leave it to our fancy or to
our fingers what the result of our labor shall be.
The inventor of the aerostatic balls was perfectly

warranted in calculating the relation of the gas in the balls to the weight of the atmosphere, and thus to discover the velocity of movement of his machine, although he did not know yet whether he would ever be able to discover a gas sufficiently lighter than air ; and Archimedes was able to calculate the machine by which he could move the globe out of its place, although he knew well enough that he could find no place beyond the attraction of the earth from which to operate with his machine. Thus, also, with our science of knowledge. It is not as such something which exists independent of us, but rather something which must first be produced by the freedom of our mind, working in a certain direction, that is, if there is such a freedom, which, of course, can also not be known as yet. Let us determine this direction in advance, and obtain a clear conception of *what* is to be our work. Whether we can produce it or not will appear from the fact whether we *do* produce it, but this is not yet our purpose. We at present merely wish to see *what* it really is we intend to do.

1st. First of all, the described science is to be a *science of science generally.* Every possible science has *one fundamental principle*, which can not be proven in it, but must be certain in advance of it. But where, then, is this first principle to be proven ? Evidently in that science which is to be the ground of all possible sciences. In this respect the science of knowledge would have a twofold object : Firstly, to show the possibility of fundamental principles generally ; to show how, to what extent, and under what conditions, and perhaps in what degree something can be certain, and indeed to show what it really means to be certain ; and, secondly, to prove particularly the fundamental principles of all possible sciences, which can not be proven in those sciences themselves.

Every science, which is to be a whole of component parts, has a *systematic form.* This form—the condition of the connection of the deduced propositions with the fundamental principle, and the ground which justifies us in drawing conclusions from this connection, that the deduced propositions have necessarily the same certainty which pertains to the fundamental principle—can also, like the truth of the fundamental principle, *not* be demonstrated in the particular science itself, but is presupposed as the possibility of its form. Hence, a general science of knowledge must, moreover, show up the ground for the systematic form of all possible sciences.

2d. The science of knowledge is itself *a science.* Hence it must also have one *fundamental principle,* which can not be proven in it, but must be presupposed for its very possibility as a science. But this fundamental principle can not be proven in another higher science, since otherwise this other higher science would be the science of knowledge. This fundamental principle of the science of knowledge, and hence of all sciences and of all knowledge, is, therefore, absolutely not to be proven ; that is, it can not be deduced from a higher principle, the relation to which might demonstrate its certainty. Since, nevertheless, it is to be the basis of all certainty, it must be certain in itself, through itself, and for the sake of itself. All other propositions will be certain, because it can be shown that they are in some respect related to it, but this one must be certain merely because it is related to itself. All other propositions will only have a mediated certainty derived from it, but itself must have immeate certainty. Upon it all knowledge is grounded, without it no knowledge were indeed possible ; but itself has its ground in no other knowledge, being, on the contrary, itself the ground of all knowledge. This fundamental principle is absolutely certain ; that is, it is certain *because* it is certain. You can not inquire after its ground without contradiction. It is the ground of all certainty ; that is, every thing which is certain is certain, because this fundamental principle is certain, and nothing is certain if it is not certain. It is the ground of all knowledge ; that is, you know what it asserts, simply because you know any thing at all ; you know it immediately when you know any thing at all. It accompanies all knowledge, is contained in all knowledge, and is presupposed by all knowledge. The science of knowledge, in so far as it is a science, and is to consist of more than its fundamental principle—which seems necessary, since it is to furnish the fundamental principles of all sciences—must have a *systematic form.* It is evident that it can not derive this form, either in regard to its *determinateness* or in regard to its *validity*, from any other science, since itself is to furnish all other sciences their systematic form. Hence, the science of knowledge must contain this form within itself, and must itself show up the ground of this form. Let us consider this a little, and it will directly appear what this assertion means. That whereof any thing is known we will, in the mean while, call the *content*, and that which is known thereof the *form* of a proposition. (In the proposition, gold is a body ; that whereof is known is gold and the body ; that which is known of them is, that they are in a certain respect equal, and might in so far replace each other. It is an affirmative proposition, and this relation is its form.)

No proposition is possible without content or without form. It must contain something whereof we know, and something which is known thereof. Hence, the first principle of the science of knowledge must have both content and form. Now, this first principle is to be immediately and of itself certain, and this can only signify : its content must determine its form, and its form its content. Its form can only fit its content, and its content can only fit its form ; every other form connected with that content, or every other content connected with that form, would cancel that principle itself, and thus annihilate all knowledge. Hence, the form of the absolute first principle of the science of knowledge is not only contained in that principle itself, but is

also presented as absolutely valid for the content of
that principle. Again : if there should be, besides
this absolute first principle, still other fundamental
principles of the science of knowledge—which in
that case can only be partly absolute, and must be
partly derived from the first principle, since otherwise in the first case they would not be fundamental principles, and in the latter case not connected
with the first and highest principle—then the absolute part of these other fundamental principles could
only be either the content or the form ; and, likewise, the conditioned or derived part of these principles could only be either the content or the form.
If the *content* of these other fundamental principles
be their absolute or unconditioned part, then the
absolute first principle of the science of knowledge
must condition the *form* of those contents ; or if
the *form* of those other principles be the unconditioned part, then their *content* must be conditioned
by the first principle of the science of knowledge ;
and thus indirectly also their form, that is, in so far
as the form is to be form of the content. In either
case, therefore, the *form* would be determined by
the first absolute principle of the science of knowledge. And since it is impossible that there should
be a fundamental principle not determined either in
form or in content by the first absolute principle,
(that is, if we are to have a science of knowledge at
all,) it follows that there can only be three fundamental principles : one absolutely in and through
itself determined both in form and in content ; a

second one determined through itself in form ; and a third one determined through itself in content. If there are still other propositions in the science of knowledge, they must be determined both in regard to form and content by the fundamental principle. Hence, a science of knowledge must determine the form of all its propositions, in so far as they are separately considered. But such a determination of the separate propositions is only thus possible : that they reciprocally determine each other. But each proposition must be *perfectly* determined, that is, its form must suit only its and no other content, and its content must only suit its and no other form ; for else such a proposition would not be *equal* to the first principle, in so far as that first principle is certain, and hence would not be certain. If, nevertheless, all the propositions of a science of knowledge are to be different, which they must be if they are to be many propositions and not one proposition, then no proposition can obtain its complete determination otherwise than through a single one of all propositions. And thus the whole series of propositions becomes determined, and no proposition can occupy another place in the system than that which it occupies. Each proposition in the science of knowledge has its position determined by a determined other proposition, and on its part determines the position of a determined third proposition. Hence, the science of knowledge establishes itself the form of its whole for itself.

This form of the science of knowledge is neces-

sarily valid for its content. For if the absolute first
principle was immediately certain, that is, if its
form was fit only for its content, and its content
only for its form, and if through this first principle
all possible subsequent propositions are determined,
immediately or mediately, in form or content; if
all subsequent theorems, in other words, are, as it
were, contained already in the first one, then it follows that what holds good for the first must also
hold good in regard to the others ; that is, that
their form is only fit for their content, and their
content only for their form. It is true, this relates
only to the separate propositions ; but the form of
the whole is nothing but the form of the separate
propositions, thought in one ; and what is valid for
each separate must be valid for all, thought as one.

But the science of knowledge is to give not only
itself its own form, but is also to give *all other possible sciences their form ;* and is to make certain the
validity of this form for all other sciences. This
can only be thought possible on condition that
every thing which is to be a proposition of any
other science must be already involved in some
proposition of the science of knowledge, and hence
must have obtained its proper form already in that
science. This opens to us an easy way of getting
back to the content of the absolute first principle
of the science of knowledge, of which we can now
say something more than was possible before. If
we assume for the present that *to be certain* means
simply to have an insight into the inseparability

of a determined content from a determined form, (which is to be only a definition of a name, since a real definition of knowledge is simply impossible,) then we might understand already to some extent how the fact that the fundamental principle of all knowledge determines its form only through its content, and its content only through its form, could determine the form of *all* the content of knowledge ; that is to say, if all possible content were contained in the content of that first principle. If, therefore, there is to be an absolute first principle of all knowledge, this assumption must be correct ; that is, the content of this first principle must contain all other possible content, but must itself be contained in no other content. In short, it must be the absolute content.

It is easy to remember that, in presupposing the possibility of a science of knowledge, and particularly of its first principle, we always presuppose that there is really a system in human knowledge. If such a system, however, is to be in it, it can be shown—even apart from our description of the science of knowledge—that there must be such an absolute first principle. If there is not to be any such system, two cases only are possible. Either there is no immediate certainty at all, and then our knowledge forms many series or one infinite series, wherein each theorem is derived from a higher one, and this again from a higher one, etc., etc. We build our houses on the earth, the earth rests on an elephant, the elephant on a tortoise, the tor-

toise again—who knows on what ?—and so on *ad*
infinitum. True, if our knowledge is thus constituted, we can not alter it ; but neither have we,
then, any firm knowledge. We may have gone
back to a certain link of our series, and have found
every thing firm up to this link ; but who can guarantee us that, if we go further back, we may not
find it ungrounded, and shall thus have to abandon
it ? Our certainty is only assumed, and we can
never be sure of it for a single following day.

Or the second case : Our knowledge consists of
finite series, but of many finite series, each series
ending in a fundamental principle, which has its
ground in no other one, but only in itself; all
these fundamental principles having no connection
among each other, and being perfectly independent
and isolated. In this case there are, perhaps, several inborn truths in us, all more or less inborn,
and in the connection of which we can expect no
further insight, since it lies beyond these inborn
truths ; or there is, perhaps, a manifold simple in
the things outside of us, which is communicated to
us by means of the impression produced upon us
by the things, but into the connection whereof we
can not penetrate, since there can not be any thing
more simple than the simplest in the impression.
If this second case is the truth, if human knowledge is in itself such a piecework — as the real
knowledge of so many men unhappily is—if originally a number of threads lie in our minds, which
are or can be connected with each other in no

point, then again we may not be able to alter this
state of things, and our knowledge is, as far as it
extends, certain enough ; but it is no *unit*, it is a
manifold knowledge. Our building stands firm,
but, instead of being a connected structure, it is an
aggregate of chambers, from none of which we can
enter the other ; a building wherein we always get
lost, and never feel ourselves at home. There is
no light in it ; and in spite of our riches we always
remain poor, because we can never calculate them,
never consider them as a whole, and hence never
know what we really possess ; we can never use
part of it to improve the rest, because no part is
relatable to the rest. Nay, more : our knowledge
will never be completed ; we must expect every
day that a new inborn truth may manifest itself in
us, or that experience may furnish us with a new
simple. We must always be prepared to build a
new house for ourselves. No general science of
knowledge will be possible as containing the
ground of other sciences. Each will be grounded
in itself. There will be as many sciences as there
are separate immediately certain propositions. But
if neither the first case is to be correct, namely,
that there are one or more mere fragments of a
system, nor the second, that there are to be a
manifold of systems, then a highest and absolute
first fundamental principle must exist as the basis
of a complete and unit-system in the human mind.
From this first principle our knowledge may expand into ever so many series, each of which again
may expand into series, etc., still all of them must

rest firm upon one single link, which is not dependent upon another one, which holds itself and the whole system by virtue of its own power. In this link we shall possess a globe, holding itself firm by virtue of its own gravitation, the central point whereof attracts with almighty force whatsoever we have but erected upon its surface and perpendicularly, and not in the air or obliquely, and which allows no grain of dust to be torn away from its sphere of power.

Whether such a system and its condition, a first principle, exist, can not be decided in advance of the investigation. This fundamental principle can neither be proven as mere principle, nor as the basis of all knowledge. Every thing depends upon the attempt. If we shall find a proposition which has the internal conditions of the fundamental principle of all human knowledge, we shall try to discover whether it has also its external conditions, whether every thing we know or believe to know can be traced back to it. If we succeed in this, we shall have proven by the realization of the science of knowledge that it is possible, and that there is a system of human knowledge, whereof it is the representation. If we do not succeed in this, there either is no such system or we have merely failed in discovering it, and must leave the discovery to more fortunate successors. To maintain that there is no such system merely because *we* have failed to discover it would be an assumption, the refutation whereof is beneath the dignity of earnest investigation.

PART SECOND.

§ 3.—DEVELOPMENT OF THE CONCEPTION OF THE SCIENCE OF KNOWLEDGE.

To develop a conception scientifically is to assign to it its place in the system of human sciences generally, that is, to show what conception determines its position in the system, and of which conception it determines the position. But the conception of the science of knowledge generally, as well as of knowledge generally, can evidently have no position in the system of all sciences, since it is itself rather the place for all scientific conceptions, and assigns to all their positions in itself and through itself. It√ is clear, therefore, that we can speak here only of a hypothetical development ; that is, the question is, If we assume that there are sciences, and that there is truth in them, (which can not be known in advance of the science of knowledge,) how is the science of knowledge related to these sciences ?

This question also is answered by the mere conception of that science. The latter sciences are related to it as the grounded is to its ground ; they do not assign to it its place, but it assigns to them their places in itself and through itself. All we can, therefore, propose to ourselves here is a further explanation of this answer.

1. The science of knowledge is to be a science of all sciences. Here arises the question: How can the science of knowledge guarantee that it has furnished the ground, not only of all as yet discovered and known, *but also of all discoverable and knowable* sciences, and that it has *completely* exhausted the whole field of human knowledge?

2. As the science of all sciences, the science of knowledge is to furnish to all sciences their fundamental principles. Hence, all propositions, which are fundamental principles of the particular sciences, are at the same time inherent propositions of the science of knowledge; and thus one and the same propositions may be regarded both as a proposition of the science of knowledge, and as the fundamental principle of a particular science. The science of knowledge evolves from the same proposition further deductions; and the particular science whereof it is the fundamental principle also evolves from it further deductions. Hence, either the deductions of both sciences are the same—and then there is no such a thing as a particular science—or both sciences have a distinct and peculiar mode of deduction; and this is impossible, because the science of knowledge is to furnish the *form* of all *sciences;* or something is added to a proposition of the science of knowledge, which something must,

of course, be derived from the same science, whereby it becomes fundamental principle of a particular science. Here the question arises : What is this which is added ? or, since this additional is to frame the distinction, what is the definite boundary between the general science of knowledge and every particular science ?

3. Again, the science of knowledge is to determine the form of all sciences. How this can be done we have shown above. But another science, under the name of logic, pretends to have this same object. Sentence must be passed upon the claims of both sciences, that is, it must be decided how the science of knowledge is related to logic.

4. The science of knowledge is itself a science. What it is to accomplish as such we have shown above. But in so far as it is a mere science, a knowledge, in the formal significance of the word, it is a science of a *something ;* it has an object, and it is clear from the above that this object can be no other than the system of human knowledge generally. The question arises : How is the science of knowledge, as science, related to its object as such ?

§ 4.—IN HOW FAR CAN THE SCIENCE OF KNOW-LEDGE BE SURE OF HAVING EXHAUSTED HUMAN KNOWLEDGE GENERALLY ?

The *hitherto* true or imaginary human knowledge is not human knowledge generally ; and, though a philosopher had really exhausted the former, and shown by a perfect induction that it were contained in his system, he would yet by no means have satisfied the task imposed upon philosophy ; for how could he prove by his induction from present experience that in the future some discovery might not be made which would not fit into his system ?

Quite as unsatisfactory would be the excuse that he only intended to exhaust the knowledge possible in the present sphere of human existence ; for if his philosophy is only valid for this sphere, he clearly confesses that he knows no possible other sphere, and hence, also, not the limits of that sphere which his philosophy claims to exhaust. Hence, he has arbitrarily drawn a limit, the validity whereof he can only prove by past experience, and which may, therefore, be contradicted by any possible future experience even within his own posited sphere. Human knowledge generally is to be exhausted, signifies : it is to be absolutely and unconditionally determined what man can know not only on the present stage, but on all possible and conceivable stages of his existence.

This is only possible if it can be shown, firstly, that the accepted fundamental principle is exhausted ; and, secondly, that no other fundamental principle is possible than the accepted one: A fundamental principle is exhausted when a complete system has been erected upon it, that is, when that fundamental principle necessarily leads to *all* the propositions deduced from it, and when, again, *all* deduced propositions necessarily lead back to it. When no proposition occurs in the whole system which could be true if the fundamental principle were false, or false if the fundamental principle were true ; then this is the negative proof that no *superfluous* proposition has been accepted in the system ; for the superfluous one, which did not belong to the system, might be true though the fundamental principle were false, 'or false though the latter were true. When the fundamental principle is given, *all* propositions must be given. Each particular one is given in and through the fundamental principle. This connection of the separate propositions of the science of knowledge proves that the science has the required negative proof in and through itself. This negative proof shows that the science is *systematic*, that all its parts are connected in a single fundamental principle.

Again, the science is a *system*, or is completed, if no further proposition can be deduced ; and this furnishes the positive proof that *all* the propositions of the system have been admitted. Still, of this there must be other evidence ; for the mere relative and negative assertion, *I* do not see what other deductions might be made, is not sufficient. Some one else might arise hereafter, and see what I did not see. We need, therefore, a positive proof that no other propositions could possibly follow, and this proof can only arise if the same fundamental principle from which we started shall also show itself to be the final result ; since, then, we could not pro-

ceed without describing the same circle we should
have already drawn. When the time comes to represent this science, it will be shown, also, that it
really describes this circle, leaving the student precisely at the point from which it started, and thus
furnishing also the second positive proof in and
through itself.*   But although the fundamental
principle be exhausted and a complete system
erected upon it, it does not follow that thereby human knowledge generally is exhausted, unless we
presuppose what ought first to be proven, namely,
that this fundamental principle is the fundamental
principle of human knowledge generally. Of course,
nothing can be added or taken away from the completed system which has been erected ; but why
might not the future, through augmented experience, cause propositions to arise in human consciousness which can not be grounded upon that fundamental principle, and which, therefore, presuppose one or more other fundamental principles ?
In short, why could not one or more other systems
coexist in the human mind with the first one ? To
be sure, they would be neither connected with the
first one nor with each other in any common point ;
but neither is this *required*, if they are to form many

* The science of knowledge has absolute totality. In it one leads
to all, and all to one. But it is also the *only* science which can be
completed. Completion is, therefore, its distinguishing characteristic. All other sciences are infinite, and can not be completed, for
they do not return to their fundamental principles. This the science
of knowledge has to prove for all other sciences, and show up the
ground of it.

systems. Hence, if the impossibility of new dis-
coveries is to be satisfactorily proven, it must be
shown *that only one system can be in human knowledge.* Now, since the proposition that all human
knowledge results only in one in itself connected
knowledge—is itself to be a component of human
knowledge—it can not be grounded upon any other
principle than the one assumed as the fundamental
principle of all human knowledge, and can only be
proven by it. By this we have gained, at least for
the present, so much that we see how such a future
proposition as we supposed might possibly arise in
consciousness would not only be *another* one, different from the fundamental principle of our system, but would also be contradictory of the latter
in form. For, according to all we have said, the
fundamental principle of our system must involve
the proposition that there is a unit-system in human knowledge. Every proposition, therefore, which
is not to belong to this system must not only be a
different system, but must be a direct contradiction
of it, in so far as the former system asserts itself
to be the only possible one. It must be a contradiction of the deduced proposition of the unity of
the system ; and, since all its propositions are inseparably connected, of each single theorem, and
particularly of the fundamental principle thereof.
Hence, it would have to rest on a fundamental
principle directly opposed to the first fundamental
principle. If, for instance, the first fundamental

principle should turn out to be : I am I ; this
second one would have to be : I am not I.

Now, it would be wrong to conclude from this
contradiction the impossibility of such a second
fundamental principle. If the first fundamental
principle involves the proposition that the system
of human knowledge is a unit, it involves also, it is
true, that nothing must contradict this system. But
both these propositions are merely deductions from
the first fundamental principle, and hence, by ac-
cepting the absolute validity of the deductions, we
already assume that itself is the absolute first and
only fundamental principle of human knowledge.
Here, therefore, is a circle which the human mind
can never get out of ; and it is well to confess this
circle plainly, lest its unexpected discovery at some
time might confound men. This circle is as follows : If the proposition X is the first, highest, and
absolute fundamental principle of human knowledge, then there is in human knowledge a unit-
system, for the latter is the result of the proposition
X. Now, since there is to be in human knowledge
a unit-system, the proposition X, which really does
establish such a system, is the fundamental principle of human knowledge, and the system based
upon it is that unit-system of human knowledge.

It is unnecessary to be surprised at this circle.
For to demand that it should be annihilated is to
demand that human knowledge should be utterly
groundless, that there should be no absolute certainty, and that all human knowledge should be

only conditioned ; in short, it is to assert that there
is no immediate truth at all, but only mediated truth,
and this *without any thing whereby it is mediated.*
Whosoever feels thereunto inclined may investigate as much as he pleases what he would know
if his Ego were not Ego ; that is, if he did not exist,
and if he could not distinguish a Non-Ego from
his Ego.

§ 5.—WHAT IS THE LIMIT WHICH SEPARATES THE
SCIENCE OF KNOWLEDGE FROM THE PARTICULAR
SCIENCES ?

We discovered above (§ 3) that one and the
same proposition could not be in the same respect
a proposition of the science of knowledge and of a
particular science ; and that to be the latter, it
would be necessary to have something added to it.
This character which is to be added can only be
derived from the science of knowledge, since it
contains all possible human knowledge ; but can
not, as is evident, be contained in that science in
the same proposition which is to become fundamental principle of the particular science. Hence,
it must be, perhaps, contained in another separate
proposition of the science of knowledge, which is
connected with the proposition which is to become
the fundamental principle of a particular science.
Since we have here to meet an objection which
does not arise from the conception of the science
of knowledge itself, but merely from the presuppo-

sition that there exist also other separate sciences,
we can meet it also only by a presupposition, and
shall have done enough for the present if we but
show a possibility of the required limitation.   That
it will be the true limitation — although it may,
nevertheless, turn out so—we neither care nor need
to prove here.

Let it be, therefore, assumed that the science of
knowledge contains those determined acts of the
human mind which it—be it conditioned or unconditioned — enacts necessarily and under compulsion ; but that it posits at the same time, as the
highest explanatory ground of those necessary acts,
a power to determine itself, (absolutely and without
compulsion or necessity :) *to act generally.*   Under
this assumption the science of knowledge will result in a necessary and a not necessary or free acting.   The acts of the human mind, in so far as it
acts necessarily, will be determined by the science,
but not in so far as it acts free.

Let it be further assumed that the free acts also
are to be determined from some reason or another ;
then this determination can not occur in the science
of knowledge.   But since it is a *determining,* it
must occur in *sciences ;* hence in particular sciences.
The object of these free acts can be no other than
the necessary, furnished by the science of knowledge, since it furnishes every thing and since it
furnishes only the necessary.   Hence, in the fundamental principle of a particular science, an act
which the science of knowledge left free would be

determined. The science of knowledge would thus give to the act, that is, to the fundamental principle, firstly, its necessary character, and, secondly, freedom generally ; but the particular science would give that freedom its determination ; and thus the sharply drawn line of limitation would have been discovered. As soon as an in itself free act receives a determined direction, we leave the field of the science of knowledge generally, and enter the field of a particular science.

I shall illustrate this by two examples :

The science of knowledge furnishes, as necessary, space, and, as absolute limit, the point ; but it leaves imagination perfectly free to posit the point wherever it chooses. As soon as this freedom is determined, for example, to move the point against the limit of the unlimited space, and thus to draw a line,* we are no longer on the field of the science of knowledge, but on the field of a particular science, which is called geometry. The general problem, to limit space in accordance with a rule, or the con-

---

* A question for mathematicians. Does not the conception of a line involve already the conception of straightness? Are there other lines than straight ones? And is the so-called curved line any thing but a combination of infinitely many and infinitely close connected points? The origin of the curved line as the line of limitation of the infinite space (from the Ego as central point an infinite manifold of infinite *radii* are drawn, to which our limited imagination posits an end-point, and these end-points, when thought as one, are the original line of the circle) seems to guarantee this ; and from this it becomes clear *that* and *why* the problem of measuring it by a straight line is an infinite problem. It also appears from this why the straight line can not be defined.

struction in space, is fundamental principle of geometry, which science is thus clearly divided from the
science of knowledge. Again : the science of
knowledge furnishes as necessary a nature which,
in its being and determinations, is to be considered
as independent of us ; and also furnishes as necessary the laws, according to which nature is to be
and must be observed.* But our power of judgment retains its full freedom to apply these laws or
not, or to apply whatever law it chooses to any possible object ; (for instance, to regard the human
body as inorganic, or as organic, or as living matter.) But as soon as the power of judgment is required to observe a determined object by a determined law, (for instance, whether animal life can be
explained from the mere inorganic ; whether crys-
tallization be the transition from chemical connec-
tions to organization ; whether magnetic and elec-

* Curious as it may appear to many explorers of nature, it will
nevertheless show itself to be the strict truth, that they themselves
first put the laws into nature which they believe to have learned
from her, and that the smallest as well as the most extensive law
the structure of a leaf of grass as well as the motion of the heavenly
bodies, can be deduced in advance of all observation from the fundamental principle of all human knowledge. It is true that no law
of nature, and indeed no law whatever, arises to our *consciousness*,
unless an object is given to which it can be applied ; it is true that
not all objects necessarily, and not all objects in the same degree,
must or can agree with the laws; but for that very reason is it
true that we do not learn them from observation, but posit them as
the ground of all observation, and that they are not so much laws
of independent nature as laws for ourselves how we have to observe nature.

tric powers are the same or not, etc.,) then it is no longer free, but obeys a rule ; and hence we are no longer in the science of knowledge, but on the field of another science, which is called the science of nature. The general rule, to subsume every object of experience under a given law of nature in our mind, is fundamental principle of the science of nature. That science consists throughout of experiments, (not of a passive reception of the lawless influences of nature upon us,) which are arbitrarily undertaken, and with which nature may correspond or not ; and by this characteristic the science of nature is abundantly separated from the science of knowledge.

Here, therefore, is already clearly seen why only the science of knowledge can have absolute totality, and why all particular sciences must be infinite. The science of knowledge contains only the necessary ; if this is necessary in every respect, it is necessary also in respect to quantity, that is, it is necessarily limited. All other sciences are based upon freedom, freedom of our mind as well as of the absolutely independent nature. If this is to be truly freedom, subject to no law, it is impossible to prescribe for them a limited sphere, since this could only be done by a law. Hence, their spheres are infinite. Let no one, therefore, apprehend danger from an exhaustive science of knowledge for the infinite perfectibility of the human mind ; on the contrary, instead of canceling that infinite perfectibility, the science of knowledge rather secures it against all doubt, and assigns to it a problem which can not be completed in all eternity.

§ 6.—HOW IS THE SCIENCE OF KNOWLEDGE RELATED TO LOGIC?

The science of knowledge is to determine the form for all possible sciences. According to current opinion, in which there may be something true, logic does the very same thing. How are these two sciences related to each other, particularly in respect to this problem, which each claims to solve?

By remembering that logic only pretends to determine the form of all possible sciences, whereas the science of knowledge is also to determine their content, an easy way is discovered to enter into this important investigation. In the science of knowledge the form is never separated from the content, nor the content from the form. In each of its propositions both form and content are inseparably united. If the propositions of logic are therefore to contain merely the form of possible sciences, they are not propositions of the science of knowledge; and hence the whole science of logic is not science of knowledge, nor even part of it. Curious as it may sound at the present state of philosophy, the science of logic is no philosophical science at all, but a peculiar, separate science; a fact, however, which is not to disparage the dignity of that science.

If the science of logic is such a separate science, it must be possible to show a determination of freedom by means of which the science of logic arises from the science of knowledge, and the limit of both may be ascertained. Such a determination of freedom is indeed clearly to be pointed out. In the science of knowledge, as we have said, form and content are necessarily united. Logic is to represent the pure form apart from the content ; and this separation of form and content can only—since it is not an original separation—occur through freedom. Hence, it is by the free separation of form from the content that logic arises as a science. Such a separation is called *abstraction ;* and hence logic consists essentially in abstraction from all content of the science of knowledge.

In this manner the propositions of logic would be merely form, which is impossible, for the conception of a proposition involves (see § 1) that it have both form and content. Hence, that which in the science of knowledge is mere form must be *content* in logic, and this content must again receive the general form of the science of knowledge, but which is now thought as the form of a logical proposition. This second act of freedom, whereby the form becomes its own content and returns into itself, is called *reflection.* No abstraction is possible without reflection, and no reflection without abstraction. Both acts, considered separately, are acts of freedom ; and when, in this same separation, they are placed in relation to each other, one of them is necessarily

the condition of the other. But in synthetical thinking both are only one and the same act, viewed from
two sides.

From this results the determined relation of
logic to the science of knowledge. The former is
not the *ground* of the latter ; but the latter is the
ground of the former. The science of knowledge
can not be proven from the science of logic, and no
logical proposition, not even the proposition of contradiction, must be accepted in advance as valid by
the science of knowledge ; but, on the contrary, every
logical proposition and the whole science of logic
must be proven from the science of knowledge. It
must be shown that all the forms contained in logic
are really forms of a certain content in the science
of knowledge. Thus, logic derives its validity from
the science of knowledge, and not the science of
knowledge its validity from logic.

Again, the science of knowledge is not *conditioned*
and *determined* by logic, but logic is conditioned
and determined by the science of knowledge. The
science of knowledge does not derive its form from
logic, but has that form in itself. On the contrary,
the science of knowledge conditions the validity
and applicability of logical propositions. The forms
which logic establishes must, in the common way
of thinking, and in all particular sciences, be applied
to no other content than that which they are confined to in the science of knowledge ; not necessarily to the whole of that content—for then we
should have no particular sciences—but at least to

what is part of that content. Without this condition the particular science to which such forms were applied would only be an air castle, however correct its logical deductions might be.

Finally, the science of knowledge is necessary ; not necessary exactly in so far as it is a clearly conceived and systematically arranged science, but at least necessary as a natural gift ; while logic is an artificial product of the human mind in its freedom. Without the former, no knowledge and no science would be possible ; without the latter, all sciences would have been much later developed. The former is the exclusive condition of all science ; the latter is a very beneficial invention to secure and facilitate the progress of sciences.

Let me exemplify this :

A=A is undoubtedly a correct logical proposition, and in so far as it is this it signifies : *If* A is posited, then A is posited. Two questions arise here : Is A really posited ? and in how far and why is A posited *if* it is posited, or how are the *if* and the *then* connected ?

Let us assume that A in this proposition signifies I, (*Ego,*) and that it has, therefore, its determined content, then the proposition would be this : I am I ; or, *if* I am posited, then I am posited. But since the subject of this proposition is the absolute subject, in this single case the content is posited at the same time with the form ; I am posited, *because* I have posited myself. I am *because* I am. Hence, logic says : *If* A is, then A is ; but the science of knowledge says : *Because* A (that is, this particular A=Ego) is, therefore A is. And thus the question : Is A (this particular A) really posited ? is answered thus : It is posited, since it is posited. It is unconditionally and absolutely posited.

Let us assume that in the above proposition A does not signify I, (Ego,) but something else, then the condition can be clearly realized, under which it would be possible to answer : A is posited ; and how we can be justified in drawing the conclusion : If A is posited, then it is posited. For the proposition A=A is valid *originally only for the Ego ;* it has been abstracted from the proposition of the science of knowledge, I am I. Hence, all the content, to which it is to be applicable, must be contained in the Ego. No A can, therefore, be any thing else but an A *posited in the Ego ;* and now the proposition reads : Whatsoever is posited in the Ego is posited ; if A is posited in the Ego, then it is posited, (that is, in so far as it is posited as possible, actual, or necessary ;) and thus the proposition is shown to be true, beyond contradiction, if the Ego is to be Ego. Again, if the Ego is posited because it is posited, then every thing which is posited in the Ego is posited because it is posited ; and if A alone is posited in the Ego, then it *is* posited if it is posited ; and thus our second question is also answered.

§ 7.—HOW IS THE SCIENCE OF KNOWLEDGE, AS SCIENCE, RELATED TO ITS OBJECT?

Let us first premise that this question has hitherto been utterly abstracted from, and that hence
all the foregoing must be modified by the answer-
ing of this question.

Every proposition in the science of knowledge
has form and content ; something is known, and
there is something whereof is known.   But the
science of knowledge is itself the science of something, and not this something itself.   This would
seem to prove that the science of knowledge, with
all its propositions, is form of a content which ex-
isted in advance of it.   How, then, is it related to
this content, and what follows from this relation ?

The object of the science of knowledge, we have
seen, is the system of human knowledge.   This exists independently of the science of it, and the science only shapes it into systematic form.   What,
then, may this new form be, how is it distinguished
from the form which must exist in advance of the
science, and how is the science generally distinguished from its object ?

Whatever exists in the human mind, independently
of science, we may also call the acts of that mind.
These acts are the *What* which exists ; they occur
in a certain determined manner, and by this determined manner are they distinguished from each
other.   This is the *How* of the *What.*   Hence,
there is in the human mind originally, and in ad-

5

vance of our knowledge, form and content, and
both are inseparably united ; each act occurs in a
determined manner, in accordance with a law, and
this law determines the act. Nay, there may be,
even for an outside observer, a system in these acts,
if they are mutually connected with each other, and
if they follow general, particular, and specific laws.

But it is not at all necessary that they should
actually occur (that is, in time) in that systematic
form which the outside observer frames in positing
them as dependent on each other ; it is not at all
necessary, for instance, that the act which com-
prises all others, and which furnishes the highest
universal law, should actually occur *first* in our
mind, and be followed by the one next in importance ; not necessary at all that they should all occur
in a pure and unmixed state, or that many of them
might not appear as one. Let us assume, for instance, that the highest act of the Intelligence be
this : to posit itself. It is not at all necessary that
this act should be *in time* the first act of our mind,
which arises to clear consciousness ; nor is it even
necessary that it should ever occur in consciousness
in its purity ; that is, that the Intelligence should
ever be able to think simply *I am*, without, at the
same time, thinking another, which is Not I.

Now, herein lies the whole content of a possible
science of knowledge, but not that science itself.
In order to build up this science we need a new act of
the human mind, not contained in all its other acts,
namely, the power to become conscious of its *man-*

ner of acting generally. And since this act is not to ¹
be contained in all the other acts, which are all necessary, and which are all the necessary acts, it must
be an act of freedom. Hence, the science of knowledge, in so far as it is to be a systematic science,
is built up in the same manner in which all possible
sciences, in so far as they are to be systematic, are
built up, that is, through a determination of freedom ; which freedom is in the science of knowledge particularly determined : to become conscious
of the general manner of acting of the intelligence.
Hence, the science of knowledge is distinguished ✓
from other sciences only in this, that the object of
the latter sciences is itself a free act, while the objects of the science of knowledge are necessary
acts.

Now, by means of this free act, something, which
is in itself already form, namely, the necessary act
of the intelligence, is taken up as content and put
into a new form, that is, the form of knowledge or
of consciousness ; and hence that free act is an act
of reflection. Those necessary acts are separated
from the order in which they may occur perchance,
and are thus separated each free from all mixture ;
hence, that act is also an act of abstraction. It is ✓
impossible to reflect unless you have abstracted.

The form of the consciousness, wherein the necessary and general *manner of acting* of the intelligence is to be received, undoubtedly belongs itself
to the necessary modes of acting of the intelligence.
Hence, the manner of acting of the intelligence

will undoubtedly be received in that consciousness
like all its other contents ; and the question whence
the science of knowledge is ever to get this form
would thus appear to involve no difficulty.   But, if
we escape the difficulty in the question about the
form, the whole difficulty centres in the question
about the content.   If the necessary manner of
acting of the intelligence is to be received into the
form of consciousness, it must be already known as
such, and hence must have already been received
into this form.   We are clearly in a circle.

   This manner of acting is to be separated, according to the above, by a reflecting abstraction,
abstracting from all that this manner of acting is
not. This abstraction occurs through freedom, and
in it the philosophizing judgment is not led by a
blind compulsion.   The whole difficulty, therefore,
centres in this question : What rules does freedom
follow in that separation ? or how does the philosopher know what he is to accept as the necessary
manner of acting of the intelligence, and what he
is to pass by as accidental ?

   Now, this he can not possibly know, unless that
which he is first to become conscious of is already
in consciousness, which is a contradiction.   There
is, therefore, and can be, no *rule* for this procedure.
The human mind makes many attempts ; by blind-
ly groping it first discovers dawn, and only from
dawn does it emerge to the light of day.   At first
it is led by dark feelings,* (the origin and reality of

   * Hence it follows that the philosopher requires the dim feelings

which the science of knowledge has to show up ;) and if we had not begun to feel dimly what afterward we plainly recognized, we should be to-day yet the same lump of clay which arose from the earth, lacking all clear conceptions. This indeed the history of philosophy fully proves ; and we have now stated the true ground why that which lies open in every human mind, and which every one can grasp with his hands, if it is clearly exposed to him, could only arise to the consciousness of a few, after much straying into error. All phi- ✔ losophers have proposed to themselves this same object, all have attempted to separate by reflection the necessary manner of acting of the intelligence from its accidental conditions ; all have thus separated it more or less purely and perfectly ; and, on the whole, the philosophizing judgment has steadily made progress, and drawn nearer to its final result.

But since that reflection—not in so far as it is undertaken or not undertaken, for in this respect it is *free*, as we have seen, but in so far as it is undertaken in *accordance with laws*, (that is, in so far as it is determined in character, if it is undertaken)— does also belong to the necessary manner of acting of the intelligence, its laws would necessarily occur in the system of that manner of acting ; and thus one might well observe—after the science were

of the true, or requires genius in no less degree than the poet or the artist, only it is a genius of another kind. The artist requires the sense of *beauty*, the philosopher the sense of *truth*.

finished—whether they were correct ; that is, whether they agreed with the former or not. In other words, it would seem that it were possible to furnish an evident proof of the correctness of our scientific system after it had been finished.

But the laws of reflection, which we would thus discover in the course of the science of knowledge as the only possible ones whereby a science of knowledge could be possible, are, after all—even though they agree with those laws of reflection which we had presupposed as the rules of our investigation— the result of their previous application, and we thus discover here a new circle.

Certain laws of reflection have been presupposed by us ; and now, in the course of the science of knowledge, we discover the same laws as the only correct ones ; *ergo,* our presupposition has been true, and our science of knowledge is perfectly correct in form. If we had presupposed other laws, we doubtlessly should have discovered other laws in our science of knowledge as the only correct ones, and the only question would have been whether they agreed with the presupposed laws or not. If they did not, we should be sure either that the presupposed laws were wrong, or the discovered laws, or, which is most probable, both. It is, therefore, not allowable to draw such a conclusion in a circle. We merely conclude from the *harmony* of the presupposed and the discovered laws of reflection that the system is correct. This, to be sure, is only a negative proof, which gives simply proba-

bility. If the presupposed and the discovered laws
do not agree, then the system is surely false. If
they do agree, it *may* be correct. But it must not
necessarily be correct ; for although—if there is
a system in human knowledge—such an agreement
or harmony can only be discovered in *one* way, *if
the conclusions are rightly* drawn, it always remains
possible that the harmony may be the result of two
incorrectly drawn conclusions, which cancel each
other and thus produce harmony. It is as if I
tested a calculation of division by multiplication.
If I do not obtain the desired sum as product, I
may be sure that I have made a mistake in calculating ; but if I do obtain it, it is merely *probable*
that I have calculated correctly ; for I might have
made both in division and multiplication the same
mistake ; for instance, might in both have counted
$5 \times 9 = 36$. It is thus with the science of knowledge. That science is not only the rule, but, at
the same time, the calculation. Whosoever doubts
the correctness of our product, does not on that
account doubt the ever-valid law that we must
posit the one factor as many times as the other one
has units ; he only doubts whether we have correctly observed this law.

Hence, even the highest unity of the system,
which is the negative proof of its correctness, leaves
always something which can never be strictly prov-
en, but only accepted as probable ; namely, that this
unity has not been the result of chance, or of incorrect conclusions. Various means may be devised

to heighten this probability ; the series of propositions may be gone over in thought again and again ;
one may reverse the method and compare the
account from the result back to the fundamental
principle ; or one may reflect again upon the reflection, etc., etc. ; the probability always becomes
greater, but never becomes certainty. If one is
only conscious of having investigated honestly, and
not having had in mind the final results one wished
to discover, this probability may well suffice, and an
objector to the correctness of our system may well
be required *to show up the error in our conclusions;*
but it will never do to claim infallibility. The system of the human mind, whereof the science of
knowledge is to be the representation, is absolutely
certain and infallible ; every thing grounded in it is
absolutely true ; it never errs, and whatever has
ever *necessarily* been, or ever *necessarily* will be, in
any human soul, is true. If *men* erred, the fault
lay not in the necessary, *but in the freedom of reflection,* which substituted one law for another. And
if our science of knowledge is a correct representation of this system, it is absolutely certain and infallible as that system ; but the very question is,
whether our representation is or is not correct, and
of this we can never furnish a strict conclusion, but
only a probable proof. Our science of knowledge
has truth only on the condition and in so far as its
representation is a correct one. We are not the
legislators of the human mind, but its historians ;
not newspaper writers, it is true, but pragmatic his-
tory-writers.

Add to this the circumstance that a system may really be correct as a whole, though its separate parts have not complete evidence. Here and there an incorrect conclusion may have been drawn, suggestive propositions may have been left out, other propositions which can be proven may have been asserted without proof or established by incorrect proof ; and yet the most important results may be correct. This seems impossible ; it seems as if a hair-breadth deviation from the straight line would necessarily lead to infinitely increasing deviation ; and thus indeed it would be if man had to produce all his knowledge by clear conscious thinking ; whereas rather the fundamental genius of reason unconsciously guides him and leads him by new errors from the straight path of his *formaliter* and logically correct argument back to the *materialiter* only correct result, which he would never have reached again had he persisted in logically carrying out his wrong proposition.

Even, therefore, if a universally valid science of knowledge should be established, the philosophical judgment will still have an infinite field wherein to work its ultimate perfection ; it will have to fill up blanks, to make more strict the proofs, and clearer to determine the determinations.

I have two more remarks to add :

The science of knowledge presupposes the rules √ of reflection and abstraction as well known and valid ; it must do so necessarily, and need not be ashamed or make a secret of it. That science may

express itself and draw conclusions like any other
science, it may presuppose all logical rules and apply all conceptions which it needs. But these presuppositions are merely made to make itself intelligible ; hence, without drawing any consequences
therefrom. Every thing provable must be proven ;
with the exception of that first and highest fundamental principle, all propositions must be deduced.
Hence, for instance, neither the logical proposition
of opposition or contradiction, which is the ground
of all analysis, nor the logical proposition of the
ground, (nothing is opposite which is not related
in a third, and nothing is related which is not opposed in a third, the proposition which is the
ground of all synthesis,) is deduced from the absolute first principle, though they are deduced from
the two fundamental principles which rest upon it.
These two latter principles are also fundamental
principles, it is true, but they are not absolute, only
part of them is absolute ; hence, these fundamental
principles as well as the logical propositions which
rest upon them need not be proven, but must be
deduced. I explain myself clearer.

That which the science of knowledge establishes
is a proposition, thought and put into words ; that
in the human mind which corresponds to it is an
act of that mind, which in itself need not be *thought*
at all. Nothing must be presupposed to this act
than that without which the act *as* act would be
impossible ; and this is not tacitly presupposed, but
the science of knowledge has to establish it clearly

and distinctly *as* that without which the act would be impossible. Let the act be, for instance, D, the fourth in the series A, B, C, D; then the act C must be preposited to the act D, and shown as the exclusive condition of the act D; to the act C, again, the act B must be preposited, etc., etc. But the act A, the first act, is absolutely and unconditionally possible; and hence nothing is to be preposited as the condition of its possibility.

The *thinking* of this act A is, however, a quite different act, which presupposes far more. Suppose this thinking of A to be, in the series of acts about to be established, D, then A, B, and C must necessarily be presupposed as grounds of its possibility; and since that thinking (of A) is to be the first business of the science of knowledge, A, B, and C must be *tacitly* presupposed. It is not till you get to D that the presuppositions of the first can be proven; but as soon as you get this proof, you will have presupposed something else. The form of the science is thus always in advance of its content; and this is the reason why the science as such can only attain probability. The represented and the representation are in two different series. In the first series nothing is presupposed which is not proven; but for the possibility of the second you always must presuppose what can not be proven till later. The reflection which rules in the whole science of knowledge, in so far as it is a science, is a *representing*. But from this it does not follow that every thing about which it reflects must also be merely a representing. In the science of knowledge the Ego *is represented;* but from this it does not follow that the Ego is represented *as* merely representing ; for other determinations of the Ego may be discovered in it. The Ego as philosophizing *subject* is undoubtedly merely representing ; but the Ego as *object* of the philosophizing may be something more. Representing is the highest and absolute first act of the philosopher as such ; but the absolute first act of the human mind may well be of another kind. That it will turn out to be so appears probable, in advance of all experience, from simply this reason : that the representation may be completely exhausted, and that its acting is altogether necessary, and must, therefore, have a final ground of its necessity, which, as final ground, can have no higher one. A science, therefore, which is erected on the conception of representation, might well be a very useful introduction to the science, but could not be the science of knowledge itself. But this much follows certainly from the above, that the collective modes of acting of the intelligence, which the science of knowledge is to exhaust, can be received in consciousness only in the form of representation ; that is to say, only in so far as they are represented.

FUNDAMENTAL PRINCIPLES

OF THE WHOLE

SCIENCE OF KNOWLEDGE.

6

SCIENCE OF KNOWLEDGE.

———◆———

§ I. — FIRST AND ABSOLUTELY UNCONDITIONED FUNDAMENTAL PRINCIPLE.

WE have to *search for* the absolute, first, and unconditioned fundamental principle of human knowledge. It can not be *proven* nor *determined* if it is
to be absolute first principle.

This principle is to express that *deed-act* which
does not occur among the empirical determinations
of our consciousness, nor can so occur, since it is
rather the basis of all consciousness, and first and
alone makes consciousness possible. In representing this deed-act it is not so much to be feared that
my readers will *not* think what they ought to think,
as that they will think what they ought not to think.
This renders necessary a *reflection* on what may
perhaps for the present be taken for that deed-act,
and an *abstraction* from all that does not really
belong to it.

Even by means of this abstracting reflection, that
deed-act, which is not empirical *fact* of conscious-

ness, can not become fact of consciousness ; but by means of this abstracting reflection we may recognize so much : that this deed-act must necessarily be *thought* as the basis of all consciousness.

The laws* according to which this deed-act must necessarily be thought as basis of human knowledge, or, which is the same, the rules according to which that abstracting reflection proceeds, have not yet been proven as valid, but are for the present tacitly presupposed as well-known and agreed upon. As we proceed we shall deduce them from that fundamental principle, the establishment whereof is correct only if they are correct.   This is a circle, but an unavoidable circle. (See our Introduction, § 7.)   And since it is unavoidable and freely admitted, it is also allowable to appeal to all the laws of general logic in establishing this highest fundamental principle.

In undertaking this abstracting reflection we must start from some proposition which every one will admit without dispute.   Doubtless there are many such.   We choose the one which seems to us to open the shortest road to our purpose.

In admitting this proposition, the deed-act, which we intend to make the basis of our whole science of knowledge, must be admitted ; and the reflection must show *that* this deed-act is admitted the moment that proposition is admitted.

Our course of proceeding in this reflection is as

---

* The laws of general logic.

follows : Any fact of empirical consciousness, admitted as such valid proposition, is taken hold of, and from it we separate one of its empirical determinations after the other, until only that remains, which can no longer be separated and abstracted from.

As such admitted proposition we take this one : A is A.

Every one admits this proposition, and without the least hesitation. It is recognized by all as completely certain and evident.

If any one should ask a proof of its certainty, no one would enter upon such a proof, but would say : This proposition is *absolutely* (that is, *without any further ground) certain ;* and by saying this would ascribe to himself the power of *absolutely positing something.*

In insisting on the in itself certainty of the above proposition, you posit *not* that A *is.* The proposition A is A is by no means equivalent to A *is.* (*Being* when posited without predicate is something quite different from being when posited with a predicate.) Let us suppose A to signify a space inclosed within two straight lines, then the proposition A is A would still be correct ; although the proposition A *is* would be false, since such a space is impossible.

But you posit by that proposition : *If* A is, *then* A is. The question *whether* A is at all or not, does not, therefore, occur in it. The *content* of the proposition is not regarded at all,: merely its *form.* The
6*

question is not whereof you know, but *what* you know of any given subject. The only thing posited, therefore, by that proposition is the *absolutely* necessary connection between the two As. This connection we will call X.

In regard to A itself nothing has as yet been posited. The question, therefore, arises : Under what condition *is* A ?

X at least is in the Ego, and posited *through* the Ego, for it is the Ego which asserts the above proposition, and so asserts it by virtue of X as a law, which X or law must, therefore, be given to the Ego ; and, since it is asserted absolutely, and without further ground, must be given to the Ego through itself.

Whether and *how* A is posited we do not know ; but since X is to designate a connection between an unknown positing of A (of the first A in the proposition A is ·A) and a positing of the same A, which latter positing is absolute on condition of the first positing, it follows that A, *at least in so far as that connection is posited*, is posited *in* and *through* the Ego, like X. Proof: X is only possible in relation to an A ; now X is really posited in the Ego ; hence, also, A must be posited in the Ego, in so far as X is related to it.

X is related to that A, in the above proposition, which occupies the logical position of subject, and also to that A which is the predicate, for both are united by X. Both, therefore, are posited in the Ego, in so far as they are posited ; and the A of the predicate is posited *absolutely* if the first one is posited. Hence, the above proposition may be also expressed : If A is posited *in the Ego*, then *it is posited*, or then it *is*.

Hence, by means of X, the Ego posits : that A *is* absolutely for the asserting Ego, and *is* simply because it is posited in the Ego ; or that there is something in the Ego which always remains the same, and is thus able to connect or posit ; and hence the absolutely posited X may also be expressed, Ego=Ego, or I am I.

Thus we have already arrived at the proposition *I am ;* not as expression of a deed-act, it is true, but, at least, as expression of a *fact*.

For X is absolutely posited ; this is a fact of empirical consciousness, as shown by the admitted proposition. Now, X signifies the same as I am I ; hence, this proposition is also absolutely posited.

But Ego is Ego, or I am I, has quite another significance than A is A. For the latter proposition had content only on a certain condition, namely, *if* A is posited. - But the proposition I am I is unconditionally and absolutely valid, since it is the same as X ; it is valid not only in form, but also in content. In it the Ego is posited not on condition, but absolutely, with the predicate of self-equality ; hence, it is posited, and the proposition may also be expressed, *I am*.

This proposition, *I am*, is as yet only founded upon a fact, and has no other validity than that of a fact. If "A=A" (or X) is to be certain, then

" I am " must also be certain. Now, it is fact of empirical consciousness that we are compelled to regard X as absolutely certain ; hence, also, " I am " is certain, since it is the ground of the X. It follows from this, that the *ground of explanation of all facts of empirical consciousness is this : before all positing, the Ego must be posited through itself.*

(I say of *all* facts ; and to prove this I must show that X is the highest fact of empirical consciousness, is the basis of all others, and contained in all other facts ; which, perhaps, would be admitted by all men without proof, although the whole science of knowledge busies itself to prove it.)

The proposition A=A is *asserted.* But all asserting is an act of the human mind ; for it has all the conditions of such an act in empirical consciousness, which must be presupposed as well known and admitted in order to advance our reflection. Now, this act is based on something which has no higher ground, namely, X or I am.

Hence, that which is *absolutely posited and in itself grounded* is the ground of *a certain* (we shall see hereafter of *all)* acting of the human mind ; hence its pure character ; the pure character of activity in itself, altogether abstracting from its particular empirical conditions.

The positing of the Ego through itself is, therefore, the pure activity of the Ego. The Ego *posits itself;* and the Ego is by virtue of this its mere self-positing. Again, *vice versa :* the Ego *is* and *posits* its being, by virtue of its mere being. It is both the acting and the product of the act ; the active and the result of the activity ; deed and act in one ; and hence the *I am* is expressive of a deed-act ; and of the *only possible* deed-act, as our science of knowledge must show.

Let us again consider the proposition *I am I.* The Ego is absolutely posited. Let us assume that the first Ego of this proposition (which has the position of formal subject) is the *absolutely posited* Ego, and that the second Ego (that of the predicate) is the *being* Ego ; then the absolutely valid assertion that both are one signifies : the *Ego* is, *because* it has posited itself.

(This is, indeed, the case according to the logical form of the proposition. In A=A the first A is that which is posited in the Ego, (either absolutely, like the Ego itself, or conditionally, like any non-Ego ;) and in this positing of A the Ego is absolute subject ; and hence the first A is also called the subject. But the second A designates that which the Ego, in now making itself the object of its own reflection, discovers thus *as* posited in itself, (since it has just before itself posited the A in itself.) The Ego, in asserting that proposition A=A, predicates in truth not something of A, but of itself, namely, that it has found an A posited in itself ; and hence the second A is called predicate.)

The Ego in the former and the Ego in the latter significance are to be absolutely equal. Hence, the above proposition may be turned around, and then it reads : The Ego posits itself simply *because* it is.

It posits itself through its mere being, and *is* through its mere being posited.

This, then, will explain clearly in what significance we here use the word Ego, (I,) and will lead us to a definite explanation of the Ego as absolute subject. The Ego as absolute subject is *that, the being (essence) whereof consists merely in positing itself as being.* As soon as it posits itself, it is; and as soon as it is, it posits itself; and hence the Ego is for the Ego absolute and necessary. Whatsoever is not for itself is not an Ego.

Illustration.

The question has been asked, What *was* I before I became self-conscious? The answer is, *I* was not at all, for I was not I. The Ego is only, in so far as it is conscious of itself. The possibility of that question is grounded upon a mixing up of the Ego as *subject*, and the Ego as *object* of the reflection of the absolute subject; and is in itself altogether improper. The Ego represents itself, and in so far takes itself up in the form of representation, and now first becomes a *somewhat*, that is, an object. Consciousness receives in this form of representation a substrate, which *is*, even without the real consciousness, and which, moreover, is thought bodily. Such a condition is thought, and the question asked, *What* was the Ego at that time? that is, what is the substrate of consciousness? But even in this thought you unconsciously *add in thinking* the *absolute subject* as looking at that substrate ; and hence you unconsciously add in thought the very thing whereof you wanted to abstract, and thus you contradict yourself. The truth is, you can not think any thing at all without adding in thought your Ego as self-conscious ; you can not abstract from your self-consciousness ; and all questions of the above kind are not to be answered, since, maturely considered, they can not be asked.

If the Ego *is* only in so far as it posits itself, then it also is only *for* the positing, and posits only for the being Ego. *The Ego is for the Ego;* but if it posits itself absolutely, as it is, then it posits itself necessarily, and is necessary for the Ego. *I am only for me; but for me I am necessarily.* (By saying *for me,* I already posit my being.)

To posit itself and *to be* is, applied to the Ego, the same. Hence, the proposition I am because I have posited myself, can also be expressed : *I am absolutely because I am.*

Again, the Ego as positing itself and the Ego as being are one and the same. The Ego is as *what* it posits itself, and posits itself as *what* it is. Hence, *I am absolutely what I am.*

The immediate expression of the thus developed deed-act may be given in the following formula : *I am absolutely because I am, and I am absolutely what I am for myself.*

If this narration of the original deed-act is to be placed at the head of a science of knowledge

as its highest fundamental principle, it may perhaps
be best expressed thus :

THE EGO POSITS ORIGINALLY ITS OWN BEING.

(In other words, the Ego is necessarily identity
of subject and object ; is itself subject-object ; and
it is this without further mediation.)

We started from the proposition A=A, not as if
the proposition, I am, could be proven by it, but because we had to start from some one certain proposition, given in empirical consciousness.   And our
development, also, has shown that A=A does not
contain the ground of " I am," but, on the contrary,
that the latter proposition is the ground of the
former.

By abstracting from the content of the proposition I am, and looking merely to its form, namely,
the form of drawing a conclusion from the being
posited of something to its being, as we must abstract for the sake of logic, we thus obtain as *fundamental principle of logic* the proposition A=A,
which can only be proven and determined through
the science of knowledge.   *Proven :* for A is A because the Ego which has posited A is the same as
the Ego in which A is posited.   *Determined :* for
whatever is, is only in so far as it is posited in the
Ego, and there is nothing outside of the Ego.   No
possible A (no *thing*) can be any thing else but an
A posited in the Ego.

By abstracting, moreover, from all asserting as a
determined acting, and looking merely to the general *manner* of acting of the human mind, which is

given through that form, we obtain the *category of reality.* Every thing to which the proposition A=A is applicable has reality, *in so far as that proposition is applicable to it.* That which is posited through the mere positing of any thing (in the Ego) is its reality, its essence.

Remarks.

Kant, in his deduction of the categories, has hint- ᵥ ed at our proposition as absolute fundamental principle of all knowledge ; but he has never definitely established it *as* fundamental principle. Before Kant, Descartes has suggested a similar one, *Cogito, ergo sum ;* which, however, is not necessarily the *minor* and conclusion of a syllogism, of which the *major* would have to be, *Quodcunque cogitat, est ;* but which he may also have viewed as immediate fact of consciousness. In that case it would signify, *Cogitans sum, ergo sum,* (or, as we should say, *Sum, ergo sum.*) But in that case the word *cogitans* is completely superfluous ; you do not *think* necessarily when you *are,* but you are necessarily when you think. Thinking is not the essence, but merely aᴹˡ particular determination of the Ego ; and there are many other determinations of the Ego.

Reinhold speaks of representation, and his fundamental principle would read in the Cartesian form, *Repræsento, ergo sum ;* or, more correctly, *Repræsentans sum, ergo sum.* He goes considerably further than Descartes, but not far enough ; for representa-

tion, also, is not the essence of the Ego, but merely
a particular determination of the Ego ; and there
are many other determinations of the Ego, *although
they certainly must pass through the medium of representation in order to enter empirical consciousness.*

Spinoza, on the other hand, goes beyond our
proposition in its established significance. He does
not deny the unity of empirical consciousness, but
he utterly denies its pure consciousness. According
to him the whole series of representations of a single empirical subject is related to the only one pure
subject, as a single representation is related to the
whole series.   In his view the Ego (that is, that
which he calls *his* Ego, or which I call *my* Ego)
is not absolutely *because* it is, but because *something
else* is.   True, he considers the Ego to be Ego *for*
the Ego ; but he asks what it may be for something
outside of the Ego.   Such an " outside of the Ego"
would also be an Ego, of which the posited Ego
(for instance, *my* Ego) and all possible Egos would
be modifications.   He separates the *pure* and the
empirical consciousness. The first he posits in God,
who never becomes self-conscious, since pure consciousness never attains consciousness ; the latter
he posits in the particular modifications of the Godhead.   His system, thus established, is perfectly
logical and not to be refuted, because he has entered
a sphere where reason can not follow him ; but his
system is also groundless, for what justified him
in going beyond the pure consciousness given in
empirical consciousness ?

§ 2.—SECOND, AND IN REGARD TO ITS CONTENT,
CONDITIONED FUNDAMENTAL PRINCIPLE.

For the same reason why the first fundamental
principle could not be proven or deduced, the second, also, can not be proven. Hence, we here, also,
proceed from a fact of empirical consciousness in
the same manner.

The proposition not A is not A will doubtless be
recognized by every one as certain, and it is scarcely to be expected that any one will ask for its
proof.

If, however, such a proof were possible, it must
in our system be deduced from the proposition
A=A.

But such a proof is impossible. For let us assume, at the utmost, that the above proposition is the
same as —A is —A, (and hence that —A is equal to
some Y posited in the Ego,) and that for this reason
our proposition signifies now : *if* the opposite of A is
posited, *then* it is posited ; still we should only have
the same connection posited (X) which we obtained in our § 1, and our proposition, —A is not A, instead of being derived from A=A, would, after all,
be only the very same proposition. The chief
question, *Is* the opposite of A posited, and under
what condition *of form of mere acting* is it posited ?
is altogether ignored. If our second proposition
were a derived one, then this condition of the form
of acting would have to be derived from the proposition A=A. But how can the proposition A=A,

which involves only the form of positing, also involve the form of oppositing? Hence, that form of acting, the oppositing, is posited absolutely, and with no attached condition. —A is posited *as* such simply *because* it is posited.

Hence, as sure as the proposition —A not = A occurs among the facts of empirical consciousness, there occurs among the acts of the Ego an *oppositing;* and this oppositing, as far as its *form* is concerned, is absolutely and unconditionally possible, and is an acting which has no higher ground.

Through this absolute act the opposite, *as mere* opposite, is posited. Every opposite, in so far as it is merely opposite, is simply by virtue of an absolute act of the Ego, and has no other ground. Opposition generally is simply posited through the Ego.

But if any —A is to be posited, an A must be posited. Hence, the act of oppositing is also, in another respect, conditioned. Whether the act at all is possible depends upon another act ; hence, the act in its *content*, as acting generally, is conditioned ; it is an acting in relation to another acting. The *form* of the act, however, (the How ? namely, that it is not an act of positing, but of oppositing,)is unconditioned.

(Opposition is only possible on condition of the unity of consciousness of the positing and the oppositing. For if the consciousness of the first act were not connected with that of the second, then the second positing would not be an *op*-positing, but an absolute positing. Oppositing it becomes only through its relation to a positing.

As yet.we have only spoken of the act, as mere act, of the *manner* of acting. Let us now examine its product, $= -A$.

In $-A$ we can again distinguish *form* and *content.* Through the form is determined, that it is an *opposite;* the content determines that it is an opposite of a determined something, (of A,) that it is *not* this something.

The *form* of $-A$ is determined simply through the act ; it is an opposite because it is product of an oppositing ; the *content* is determined through A : it is *not* what A is, and its whole essence consists in this, that it is not what A is. I know of $-A$ simply *that* it is the opposite of A. But *what* that is *whereof* I know this, I can only know by knowing A.

Originally only the Ego is posited, and this alone is absolutely posited. (§ I.) Hence, an absolute oppositing can only refer to the Ego. The opposite of the Ego we call *Non-Ego.*

As sure as the proposition $-A$ is not A is unconditionally admitted as fact of empirical consciousness, *a non-Ego is absolutely opposited to the Ego.* All we have said above in reference to oppositing generally, is deduced from this original oppositing, and hence is valid for it ; it is, therefore, unconditioned in form, but conditioned in content. And thus we have also found the second principle of all human knowledge.

7*

Whatsoever appertains to the Ego, of that the opposite must appertain to the non-Ego.

(The general opinion is, that the conception of the non-Ego is a discursive conception, obtained by abstracting from all objects of representation. But the foolishness of this explanation can be easily demonstrated. If I am to represent an object, I must posit it in opposition to the representing subject. Now, it is true that in the object of representation there can and must be an X, whereby it discovers itself to be not the representing, but a represented; but no object of representation can possibly teach me, that every thing wherein this X occurs is represented object, and not representing subject; on the contrary, only by presupposing this law do I attain any object.)

By undertaking the same abstraction with this proposition, which we undertook with the first, we obtain the logical proposition —A is not A, which I should call the proposition of *oppositing*. In the present place, this proposition can not yet be properly determined, or expressed in a formula, the reason whereof will appear in the following section.

By abstracting from the determined act of asserting this proposition, and looking merely to the form of drawing a conclusion from the being opposited of something to its being, we obtain the *category of negation*. This also can not be clearly developed till in the following section.

§ 3.—THIRD, IN ITS FORM CONDITIONED FUNDA-MENTAL PRINCIPLE.

Every step we take in our science brings us nearer to the point where every thing can be proven. In the first principle, nothing could be nor was to be proven ; in the second, only the *act of oppositing* was not provable ; but, this act once admitted, it was strictly shown that the opposite must be a Non-Ego. The third principle is almost throughout capable of proof, since it is not, like the second, conditioned in content, but only in form, and, moreover, conditioned in form by the *two* foregoing propositions.

It is conditioned in form signifies, the *problem of the act* it establishes is given by the two foregoing propositions, but not the *solution* of the problem. The solution is the result of an unconditioned and absolute act of reason.

We therefore commence with a deduction, and proceed as far as we can go. When we can go. no further, we shall have to appeal to this absolute act.

1. In so far as the Non-Ego is posited, the Ego is not posited ; for the Non-Ego completely cancels the Ego.

Now, the Non-Ego is posited *in* the Ego, for it is opposited ; and all oppositing presupposes the identity of the Ego.

Hence, the Ego is not posited in the Ego in so far as the Non-Ego is posited in it.

2. But the Non-Ego can only be posited in so far as an Ego is posited in the Ego, (in the identical consciousness,) as the opposite of which it is posited.

Hence, in so far as the Non-Ego is posited in the Ego, the Ego also must be posited in it.

3. The conclusions of our 1st and 2d are opposed to each other; yet both are developed from the second fundamental principle; hence, that second principle is opposed to itself and cancels itself.

4. But it cancels itself only in so far as the posited is canceled by the opposited, hence in so far as itself is valid.

Hence, it does not cancel itself. The second fundamental principle cancels itself and does not cancel itself.

5. If this is the case with the second principle, it must also be with the first principle. That first principle cancels itself and does not cancel itself. For,

If Ego is = Ego, then all is posited, which is posited in the Ego.

Now, the second principle is to be posited and not to be posited in the Ego.

Hence, Ego is not = Ego, but Ego is = to the Non-Ego, and Non-Ego = Ego.

All these results have been deduced from the established principles according to the laws of reflection presupposed as valid; they must be correct, therefore. But if they are correct, the identity of consciousness, the only absolute foundation of our knowledge, is canceled. This determines our problem. We must find an X, by means of which all these results may be correct, without destroying the identity of consciousness.

1. The opposites, to be united, are in the Ego as consciousness. Hence, X must also be in consciousness.

2. Both the Ego and Non-Ego are products of original acts of the Ego, and consciousness itself is such a product of the first original act of the Ego, of the positing of the Ego through itself.

3. But our above results show that the act of which the Non-Ego is the product, that is, the oppositing, is not at all possible without X. Hence, X itself must be a product of an original act of the Ego. There must be, accordingly, an act of the human mind = Y, the product of which is X.

4. The form of this act Y is determined by the above problem. It is to be a uniting of the opposites (the Ego and the Non-Ego) without their mutually canceling each other. The opposites are to be taken up into the identity of consciousness.

5. But the problem does not determine the How, or the manner of this uniting, nor even suggests it at all. We must, therefore, make an experiment, and ask: How can A and —A, being and not being, reality and negation, be thought together, without their mutually canceling each other?

6. It is not to be expected that any one will reply otherwise but: They must mutually *limit* each other. If this answer is correct, the act Y is a

limiting of both opposites through each other, and X would signify the *limits*.

(Let me not be understood as asserting that the conception of limits is an analytical conception, involved in, and to be developed out of, the union of reality and negation. It is true our two fundamental principles have given us the opposite conceptions, and our first principle has given us the requirement to unite them. But the *manner* of uniting them has not been given, and is determined by a *particular* law of our mind, which law our experiment was only to make us conscious of.)

7. The conception of limits, however, involves more than the required X; for it involves also the conceptions of reality and negation, which are to be united. Hence, to get X pure, we must undertake another abstraction.

8. To *limit* something signifies to cancel the reality thereof not *altogether*, but only *in part*. Hence the conception of limits involves, besides the conceptions of reality and negation, that of *divisibility*, (of *quantitability generally*, not of a *determined* quantity.) This conception is the required X, and hence, through the act Y, *the Ego as well as the Non-Ego is posited divisible.*

9. *The Ego as well as the Non-Ego are posited divisible;* for the act Y can not *succeed* the act of oppositing, for in itself the act of oppositing has shown itself impossible; nor can it *precede* that act, for the act Y occurs merely to make the act of oppositing possible; and divisibility is nothing

but a divisible. Hence, the act Y and the act of oppositing occur in and with each other ; both are one and the same, and are only distinguished in reflection. By oppositing, therefore, a Non-Ego to the Ego, both the Ego and the Non-Ego are posited divisible.

Let us now see whether the here established act has really solved the problem and united the opposites.

The first result is now determined as follows : The Ego is not posited in the Ego in so far, that is, with those parts of reality wherewith the Non-Ego is posited. That part of reality, which is ascribed to the Non-Ego, is canceled in the Ego.

This proposition at present does not contradict the second result : in so far as the Non-Ego is posited, the Ego also must be posited ; for both are posited as divisible in regard to their reality.

And only now can you say of either, it is *something*. For the absolute Ego of the first fundamental principle is not *something*, (has no predicate and can have none ;) it is simply *what* it is. But now *all* reality is in consciousness, and of this reality that part is to be ascribed to the Non-Ego which is not to be ascribed to the Ego, and *vice versa*. Both are something. The Non-Ego is what the Ego is *not*, and *vice versa*. Opposed to the absolute Ego, the Non-Ego is *absolutely nothing*, (but it can be opposed to the absolute Ego only in so far as it is an object of representation, as we shall see hereafter ;) opposed to the divisible Ego, the Non-Ego is a *negative quantity*.

The Ego is to be = Ego, and yet it is also to be opposed to itself. But it is self-equal in regard to consciousness ; and in this consciousness the absolute Ego is posited as indivisible, and the Ego, to which the Non-Ego is opposed, as divisible. Hence, in the unity of consciousness, all the opposites are united ; for in it even the Ego, in so far as a Non-Ego is opposed to it, is opposed to the absolute Ego ; and this is, as it were, the test that the established conception of divisibility was the correct one.

According to our presupposition, which can be proven only through the completion of the science of knowledge, only one absolute unconditioned, one in its content conditioned, and one in its form conditioned principle is possible. Hence, no further principle can be possible. All that is unconditionally and absolutely certain has been exhausted, and I might express the total in this formula :

The Ego opposits in the Ego a divisible Non-Ego to a divisible Ego.

Beyond this cognition no philosophy can go ; but every thorough philosophy ought to go to it, and by doing so will become science of knowledge. Whatsoever is hereafter to occur in the system of the human mind must be deducible from what we have here established.

We have united the opposites, Ego and Non-Ego, through the conception of divisibility. By abstracting from the content (the Ego and Non-Ego) and looking at the *mere form of uniting opposites through the conception of divisibility,* we obtain the logical proposition of the *ground;* that is, A is in part —A, and *vice versa.* Every opposite is related to its opposite in one characteristic $= X$; and all equals are opposed to each other in one characteristic X. Such an X is called, in the first instance, *ground of relation;* in the second instance, *ground of distinction.* This logical proposition our third fundamental principle both *proves* and *determines.*

Proves: for every opposite $= -A$ is opposed to an A, and this A is posited. Through the positing of a —A you both cancel and do not cancel A. Hence, you only cancel A in part; and instead of the X in A, which is not canceled, you have posited in —A not —X, but X itself; and hence A is $= -A$ in X.

Again, every opposite $(= A = B)$ is self-equal by virtue of being posited in the Ego: $A = A$, $B = B$.

Now, you posit $B = A$; hence, B is not posited through A, for then it would be $= A$ and not $= B$. (You would have only posited one, and not two.)

But if B is not posited through the positing of A, then it is in so far $= -A$; and through the

8

positing of both as equal, neither A nor B, but an X, is posited, which X is = X and = A and = B.

Thus it appears how the proposition A = B can be valid, which in itself contradicts the proposition A = A. X = X, A = X, B = X; hence, A = B in so far as both is = X; but A = —B in so far as both is = —X.

Opposites are related and equals opposed to each other in only *one* part. For, if they were opposed in many parts, that is, if the opposites themselves contained opposite characteristics, one of both would belong to that wherein they are equal, and hence they would not be opposites, and *vice versa*. Every grounded judgment has, therefore, only one ground of relation and one ground of distinction. If it has more, it is not one judgment, but many judgments.

Determines: for only on condition that many things are posited at all as equals or as opposites, are they thus opposed or related in one characteristic. But it is by no means asserted that absolutely every thing which may occur in our consciousness, must be equal to another and opposed to a third.

A judgment, therefore, concerning that to which nothing can be related or opposed, does not come at all under the rule of this proposition of the ground, for it is not under the condition of its validity; it is not grounded, since, on the contrary, itself grounds all possible judgments; it has no ground, but furnishes itself the ground of all grounded. The object of all such judgments is the absolute Ego, and all judgments, whereof it is the subject, are valid absolutely and without further ground; whereof more below.

The act whereby, in comparing a twofold, you look up the mark wherein they are *opposites*, is called the *antithetical* proceeding, generally spoken of as *analytical*, which expression, however, is less proper; partly because it permits the opinion that you can develop something out of a conception which you have not previously put into it by a synthesis, and partly because the expression *antithetical* signifies more clearly that it is the opposite of synthetical. For the *synthetical* proceeding consists in this, that in opposites that characteristic is looked up wherein they are *equal*. In the mere logical form, judgments of the first class are called antithetical or negative, and judgments of the latter class synthetical or affirmative judgments.

Again: since we discovered, in the development of our third principle, that the act of uniting opposites in a third is not possible without the act of oppositing, and *vice versa*, it also follows that in logic antithesis and synthesis are inseparable. No antithesis—no positing of equals as opposites—without synthesis — without the previous positing of the equals as equals. No synthesis—no positing of opposites as equals — without antithesis — without the previous positing of the opposites as opposites. (As far as the content is concerned, mere analytical judgments have, therefore, no existence; and not only do they not carry us far, as Kant remarks, but they do not advance us a single step.)

Kant's celebrated question, which he placed at the head of his Critic of Pure Reason, How are synthetical judgments *à priori* possible ? has now been answered in the most universal and satisfactory manner. In our third principle we have established a synthesis between the opposites, Ego and Non-Ego, by means of the posited divisibility of both, concerning the possibility of which no further question can be asked nor any further ground assigned ; it is absolutely possible, and we are justified in establishing it without further ground. All other syntheses, which are to be valid, must be involved in this one ; must have been established in and with this one ; and as soon as this is proven, the most convincing proof has been shown up that they are equally valid.

Must be involved in this one; and this shows us at the same time in the most determined manner, how we must henceforth proceed in the development of our science. It is syntheses we are to obtain, and hence our whole course of proceeding hereafter will be synthetical ; every proposition will contain a synthesis. (At least in the theoretical part of our science, for in the practical part the very reverse is the case, as will appear hereafter.) But no synthesis is possible without a previous analysis ; from this analysis, however, in so far as it is an *act*, we abstract, and only look up its product— the opposites. Hence, at every proposition here-

THE SCIENCE OF KNOWLEDGE.

after we shall begin by looking up the opposites involved in it, and which are to be united. Again,
all our syntheses are to be involved in the highest synthesis, just shown up, and to be developed
out of it. Hence, it will be our task to look
up in the Ego and Non-Ego, which that synthesis
unites, some opposite characteristics, which have not
been united; and to unite these opposites through
a new ground of relation, which, again, must be involved in the highest ground of relation; next, it
will be our task to look up new opposites in the opposites united by this second synthesis, and to unite
them in a third synthesis; and to continue this
course until we arrive at opposites which can no
longer be perfectly united, whereby we shall then
be forced to enter the practical part of our science.

As antithesis is not possible without synthesis,
and *vice versa*, so neither is possible without a thesis; that is, without an absolute positing, whereby
a certain A (the Ego) is posited, not as the equal
of any other, nor as the opposite of any other, but is
absolutely posited. This, when applied to our system, gives it completeness and surety. It must be
a system and one system; the opposites must be
united so long as opposites still exist, and until the
absolute unity is produced; which absolute unity,
as will be shown hereafter, can, however, only be
produced by a completed approach to the infinite,
that is to say, never in time.

The necessity to opposit and unite in the above
determined manner, rests immediately on our third

fundamental principle ; the necessity to unite at all, rests on the first highest and absolutely uncondi- tioned principle. The *form* of the system is ground- ed in the highest synthesis ; but *that* a system is to be at all, is grounded in the absolute thesis.

There is, however, another application of our above remark which can not be left unnoticed here ; that is, its application to the form of judg- ments. For as we had synthetical and antithetical judgments, we shall also doubtless find thetical judgments, which in some respect will be utterly opposed to the former. For the correctness of an- tithetical and synthetical judgments always pre- supposed a ground, and a double ground, namely, one of relation and one of distinction. A thetical judgment would, therefore, be one wherein some- thing would not be related or opposed to another, but would only be posited as equal to itself ; hence, it would presuppose neither a ground of distinction nor of relation. But since the logical form requires some presupposition, this presupposition in theti- cal judgments could only be a *problem* to find a ground.

The highest judgment of this kind is *I am*, wherein nothing is asserted of the Ego, the place of the predicate being left empty for any possible infinite determination of the Ego. All other judg- ments (involved in this highest one) are of the same kind. For instance, Man is free. You may consider this either as a positive judgment—in which case it signifies, man belongs to the class of free

beings ; and in that case a ground of relation ought
to be shown up between man and the class of free
beings, which ground as ground of that freedom
ought to be contained in the conception of free beings generally, and particularly of man ; but, far
from being able to show up such a ground, we can
not even point out a class of free beings ; or you
may consider it as a negative judgment, in which
case you posit man in opposition to all beings, which
are subject to the law of natural necessity ; but
then you must first point out the ground of distinction between necessity and not-necessity ; and
you must show that the latter is *not* involved in the
conception of man, but is involved in the conception of the opposite beings ; and at the same time
you must show a ground of relation wherein both
are equal. But man, in so far as the predicate of
freedom can be applied to him, that is, in so far as
he is absolute, and not represented nor representa-
ble subject, has nothing in common with the beings
of nature, and hence also is not to be opposed to
them. Still, the logical form of the judgment,
which is positive, demands that both conceptions be
united. But they can not be united in any conception, and can only be united in the idea of an Ego,
the consciousness whereof is determined by nothing external, but which rather through its mere consciousness determines all external ; and such an idea
itself is not thinkable, but involves for us a contradiction. Yet it is posited for us as our highest

practical destination.   Man is to draw infinitely
nearer to the in itself unattainable freedom.

Thus, again, the æsthetical judgment : A is beautiful (that is, in A is a characteristic which is also
in the idea of the beautiful) is a thetical judgment ;
for I can not compare that characteristic with the
ideal, since I do not know the ideal.   It is rather a
problem given to me, which is the result of my absolute self-positing, to discover that ideal ; but this
problem can only be solved in a completed attainment of the infinite, that is, never in time.

Hence, Kant and his successors have called these
judgments very properly *infinite* judgments ; although not one, so far as I know, has explained
them in a clear and definite manner.

It appears, therefore, that for thetical judgments
no *ground* can be adduced ; but their general possibility and validity is grounded in the absolute
self-positing of the Ego.   It is useful, and will furnish the clearest insight into our science, if this
manner of grounding thetical judgment is compared
with that of grounding antithetical and synthetical
judgments.

All opposites, which are opposed in a conception
expressing their ground of distinction, agree in a
higher (more universal) conception, which is called
the conception of species ; that is, a synthesis is
presupposed, which contains both opposites, and in
so far as they are equal to each other.   Gold and
silver, for instance, are contained in the higher conception of metal.   (Hence, the logical rule of defi-

nition, that it must state the higher conception, the ground of relation, and the specific difference, which constitutes the ground of distinction.)

Again, all equals are opposed to each other in a *lower* conception, expressive of some particular determination abstracted from in the higher conception ; that is, all synthesis presupposes a previous antithesis. For instance, in the conception Body, you abstract from the peculiar determination of color, weight, smell, etc. ; and hence any thing which fills space, and is impenetrable, and has weight, may now be a body, however different in regard to those specific determinations. (The science of knowledge determines *what* determinations are more universal or more special, and hence what conceptions are higher or lower. A conception is higher in proportion as the mediating conceptions, whereby it is deduced from the highest, (that of reality,) are less. Y is a lower conception than X, if X occurs first in the series of its deduction from the highest conception, and *vice versa.*)

Quite different is it in regard to the absolutely posited, the Ego. A Non-Ego is posited in relation to it, and at the same in opposition to it, not in a *higher* conception, however, (which in that case would contain both, and would presuppose a higher synthesis, or at least a higher thesis,) but in a *lower* conception. The Ego itself is posited into a lower conception, that of divisibility, so that it may be posited in relation (equality) to the Non-Ego ; and in the same conception of divisibility it is also opposited to the Non-Ego. Hence, there is here no ascent, as in every other synthesis, but a *descent*. The Ego and the Non-Ego, as posited in equality and opposition to each other, are both something (accidences) in the Ego, as divisible substance, and posited through the Ego as absolute and unli-/ mitable substance, to which nothing is equal and nothing opposed. Hence, all judgments, of which the limitable or determinable Ego is logical sub-ject, or of which something that determines the Ego is logical subject, must be limited or deter-mined through something higher ; but all judg-ments, of which the absolute, undeterminable Ego is logical subject, can be determined by nothing higher, because the absolute Ego is determined through nothing higher ; they have their ground and their determination altogether in themselves. Now, in this consists the essence of critical philo-sophy, that an absolute Ego is established as abso-lutely unconditioned and determinable by nothing higher than itself ; and in following up the results of this fundamental principle that philosophy be-comes science of knowledge.

On the other hand, that philosophy is called dog-matic, which establishes something else as both equal and opposed to the Ego ; which something else is its pretendedly higher conception of the *thing (ens)* arbitrarily established by that philo-sophy as the *highest* of all conceptions. In critical philosophy the thing is posited in the Ego, in dog-matic philosophy the Ego in the thing ; critical phi-

losophy is, therefore, *immanent*, because it posits all
in the Ego; dogmatism is, on the contrary, transcendent, because it proceeds beyond the Ego. In so far
as dogmatism can be logical, Spinozism is its most
logical product. If you wish to treat dogmatism
from its own stand-point, as should be done, ask it
why it assumes a thing in itself without higher
ground, whereas it did ask for a higher ground in
the case of the Ego. Ask the dogmatist, Why do
you accept the thing as absolute, since you would
not accept the Ego as absolute? He can show no
warrant for so doing, and you are perfectly justified
in requiring him to hold fast to his own principles,
and to assume nothing without a ground; hence,
to give you again a higher conception as the
ground of the thing, and then again a higher conception for that higher conception, and so on *ad
infinitum.*

A thorough dogmatism either denies altogether
that our knowledge has a ground, and that there is
a system in the human mind, or it contradicts itself. A logical dogmatism is a skepticism, which
doubts that it doubts, for it must cancel the unity
of consciousness, and hence the whole logic. It is,
therefore, no dogmatism, and contradicts itself by
pretending to be one.

Thus Spinoza posits the ground of the unity of
consciousness in a substance wherein it is necessarily determined as well in regard to its content
(that is, in regard to its determined series of representation) as in regard to its form of unity. But I

ask him : What, then, is that, again, which contains
the ground of the necessity *of this substance*, as
well in regard to its content (in regard to the different series of representations contained in it) as
in regard to its form, (the form that in it *all* possible
series of representation are to be exhausted, and
to constitute a complete whole?)   Now for this necessity he gives no further ground, but says : It is
so absolutely ; and he says this because he is compelled to assume some absolute first, some highest
unity ; but if he wants to do this, why did he not
stop at the unity given in consciousness ?   Why
did he go beyond and imagine a higher unity, since
nothing forced him to do so ?*

It would be absolutely impossible to explain how
thinkers ever could have gone beyond the Ego, or,
if they once went beyond it, how they ever could
have come to a stand-still, if there were not a practical reason which explains this phenomenon.   It
was a practical and not a theoretical ground, as
they believed, which drove dogmatists to transcend
the Ego ; namely, a feeling of the dependence of
our Ego, in so far as it is practical, upon a Non-
Ego, which is in so far absolutely not subject to
our legislation, and which is hence in so far free.
Again, it was a practical reason which compelled

(*Translator's Note.*—This criticism of Spinoza applies with equal
force to the school of dogmatic idealists which followed Fichte, and
which found its highest representatives in Schelling and Hegel.
Believing that they must go beyond the Ego and discover some
other absolute—not so " subjective," as they foolishly fancied the
Ego to be—they fell into the same pit.)

them to come to a stand-still somewhere ; namely, the feeling of necessary subordination of the Non-Ego to the practical laws of the Ego. But this subordination has not at all existence as object of a conception, but simply as object of an idea ; as something which is to be effected through us in an endless time, as will appear hereafter.

And thus it appears, after all, that dogmatism is not at all what it pretends to be, and that we have done it wrong in logically carrying out its principles. Its highest unity is indeed no other one than the unity of consciousness, and can be no other one ; and its thing is the substrate of *divisibility* generally, or the highest *substance*, wherein both the Ego and the Non-Ego *(Spinoza's* Intelligence and Extension) are posited.

Far from going beyond the absolute Ego, it never reaches even so far ; at the utmost, as in Spinoza's system, it goes to our second and third principles, but not to the first unconditioned one. It was reserved for critical philosophy to take this last step, and thus to complete the science.

The first part of our system (the theoretical) is really, as will be seen hereafter, systematic Spinozism ; but our system also has a second, practical part, through which the first part is grounded and determined, the whole science of knowledge completed, every thing which occurs in the human mind exhausted, and thus common-sense, which all pre-Kantian philosophy insulted, and which our theoretical system seems to bring into a collision

9

with philosophy, which has no hope of ever being settled, forever reconciled with our science.

By completely abstracting from the *determined* form of the judgment in our third principle, namely, that it is an *oppositing* or *relating* judgment, and looking only at the general manner of acting in it, namely, to limit one through another, we obtain the category of *determination*, (or, as Kant calls it, *limitation.*) For the positing of quantity generally, be it quantity of reality or of negation, is called *determining*.

II.

THEORETICAL PART

OF THE

SCIENCE OF KNOWLEDGE.

THEORETICAL PART

SCIENCE OF KNOWLEDGE.

INTRODUCTORY.

WE have now established three logical propositions : that of *Identity,* which grounds all others ;
and those of *Opposition* and of the *Ground,* which
mutually ground each other in the first. The latter
two make synthesis generally possible, establish
and furnish the ground of its form. Hence, we
need nothing more to be certain of the formal
validity of our future reflection. On the other
hand, the first synthetical act, whereby we have
united the Ego and the Non-Ego, has given us a
content for all future syntheses ; and, hence, we also
need nothing further from this side. Our whole
science of knowledge must be developed out of that
first synthesis.

But, if any thing is to be developed out of it, the
conceptions united in that synthesis must contain
other conceptions not yet established or united,
and our task is, therefore, now to discover them ;
which is done by looking up opposite character-

istics in the conceptions of that synthesis, (which opposites were the Ego and Non-Ego, as mutually determining each other,) and this looking up is done through reflection, which is an arbitrary act of our mind. Our task is to *discover* them now, I said ; and this expression involves the presupposition that they exist already, and are not, therefore, to be artificially made and produced by our reflection, (which, indeed, reflection *could* not do.)   In other words, an originally necessary antithetical act of the Ego is presupposed. Reflection has to discover that act ; and is in so far analytical. For to become conscious of opposite characteristics contained in a cĕrtain conception = A, *as* opposites, is, to analyze that conception A.   In the present instance, however, our reflection is to analyze a conception, not at all given, but which must first be found through the analysis ; and the question arises here, therefore, How can an unknown conception be analyzed ?

No antithetical act without a synthetical act, (§ 3.) Both are one and the same act, distinguished only in reflection.   Hence, from the antithesis we can conclude as to the synthesis, and the third, wherein both are related, we can also establiŝh ; not as pro-. duct of the reflection, but as its discovery ; and as product only of that original synthetical act of the Ego ; which, for the very reason that it is such act, can not enter empirical consciousness.   Hence, we shall hereafter meet only such synthetical acts, but which are not unconditional acts like the first.

Our deduction proves, however, that they are acts of the Ego; for this they are as sure as the first synthesis, from which they result, and with which they constitute one and the same, is an act of the Ego; and that first synthesis is such an act as sure as the highest deed-act of the Ego, that is, its self-positing, is such an act.

Hence, the acts we shall hereafter establish are *synthetical*, although the reflection which establishes them is *analytical*.

Those antitheses, however, which have been pre-supposed for the possibility of an analysis through reflection, must be thought as presupposed, that is, as such from which the possibility of our future synthetical conceptions is dependent. But no anti-thesis is possible without synthesis. Hence, a higher synthesis is presupposed in advance of them, and our first business must be to look this synthesis up and establish it definitely. True, it has been already established in our § 3. But it may appear necessary to determine it in this part of our work more definitely.

DIREMPTION OF THE SYNTHESIS.

The synthesis of our § 3 was this:

In and through the Ego both the Ego and the Non-Ego are posited as each limitable through the other; that is, the reality of the one canceling that of the other, and vice versa.

This synthesis involves the following two pro-positions

1. *The Ego posits the Non-Ego as limited through the Ego.*

This proposition, which, in the practical part of our science will be of vast importance, seems use-less to us here. For as yet the Non-Ego is noth-ing, has no reality ; and it is, therefore, inconceiv-able how the Ego can limit a reality in the Non-Ego, which the Non-Ego has not got as yet. True, the proposition from which it results, the Ego and Non-Ego mutually limit each other, is posited ; but whether that proposition really involves the present one is the as yet problematical part. Perhaps the Ego can only be limited by the Non-Ego, in so far as it has first limited the Non-Ego, as the limiting has first proceeded from the Ego. Perhaps the Non-Ego does not limit the Ego in itself at all, but only the *limiting of* the Ego ; in which case our synthesis would remain true, although no reality were ascribed to the Non-Ego, and although the above problematical proposition were not involved in the synthesis.

2. *The Ego posits itself as limited through the Non-Ego.*

Of this proposition we can make use, and it must be accepted as certain, since it follows from the synthesis. For in it the Ego is posited first as ab-solute reality, and next as limitable reality, and limitable through the Non-Ego.

It will appear that the second proposition grounds the theoretical part of our science, of course only after its completion ; and that the first one grounds the practical part of our science. But since the first one is itself problematical, the possibility of such a practical part also remains as yet problematical. Hence, our reflection must proceed from the theoretical part, although it will appear hereafter that, far from it making possible the practical part, the practical part, on the contrary, makes possible it. (Reason is in itself only practical, and becomes theoretical only in applying its laws to a limiting Non-Ego.) In other words, this seeming subordination in our system of the practical to the theoretical part results from this : That the *think-ability* of the practical principle is grounded in the thinkability of the theoretical principle. And in reflection we only have to do with thinkability. We now begin our task.

A.

GENERAL SYNTHESIS OF THE OPPOSITES OF OUR PROPOSITION.

The Ego posits itself as determined through the Non-Ego. This proposition has been deduced from our synthesis, and hence must be equally valid ; and that synthesis must be valid if the unity of consciousness is to remain, and the Ego is to be Ego. Let us now analyze it, that is, see what opposites it involves. The Ego posits itself as *determined through the Non-Ego.* Hence, the Ego is not to determine, but to be determined ; and the Non-Ego is to determine, that is, to limit the reality of the Ego. Our proposition involves, therefore,

1st. *The Non-Ego determines* (actively) *the Ego*, (in so far passive.)

But, again, *the Ego posits itself*, as determined, through absolute activity. It posits itself, it posits the Non-Ego, it posits both as limitable. It posits itself as determined signifies, therefore, the same as,

2d. *The Ego determines itself*, (through absolute activity.)

Both results evidently contradict each other ; they, therefore, cancel each other, and the proposition which involves them cancels itself. But that proposition can not be canceled if the unity of consciousness is to remain. Hence, we must seek to unite the opposites involved in it. (To unite them, not through an arbitrary invention of reflection, but simply, as we said above, by *discovering* the point of union of these opposites in our consciousness, where this point of union must be, since the opposites must be in it.)

The one proposition affirms what the other denies. Reality and negation are, therefore, to be united, and this is done through limitation or determination.

The Ego determines itself, involves : The Ego is absolute totality of reality. It can determine itself only as reality, for it is posited absolutely as reality, (§ 1,) and no negation is posited in it. And yet it is to *determine* itself. This can not signify, therefore, the Ego cancels part of its reality, for then it would be a self-contradiction ; but it must

signify : The Ego determines the reality, and by
means thereof determines itself. It posits all reality as an absolute quantum, and this reality is posited in the Ego, and there is no other reality but it.
The Ego is, therefore, determined, in so far as the
reality is determined. (This absolute act of the
Ego, whereby it thus determines itself, is indeed
the same as already established in § 3, but in the
present place it was necessary more clearly to de-
fine it.)

Now, the Non-Ego is opposed to the Ego ; and
in it is negation, as reality is in the Ego. If, therefore, absolute totality of reality is posited in the
Ego, absolute totality of negation must be posited
in the Non-Ego ; and the negation itself must be
posited as absolute totality.

Both totalities are to be united through determination. Hence, the Ego *in part determines itself,*
and *in part is determined.*

But both must be thought as one and the same ;
that is, in the same respect in which the Ego is
determined, it must determine itself, and *vice versa.*

The Ego *is determined* signifies : Reality is canceled in the Ego. Hence, if the Ego posits in itself only part of the absolute totality of reality, it
thereby cancels the rest of that totality in itself,
positing this rest, by virtue of the law of opposition, (§ 2,) and of equality of itself and all quantity,
in the Non-Ego, (§ 3.) In other words, whatever
parts of negation the Ego posits in itself, so many
parts of reality it posits in the Non-Ego ; which

reality in the opposite for that very reason cancels the same reality in itself.

The Ego, therefore, posits negation in itself, in so far as it posits reality in the Non-Ego, and *vice versa ;* it therefore posits itself as *determining itself* in so far as it is *determined,* and as *determined* in so far as it *determines* itself, and our problem seems solved.

We have thus undertaken a new synthesis. The conception it establishes is involved under the higher conception of *determination,* for it posits quantity. But if it is to be a new and other conception, it must have a ground of distinction from the higher one. This its specific difference is, that, while the higher conception of *determination* generally *establishes quantity,* without investigating the How ? or In what manner ? our present synthetical conception establishes the *quantity of the one through that of its opposite,* and *vice versa.* This more determined determination may, therefore, be called, *Reciprocal Determination.* (Kant calls it *Relation.*)

B.

PARTICULAR SYNTHESIS OF THE OPPOSITES CONTAINED IN THE FIRST OF THE OPPOSITES OF OUR PROPOSITION, THROUGH THE CONCEPTION OF RECIPROCAL DETERMINATION.

If the fundamental proposition of our theoretical part is to involve all the opposites, which are here to be united, and if, moreover, we could unite these opposites generally through the conception of reciprocal determination, then the opposites again involved in these first opposites must also be already indirectly united through that conception ; or, in other words, the synthetical conception, which unites these new opposites, must already be involved in the higher conception of reciprocal determination.

Hence, we must proceed with this conception precisely as we did with the conception of *determination* generally, that is, restrict its sphere to a smaller extent by an additional condition ; whereby we shall obtain synthetical conceptions, involved under the higher conception of reciprocal determination.

The first opposite discovered in our proposition was this : *The Non-Ego is to determine the Ego ;* that is, to cancel reality in the Ego. This it can only on the condition that it has in itself the same part of reality to be canceled in the Ego. Result : *The Non-Ego has in itself reality.*

But *all reality is posited in the Ego ;* and the non-Ego is opposed to the Ego, and hence has only negation. All Non-Ego is negation, and *it, therefore, has no reality at all in itself.*

Both results cancel each other ; but they are involved in the result : the Non-Ego determines the Ego. Hence, that result cancels itself. But it can not cancel itself without destroying the unity of consciousness. Hence, it can not cancel itself ; and the opposites must be unitable.

Our conception of reciprocal determination did
10

not unite them ; for by it we only obtained this result : *If* the absolute totality of reality is posited as *divisible*, then we can certainly take parts from the Ego, and *must*, under that condition, posit these parts in its opposite, the Non-Ego. But the question, *How can we posit the reality of the Ego as divisible and abstract parts from it ?* or, What justifies and compels us to establish any reciprocal determination ? was left unanswered.

In other words, Reality is absolutely posited in the Ego. But our § 3 posited the Non-Ego as a *quantum*, and every quantum is a *something*, hence also *reality*. Now, the Non-Ego is to be negation ; hence, as it were, a real negation, a negative quantity.

According to the conception of mere relation, it is altogether the same to which of the two opposites you ascribe reality and to which negation. It all depends from which of the two reflection starts. (It is thus in mathematics, a science which completely abstracts from quality, and looks only to quantity.) So also here, as far as the result established by reciprocal determination is concerned. That conception says only, Whatever is negation in the Ego is reality in the Non-Ego, and *vice versa ;* leaving it altogether in my discretion to call the Ego reality or negation. That conception establishes only a *relative* reality. This ambiguity must be removed, or the whole unity of consciousness is canceled ; for, if it is not removed, the Ego is reality and the non-Ego is also reality ; both are no longer opposites, and the Ego is not $=$ Ego, but is $=$ Non-Ego.

We must, therefore, try to remove this ambiguity ; and by removing it we shall probably be enabled to unite the contradiction discovered in the proposition : *the Non-Ego determines the Ego.*

The Ego is the source of all reality. But the Ego *is* because it *posits itself*, and *vice versa.* Hence, to *posit itself* and *to be* is the same. But the conceptions of *self-positing* and of *activity* generally are also one and the same. All *reality* is, therefore, *active ;* and every thing *active* is reality. Activity is *positive* (in opposition to mere *relative*) reality.

It is important to think this conception of activity here *pure.* It is to signify nothing not contained in the absolute self-positing of the Ego ; nothing not immediately contained in the *I am.* Hence, not only all *conditions of time*, but also all *object* of activity, must here be abstracted from. In positing itself, the deed-act of the Ego is not directed upon any object at all, but simply returns into itself. Only when the Ego arrives at representing itself does it become object.

The Ego is to be determined, that is, reality or *activity* is to be canceled in it. Hence, the opposite of activity is posited in it, namely, *passivity.* For passivity is positive negation, in opposition to, mere relative negation. (Of course, here also all *conditions of time* must be abstracted from, as well as an activity producing this passivity. For passivity is as yet the mere negation of the above pure conception of activity, and, of course, its *quantita-*

tive negation, since that conception of activity is
also quantitative ; and since the mere negation of
activity, without regard to quantity, would be = O
or *rest.* Every thing in the Ego, which is not thus
immediately in virtue of the *I am,* which is not immediately posited in the self-positing of the Ego, is
for the Ego *passivity,* or affection generally.)

If the absolute totality of reality is to remain
when the Ego is passive, then, by the law of reciprocal determination, an equal degree of activity
must be transferred into the Non-Ego.

And this solves the above contradiction. The
*Non-Ego has no reality in itself as Non-Ego, but it
has reality in so far as the Ego is passive,* by the law
of reciprocal determination.

This result, that the Non-Ego has (at least as yet)
no reality for the Ego, except in so far as the Ego
is affected, is very important in its consequences.

The here deduced synthetical conception is involved in the higher one of reciprocal determination, for the quantity of the one is in it determined
through that of the other. But it is also specifical-
ly different from it. For under the conception of
reciprocal determination, it was all the same to
which of the two reality or negation was ascribed ;
only quantity and mere quantity was determined.
Whereas here it is not the same, but decided which
of the two has reality and which negation ? The
present synthesis posits, therefore, *activity ;* and the
same degree of activity in the one as of passivity
in its opposite.

This synthesis is called the synthesis of *causality.* That to which activity is ascribed, and in so far *not passivity,* is called *cause,* (original reality ;) that to which *passivity* is ascribed, and in so far *not activity,* is called *effect,* (dependent reality.)

(Here also empirical time conditions must be altogether abstracted from. Partly because we have not yet deduced time, and have, therefore, no right to use its conception ; partly because it is untrue that the cause, *as* such, that is, as active in the effect, must be thought in time in advance of the effect. Cause and effect, by virtue of their synthe- ᴠ tic unity, are to be thought as one and the same. Not the cause, as such, but the substance, to which the causality is attributed, precedes the effect in time, from reasons which will appear hereafter. But in this respect the substance in which the effect occurs also precedes the effect produced in it.)

C.

PARTICULAR SYNTHESIS OF THE OPPOSITES CONTAINED IN THE SECOND OF THE OPPOSITES OF OUR PROPOSITION, THROUGH THE CONCEPTION OF RECIPROCAL DETERMINATION.

The second opposite discovered in our fundamental proposition was this :

The Ego determines itself. This proposition contains itself two opposites, namely :

1st. The Ego *determines* itself ; is *active.*

10*

2d. It determines *itself;* is that which is determined, and hence is *passive.*

That is to say, the Ego is, in one and the same
act, both active and passive ; which doubtless is a
contradiction.   This contradiction must be solved
through the conception of reciprocal determination.
It would be completely solved if its two opposites
could be thus interpreted : *The Ego determines its
passivity through its activity, and vice versa.*   For
in that case it would be both active and passive in
one and the same act.   The question is, *Is* that in-
terpretation correct, and *how* can it be correct ?

The possibility of all determination (measuring)
presupposes a standard of a measure.   This standard can only be the Ego, because only the Ego is
absolutely posited.

Now, in the Ego is posited reality.   Hence, the
Ego must be posited as *absolute totality* (hence, as
a *quantum,* containing all *quanta,* and being, therefore, a measure for all quanta) of reality ; and it
must be thus posited originally and absolutely, if
our problematical synthesis is to be possible, and the
contradiction satisfactorily solved.

The Ego, therefore, posits absolutely—without
any ground, and under no possible condition—*absolute totality of reality* as a quantum, beyond which
no greater quantum is possible ; and this absolute
maximum of reality it posits *in itself.*   (Every
thing posited in the Ego is reality ; and all reality
which is, is posited in the Ego.   (§ 1.)   But this

reality is a quantum, and an absolutely posited quantum. (§ 3.))

Through this absolutely posited standard, the quantity of a deficiency of reality is to be determined. But deficiency is nothing, and the deficient is nothing, (is not determined.) Hence, it can only be thus determined, that the *remaining reality* be determined. The Ego can, therefore, only determine the restricted quantity of its *reality ;* and only through this determination of a quantity of reality is it possible to determine the quantity of *negation,* (by means of reciprocal determination.)

A determined quantum of reality is itself negation, namely, *negation of the totality.* Every determined quantum is Non-Totality.

But if such a quantum is to be *opposited* to totality, and hence *related* to it, a ground of relation of both must be shown up ; and this ground is the conception of *divisibility.* (§ 3.)

In the absolute totality there are no parts ; but it can be related to and opposed to parts ; and thus the above contradiction is solved.

To show this more clearly, let us reflect on the conception of reality. This conception is equal to the conception of activity. All reality is posited in the Ego signifies, all activity is posited in the Ego ; all in the Ego is reality signifies, the Ego is *only* active ; it is Ego only in so far as it is active, and in so far as it is not active it is Non-Ego.

All passivity is not-activity. Passivity can, therefore, be only determined by being related to activity. A ground of relation must, therefore, be shown up. This can only be the general ground of relation of reality and negation ; that is, quantity. Passivity is relatable to activity through quantity signifies : *Passivity is a quantum of activity.*

To think a quantum of activity presupposes a standard of activity, that is, *activity generally ;* (what we called above totality of reality.) The quantum generally is the measure.

If *all* activity is posited in the Ego, then the positing of a quantum of activity is a *lessening* of that activity ; and such a quantum, in so far as it is not the *total* activity, is passivity, although *in itself* it is activity.

Hence, through the positing of a quantum of activity, and through the opposition of this quantum to activity—not in so far as it is *activity generally,* but in so far as it is *all* (the total) activity—a passivity is posited ; that is, that quantum of activity *as* such is itself posited and *determined* as passivity.

We have now found an X which is reality and negation, activity and passivity together.

X is *activity* in so far as it is related to the Non-Ego, because it is posited in the Ego, in the positing, active Ego.

X is *passivity* in so far as it is related to the totality of activity. It is not that acting generally, but is a *determined* acting ; a particular manner of acting contained in the sphere of general acting.

Illustration.

Draw a circular line, = A ; and the whole plane inclosed by it, = X, is opposed to the infinite plane of infinite space which remains excluded.   Now, draw within A another circular line, = B, and the plane inclosed by it, Y, is, firstly, included in A, and, together with the X of A, opposed to the infinite space excluded by A ; hence, in so far, fully equal to X.   But if you regard Y as, secondly, included in B, it is opposed to the infinite space excluded by B, and hence also opposed to that part of X which is not contained in it.   Y is, therefore, opposed to itself ; it is either a part of the plane X, or it is its own plane Y.

Again, *I think* is, firstly, an expression of activity ; the Ego is posited as *thinking*, and in so far as *active.*   It is also an expression of negation, of passivity ; for thinking is a particular determination of the Ego, and the conception thereof excludes all other determinations.   Hence, the conception of thinking is opposed to itself ; it signifies an activity when related to the thought object, and a passivity when related to the Ego generally, for the Ego must be limited if thinking is to be possible.

Every possible predicate of the Ego signifies a limitation thereof.   The subject Ego is the absolutely active, or self-positing.   Through the predicate, I think, I represent, etc., this activity is included in a determined sphere.

It is now clear enough how the Ego can deter-

mine through its activity its passivity, and how it
can be both active and passive together.   It determines itself, is the *determining*, the active, in so far
as through absolute spontaneity it posits itself in
one of all the spheres contained in the totality of
its reality ; and in so far as we reflect merely on
this its absolute *positing* itself into the sphere, and
not on the limit of the sphere.

It is *determined*, passive, in so far as we look upon
it merely as posited in this limited sphere, abstracting from the spontaneity of the positing.   We have
found the original synthetical act of the Ego, whereby our contradiction has been solved ; and through
it we have discovered a new synthetical conception
which we have still to examine a little closer.   Like
the above conception of causality, it is a closer
determined reciprocal determination ; and we shall
obtain in both conceptions the completest insight
by comparing them with each other.

According to the rules of general determination,
both conceptions, that of causality and our new
one, must be, 1st, Equal to reciprocal determination ; 2d, Opposed to it ; 3d, Equal to each other ;
and, 4th, Opposed to each other.

They are equal to reciprocal determination in
this, that in them, as in it, activity is determined
through passivity, or reality through negation, and
vice versa.

Opposed to it in this, that, whereas by the conception of reciprocal determination a reciprocity is
only posited, but not determined, these two concep-

tions determine the order of the reciprocity, and fix
the rule by which to go from reality to negation, or
vice versa.

Equal to each other, because in both conceptions
the *order* is fixed.

Opposed to each other in regard to the order of
the reciprocity. In the conception of causality, activity is determined through passivity ; in our present conception, passivity is determined through
activity.

In so far as the Ego is regarded as embracing ˅
the whole absolutely determined sphere of all realities, it is *substance.* In so far as the Ego is posited
in a *not* absolutely determined sphere, (how such a
sphere may, nevertheless, be determined, we shall
not investigate at present,) in so far the Ego *is accidental ;* or, *there is an accidence in the Ego.* The
limit, which separates acts of this particular sphere
from the whole sphere, is that which makes the accidence accidence, or is the ground of distinction
between substance and accidence. This limit is in
the whole sphere. Hence, the accidence is *in* and
belonging to the substance ; it excludes something
from the whole sphere. Hence, the accidence is
not substance.

No substance is thinkable without relation to an
accidence ; for only through the positing of possible
spheres within the absolute sphere does the Ego
become substance ; only through possible accidences
do *realities* arise ; for otherwise the reality would
be simply one. The realities of the Ego are its ˅

modes of acting; the Ego is substance, therefore, in so far as all its possible modes of acting (all its possible modes of being) are posited in it.

No accidence is thinkable without substance; for, to know something as a *determined* reality, it must be related to *reality in general.*

The substance is *all reciprocity*, (interchange,) *thought in general;* the accidence, a *determined interchanging with another.*

Originally there is only one substance, the Ego. In it are posited all possible accidences, hence all possible realities. How several accidences, having *some particular characteristic* in common, may be comprehended together, and be themselves thought as substances, the accidences whereof are again mutually determined through the *difference* of those characteristics—this we shall see hereafter.

The conception here established is called the conception of *Substantiality.*

In the development of this conception we have left altogether unnoticed, 1st, That activity of the Ego whereby it distinguishes and relates itself as substance and accidence; and secondly, That which induces the Ego to undertake this act. (The latter, we may suppose from our first synthesis, will show itself to be induced by the Non-Ego.) Hence, as in every synthesis, every thing is properly united and connected in the centre; but the two end-points are left unconnected.

This remark shows us again, from a new side, the method of our science. We must always continue to connect the opposites by central links ; but this does not completely solve the contradiction, and only removes it further from us. True, by a new central link we remove the contradiction last shown up ; but, in order to remove it, we have been forced to assume new end-points, which are again opposites, and must again be united.

The true and highest problem to be solved is this : How can the Ego and the Non-Ego immediately determine each other, since they are both complete opposites ?

We place some X between them, upon which both may direct their causality, and thus, at least indirectly, influence each other. But we soon discover that in this X there must also be a point somewhere in which the Ego and Non-Ego immediately connect. To prevent this, we interpose a new link $= Y$. But we soon discover that in Y also there must be a point wherein the opposites immediately connect. And in this way we should continue infinitely, if reason did not interpose its absolute assertion—which the philosopher does not create, but simply show up. There *shall* be no Non-Ego ! The Ego shall be absolutely self-determined ! Whereby the knot is not untied, but cut to pieces.

Or, in so far as the Ego is limited by the Non-Ego, it is finite ; but in itself, as posited through its own absolute activity, it is infinite. These two, infinity and finity, are to be united in the Ego. But such a uniting is in itself impossible. For a

11

long time we allay the conflict through mediation ;
the infinite limits the finite.   But finally, when the
complete impossibility of the uniting is seen, finity
must be altogether canceled ; all limits must vanish,
and the infinite Ego must remain alone as the one
and as all.

Example.

Posit in space $= \Lambda$, in the point m, *light;* and
in the point n, *darkness.*   Now, since space is
continuous, and since there is no *hiatus* between m
and n, there must be between both points somewhere a point o, which point is both light and
darkness.   But this is a contradiction.   Hence, you
place between both a connecting link, *dimness.*
Let this extend from p to q, and dimness will be
limited by light in p, and by darkness in q.   But
thereby you have not solved the contradiction ; for
dimness is mixture of light and darkness.   Now,
light and darkness can limit each other in p only,
if p is both light and dimness together ; and since
dimness is distinguished from light only in this,
that it is also darkness, p must be both light and
darkness together.   So likewise in the point q.   The
contradiction can, therefore, be only solved thus :
Light and darkness are not at all opposites, but are
merely to be distinguished in degrees.   Darkness
is only a very small quantity of light.

It is precisely thus with the Ego and the Non-
Ego.

D.

SYNTHESIS OF THE OPPOSITION BETWEEN THE TWO
DISCOVERED MODES OF RECIPROCAL DETERMINA-
TION, CAUSALITY AND SUBSTANTIALITY.

*The Ego posits itself as determined through the
Non-Ego;* this was the chief synthesis from which
we started, and which could not be canceled without canceling the unity of consciousness. It involved, however, contradictions ; and these we had
to solve. First arose the question : How can the
Ego both *determine* and *be determined ?* By means
of the conception of reciprocal determination we
were enabled to say, to determine and to be determined is one and the same ; by positing a quantum
of negation in itself, the Ego posits the same quantum of reality in the Non-Ego, and *vice versa.* But
the question remained : In which is reality to be
posited, in the Ego or in the Non-Ego ?

By means of the conception of causality we were
enabled to say, negation or passivity must be posited in the Ego ; and hence the same quantum of
reality or activity is posited in the Non-Ego. Then
the question arose : But how can passivity be posited in the Ego ?

Finally, by means of the conception of substantiality we were enabled to say, passivity and activity √√
in the Ego is one and the same ; for passivity is
only a smaller quantum of activity.

But these answers have inclosed us in a circle.

If the Ego posits a smaller degree of activity in
itself, then, of course, it posits passivity in itself,
and activity in the Non-Ego. But the Ego can not
have the power to absolutely posit a lower degree
of activity in itself, since, according to the conception of substantiality, it posits all activity and nothing but activity in itself. Hence, the positing of a
lower degree of activity must be preceded by an
activity of the Non-Ego, which must have first
really canceled a part of the activity of the Ego.
But this is equally impossible, since, according to
the conception of causality, activity can be ascribed
to the Non-Ego only in so far as a passivity is posited in the Ego.

In other words, under the conception of causality
alone, it is well conceivable how an outside observer
could ascribe activity to the Non-Ego ; but not
how the Ego itself could ascribe the cause of its
passivity to the activity of the Non-Ego. The Ego
might be determined, but could never *posit itself as*
determined ; for the passivity in the Ego would be
merely posited in the Ego, but not posited in the
Ego *for itself.*

On the other hand, under the conception of substantiality, even supposing the Ego to have the
power of absolutely limiting itself independently
of any Non-Ego, and, moreover, the power of becoming conscious of this limitation ; what warrant
would the Ego have to refer its limitation to a Non-
Ego ? To assume a Non-Ego as cause of the limitation ? None at all ; on the contrary, it would re-

gard itself as the cause thereof. Hence, the Ego would be determined, but not determined *through the Non-Ego*.

Both conceptions in their separateness, therefore, do not explain what is to be explained, and the contradiction remains : If the Ego posits itself as determined, it is not determined through the Non-Ego; and if it is determined through the Non-Ego, it does not posit itself as determined.

Let us now establish this contradiction more definitely :

The Ego can not posit itself as passive without positing activity in the Non-Ego ; but it can not posit activity in the Non-Ego without positing passivity in itself. Hence, it can do neither alone.

Result :

1. The Ego does not posit passivity in itself, in so far as it posits activity in the Non-Ego, and *vice versa ;* it, therefore, does not posit at all.

(Not the *condition* is denied, but the *conditioned ;* not the rule of reciprocal determination generally, but its application to the present instance.)

2. But the Ego is to posit passivity in itself, and in so far activity in the Non-Ego, and *vice versa.*

The one proposition denies what the second one affirms ; they are, therefore, related like negation and reality. These are united through quantity. Both propositions must be valid, hence they must be valid each only *in part.* Hence :

The Ego posits *partly* passivity in itself, *in so far* as it posits activity in the Non-Ego ; but it posits

11*

partly not passivity in itself, *in so far* as it posits activity in the Ego, and *vice versa.*

The Ego posits *partly* passivity and *partly not* passivity in the Non-Ego, in so far as it posits activity in the Ego.

That is to say, an activity is posited in the Ego, to which no passivity in the Non-Ego corresponds; and an activity in the Non-Ego, to which no passivity in the Ego corresponds. Let us call this sort of activity *independent* activity. But such an independent activity in the Ego and Non-Ego contradicts the law of oppositing, which has now been closer determined by the law of reciprocal determination; hence it contradicts chiefly the conception of reciprocal determination, which rules in our present investigation. For that conception says : All activity in the Ego determines a passivity of the Non-Ego, and *vice versa ;* and our new result establishes an independent activity in the Ego, which does not determine a passivity in the Non-Ego, and *vice versa.*

But both results must be valid. Hence, they must be united in quantity. Both must be valid only in part. The conception of reciprocal determination is to be valid only in part, that is, is itself to be determined, to have its validity confined by a certain rule to a particular extent. Or the independent activity of our result is to be independent only to a certain extent.

- In the Ego is to be an activity determining and determined by a passivity in the Non-Ego ; and in the Non-Ego is also to be an activity determining and determined by a passivity of the Ego. To this activity and passivity the conception of reciprocal determination is applicable.

At the same time, there is to be in the Ego and in the Non-Ego an independent activity, not determining a passivity in the other.

Both propositions are to be valid. It must be possible, therefore, to think them as united through a synthetical conception in one and the same act.

Such a conception would be about as follows:

The *reciprocal activity and passivity determines the independent activity, and the independent activity determines the reciprocal activity and passivity.* If this be true, then,

1. The independent activities of the Ego and Non-Ego do not reciprocally determine each other *directly*, but only indirectly, through their reciprocally determined activity and passivity.

2. And the law of reciprocal determination is valid only in so far as related to the reciprocal activity and passivity and independent activity; but is not valid as related to independent activity alone.

This result involves the following three propositions:

1. An independent activity is determined through reciprocal activity and passivity.

2. An independent activity determines the reciprocal activity and passivity.

3. Both are mutually determined through each other; and it is all the same whether we proceed

from reciprocal activity and passivity to independent activity, or *vice versa*.

I.

*An independent activity is determined through re-
ciprocal activity and passivity.*

Concerning this proposition, we have first to inquire its significance, and next to apply it to the
conceptions of causality and substantiality in their
contradiction.

Its significance. We have said before, that our
present undertaking involves a restriction of the
conception of reciprocal determination. This is
done by showing the ground of the application of
that conception.

According to that conception, by positing activity in the one, (the Ego or Non-Ego,) passivity is
immediately posited in its opposite, and *vice versa*.
It is also clear from the rule of opposition, that, *if*
a passivity is to be posited, it must be posited in
the opposite of the active. But *why* is passivity to
be posited *at all*, that is, why is a reciprocal determination to occur at all?

Activity and passivity, *as* such, are opposed ; and
yet passivity is immediately posited through activity, and *vice versa*. Hence, they must be equal to
each other in a third conception, $= X$, which makes
possible the transition from the one to the other,
without destroying the unity of consciousness.
This third is the *ground of relation* between activity
and passivity in the reciprocity, (§ 3.)

This ground of relation is not dependent upon reciprocal determination, but the latter is dependent upon it, becomes possible only through that ground of relation. True, in reflection, this ground is *posited* through reciprocal determination, but also posited as independent of it and its reciprocity.

This ground is, moreover, *determined* in reflection through the reciprocity ; that is, if the reciprocal determination is posited, the ground of relation of its activity and passivity is posited in that sphere, which contains within it the sphere of reciprocal determination. In other words, through this ground of relation a higher sphere is posited round about the sphere of reciprocal determination. The ground of relation fills up the sphere of determination in general, while reciprocal determination fills up only a part of that sphere.

This ground is a reality ; or, if reciprocal determination is thought as an act, is an activity. And thus an independent activity is determined through reciprocal activity and passivity.

APPLICATION UNDER CONCEPTION OF CAUSALITY.

By means of this conception, which gave us the first instance of an activity and passivity mutually determining each other, an activity of the Non-Ego is posited through a passivity of the Ego. This first instance of a reciprocal determination (of a reciprocity, as we shall usually call it) is now to determine and posit an independent activity.

The reciprocal determination in this instance starts from passivity. Passivity *is* posited, and through and by means of passivity activity is posited. The passivity is posited in the Ego. Hence, if an activity is posited in opposition to the passivity, the activity must be posited in the Non-Ego, the opposite, according to the conception of reciprocal determination. Of course, in this transition from the Ego to the Non-Ego, there is also a ground of relation which we know already as quantity. (The absolute totality of reality or activity is always the same. If only part of it is posited in the Ego, or if passivity is posited in the Ego, the corresponding part of reality or activity is posited in the Non-Ego.) This ground of relation can be properly called here the *ideal* ground ; and, hence, the passivity of the Ego is the ideal ground of the activity of the Non-Ego. (Namely, since the whole activity is *not* posited in the Ego, the part not posited in the Ego is posited in the Non-Ego.)

But *why* is an activity to be posited at all as opposite of the *passivity in the Ego*, from which the conception of reciprocal determination starts. If it is posited, it must, certainly, as we have shown, be posited in the Non-Ego ; but why is it to be posited at all, why is the conception of reciprocal determination to be applied here at all ?

In the Ego *is posited* a passivity ; that is, a quantum of its activity is canceled. This passivity, or this *diminution* of its activity, must have *a ground ;* for the canceled activity is a *quantum,* and every quantum is determined through another quantum, by means of which it is neither a smaller nor a larger quantum, but precisely *this* quantum, according to the law of determination in general, (§ 3.)

In the Ego the ground of this diminution can not be, for the Ego only posits activity in itself, and not passivity ; it posits itself as being, not as not-being. Hence, the ground, by virtue of the law of opposition, (§ 2,) must be posited in the Non-Ego ; or the Non-Ego contains the ground of this diminution.

Here we speak no longer of mere *quantity*, but of *quality*. Passivity is opposed to the Ego here in so far as the Ego is only activity, and hence the ground of it can not be posited in the Ego, but must be posited in the Non-Ego. Now, the ground of a quality is called *real ground.* An activity of the Non-Ego, independent of the reciprocal determination of the two opposites of activity and passivity, nay, presupposed for the very possibility of that reciprocity, is thus the real ground of the passivity of the Ego ; and this independent activity is posited, so that we may have a real ground of that passivity. Hence, through the above reciprocity is posited an independent activity, (of the Non-Ego.)

We have now seen how, through the reciprocity between passivity of the Ego and activity of the Non-Ego, an independent activity of the Non-Ego is *posited* and *determined.* It is posited in order to get a ground for a passivity posited in the Ego ; and hence extends no further than this passivity. There is, hence, no original reality and activity of the Non-Ego for the Ego, except in so far as the Ego is passive. *No passivity in the Ego, no activity in the Non-Ego.* This result is valid even when this activity is spoken of as an activity, independent of the conception of causality. Even the thing in itself is only in so far as the conception of causality extends, and has validity only in so far as, at least, the possibility of passivity is presupposed in the Ego. (A result which will receive its complete determination and applicability only in the practical part of our science.)

Let it, therefore, be well remembered, that the conclusion as to the Non-Ego being real ground is valid only in so far as it is true that the passivity in the Ego is *qualitative;* which it is only in the conception of causality.

As soon as we get to the second reciprocal conception, substantiality, we shall see that under that conception the passivity of the Ego can not be thought at all as *qualitative,* but only as *quantitative,* as diminished activity ; and that under that conception, therefore, the Non-Ego again becomes merely ideal ground.

A philosophy which starts from positing the Non-Ego as cause of all representation, and the representation as its effect, and which thus posits the Non-Ego as the real ground of all, the Non-Ego being simply because it is and what it is, (Spinoza's Fate,) and the Ego being simply an accidence of the Non-Ego, and not substance at all ; such a system is a dogmatic Realism, (or material Spinoz-

ism,) a system which presupposes the impossibility of making the highest abstraction, namely,
abstraction from the Non-Ego ; and which is utterly ungrounded, as it does not establish any final
ground.

On the other hand, a system which makes the
Ego the substance of representation, and representation the accidence of the Ego, the Non-Ego being not real ground thereof at all, but merely ideal
ground, and having, therefore, no reality beyond representation—such a system is a dogmatic Idealism. In such a system no ground can be assigned
for the limitation of reality in the Ego, (for the
affection through which a representation arises.)
Such a system has certainly undertaken the highest
abstraction, and is therefore completely grounded.
But it is incomplete, because it does not explain
what is to be explained.

The true question in dispute between dogmatic
Realism and dogmatic Idealism is, therefore, in
which manner shall we explain Representation ?
Through the conception of Causality ! asserts Realism. Through the conception of Substantiality !
asserts Idealism.

In the theoretical part of our science this question will remain undecided ; or, rather, it will be
answered thus : Both modes of explanation are correct. Under certain conditions you must take the
one, and under certain conditions the other. (A
system which shows up this is a Critical Idealism,
such as Kant has established in completest form.)

But this answer involves human — that is, all finite — reason in self-contradiction ; and this con- tradiction must be solved. It is solved in the prac- tical part of our science.

The absolute being of the Ego can not be relin- quished without annihilating the Ego itself, and hence the question is finally decided in favor of the Ego, precisely as dogmatic Idealism decides it Our Idealism, however, not being dogmatic, does not assert this to be so, but shows, that it SHALL be so. In other words, our system *explains* the problem by positing the Ego (which is in so far practical) as an Ego which *shall* contain in itself the ground of the existence of the Non-Ego, through which the ac- tivity of the Ego *as intelligence* is diminished. This being an (in time) infinite idea, our explanation, in- stead of explaining, rather shows *that* and *why* what is to be explained can not be explained. (Or, that to ask for an explanation is a self-contradiction.)

APPLICATION UNDER CONCEPTION OF SUBSTAN- TIALITY.

By means of the conception of substantiality, through activity in the Ego a passivity in the Ego. is posited and determined. The reciprocal deter- mination of this activity and passivity in the Ego was the second instance of reciprocal determination. which we discovered ; and this reciprocity is also to determine an independent activity.

In themselves, passivity and activity are opposites; and we have seen how it is possible that, through one and the same act which posits a certain quantity of activity in the one, the same quantity of passivity can be posited in its opposite. But it is an evident contradiction that activity and passivity should both together be posited, not in two opposites, but in one and the same, (in the Ego.)

True, this contradiction has been partly solved in the general deduction of substantiality, by showing that passivity is in its quality nothing but diminished activity, and is in its quantity only *not* the totality of activity; and that it, therefore, can be related to the totality of activity, and can thus be posited *as* diminished activity. The ground of relation between both being thus activity.

But if the Ego posits within itself diminished activity, and if the Non-Ego is also to have diminished activity, how are both these diminished activities to be distinguished? that is, how are the Ego and Non-Ego to be distinguished? *For the ground of distinction between the Ego and the Non-Ego has been destroyed.*

Unless this distinction is possible, the required reciprocal determination is also not possible, and indeed none of our deduced determinations are possible. All our deductions would be canceled.

Hence, the diminished activity of the Ego must have a character altogether peculiar to itself, whereby it may be characterized as the activity of the Ego, and can never be taken for activity of the Non-Ego. This character is *absolute positing*, (§ 1.) But absolute signifies unlimited, and yet that activity of the Ego is to be *diminished*, limited. The diminished activity is, therefore, to be both absolute and limited. That is, in so far as it is an acting in general, it is absolute, unconditioned ; you may act or not. But in so far as it is directed upon an object, it is limited ; when you act, the act must be directed upon *this* object, and can not be directed upon any other.

We see, therefore, how this reciprocal determination *posits* an independent activity. For the activity in that reciprocity is itself independent, not however, in so far as it stands in that reciprocity, but in so far as it is *activity.* In so far as it enters the reciprocity, it is limited, and in so far passivity. We see, also, how the reciprocity *determines* this independent activity, that is, in the mere reflection. For the activity was assumed as absolute only in so far as to make possible the reciprocity. Hence, this activity is posited as absolute *only in so far as reciprocal activity and passivity are to be determined by it ;* and itself is, therefore, determined by the extent of this reciprocity. (It is not an *absolute activity in general.*) An absolute activity of this character is called *Power of Imagination,* as we shall see in time.

II.

AN INDEPENDENT ACTIVITY DETERMINES A RECI-PROCAL ACTIVITY AND PASSIVITY.

Let us first obtain the significance of this propo-sition, and its distinction from the former. The former had reference merely to the content of the reciprocity, not to its *form*. It simply said, if a reciprocity is to be, then there must be links which stand in reciprocal relation and can be interchanged. Thus the question arose : How are these links pos-sible ? And then we were led to show up an inde-pendent activity as ground of these links.

But now we have to start from that which con-stitutes the reciprocal determination *as* reciprocity, as an interchange, as a going from one opposite to another. Here, therefore, we do not seek the ground of the *content* of the reciprocity, but the ground of its *form*. This formal ground of the re-ciprocity is also to be an independent activity ; and it is this we now have to prove.

Illustration.

The magnet attracts iron ; iron is attracted by the magnet. These are two exchangeable proposi-tions; that is, through the one the other is posited. This is a presupposed fact, presupposed *as ground-ed ;* and hence, if you look to the *content* of this re-ciprocal relation, you do not ask, *Who* posits the one proposition through the other, and *how* does this

positing occur? You assume the reciprocity as *having occurred* if you look to the *content* of the reciprocity ; and you only ask, Why are *these two* propositions contained among the sphere of propositions, which can be thus posited the one through the
other? There must be something in both which
makes it possible to interchange them.   Hence,
you look up this, their material content, which
makes them interchangeable.

If, however, you look to the *form* of the reciprocity, if you reflect on the *occurring* of the interchange, and hence abstract from the propositions
which are interchanged, then the question no longer is : With what right are *these* propositions interchanged? but simply : *How* is interchange effected
at all? And then it is discovered, that there must
be an intelligent being outside of the iron and magnet, which, observing both and uniting both in its
consciousness, is compelled to give to the one the
opposite predicate of the other ; (to the one the
predicate of *attracting*, to the other the predicate
of *being attracted*.)

The first mode gives simply a reflection upon a
phenomenon ; the second mode a reflection upon
that reflection ; the reflection of the philosopher
upon the mode of observation.

APPLICATION UNDER THE CONCEPTION OF CAUSALITY.

In the reciprocity of *causality*, passivity in the
Ego posits activity in the Non-Ego. The mere
formal expression of this reciprocity is a positing

through a not-positing, that is, a transferring. Such
is the *formal* character of the reciprocity here ; and,
hence, such is the *material* character of the activity
which establishes that reciprocity. This activity
is independent of the reciprocity, since the latter
only is possible by means of it ; and is independent
also of the two links of the reciprocity *as such ;* for
only through it do they become reciprocally interchangeable, since it is the activity which inter-
changes them. But all positing belongs to the
Ego ; hence this activity of transferring, to make
possible a determination through the conception of
causality, belongs to *the Ego.* The Ego carries
over, transfers, activity from itself into the Non-
Ego ; and thus posits through activity passivity in
itself. In so far as the Ego is active in carrying
over this activity, in so far the Non-Ego is passive ;
activity is *transferred* into it.

(Of course, this contradicts our former conclusion establishing an independent activity of the
Non-Ego ; but we must wait and see how both will
be reunited.) It must also be remembered that
this activity is independent of the reciprocity which
first becomes possible through it. There might be
another reciprocity which does not become possible
through it. Our result, therefore, is this : *Even in
so far as the Ego is passive, it must also be active,
though perhaps not merely active ;* and this result
may be important enough.

In the reciprocity of *substantiality*, activity is to
be posited as limited by means of absolute totality ;
that is to say, that part of the absolute totality
which is excluded by the limit is posited as *not*
posited through the positing of the limited activity.
Hence, the mere formal character of this reciprocity is a *not-positing* by means of a positing. That
which is wanting in the limited activity is posited
in the absolute totality ; is *not* posited in the limited
activity ; it is posited as *not* posited in the reciprocity, (in the reciprocal determination of activity and
passivity.) By this conception of substantiality we
start, therefore, from an absolute positing, from a
positing of the absolute totality.

Hence, the material character of that act, which
itself posits this reciprocity, must also be a not-
positing through a positing, and through an absolute
positing. We abstract utterly from the question
whence the not-positedness in the limited activity
may come, and what may be its ground. The limited act is presupposed as existing, and the only question is: How may it interchange with unlimitedness ?

All positing in general, and particularly absolute
positing, belongs to the Ego ; the act which posits
the present reciprocity starts from absolute positing, and therefore belongs to the Ego. It is independent of the reciprocity, for that becomes possible
only through it. This not positing through a posit-

ing we may call an *externalizing*. A certain quantum of the absolute totality is excluded, externalized,
from the posited diminished activity, is posited as
not contained in it, but as outside of it. The characteristic distinction between the *externalizing* and
the previous *transferring* is this : in transferring
something is certainly also excluded from the Ego ;
but this we do not reflect upon, looking merely to
its being posited again in the opposite, the Non-
Ego. It is a transferring to another. But in externalizing we merely exclude from the Ego, and
do not say whether the excluded be posited in another, and if so in what.

To this activity of externalizing passivity must
be opposed ; and it really is thus. For a part of
the absolute totality *is* externalized, *is* posited, as
not posited. The activity has an object ; a part of
the totality is this object. To what substrate of
reality this passivity may be assigned, whether to
the Ego or to the Non-Ego, is not the question
here ; and it is very important that no other conclusions should be drawn from our result than are
contained in it, and that the form of the reciprocity
be comprehended in all its purity.

(Each thing is what it is ; it has those realities
which are posited when it is posited, (A = A.)
To call something an accidence of a thing is to say
that something is not included in the positing of the
thing, does not belong to its real nature, and is to
be excluded from its original conception. It is this
determination of the accidence which *we* have now

explained. Nevertheless, in another sense the accidence is also ascribed to the thing and posited in it.
How this is done we shall see hereafter.)

III.

BOTH THE RECIPROCITY AND THE ACTIVITY, INDE-PENDENT THEREOF, MUTUALLY DETERMINE EACH OTHER.

Let us again, as heretofore, first try to get at the
significance of this proposition, and then proceed
to apply it. As we have now, however, acquired
a twofold reciprocity, a *form* and a *content* of it, and
also a twofold independent activity, which, on the
one hand, determines the form, and, on the other
hand, is (in reflection) determined by the content of
the reciprocity; we must make more clear the above
proposition by uniting these several links through
the synthesis of reciprocal determination. Hence,
that proposition involves the following three:

(*a.*) The activity, independent of the *form* of the
reciprocity, determines the activity, independent
of its content, and *vice versa;* that is, both are synthetically united and mutually determine each
other.

(*b.*) The form of the reciprocity determines its
content, and *vice versa;* that is, both are synthetically united and mutually determine each other.

(*c.*) The reciprocity (as synthetical unity) determines the independent activity, (as synthetical unity,) and *vice versa;* that is, both determine each
other mutually and are synthetically united.

(*a.*) *The activity independent of the form, and the activity independent of the content of the reciprocity, are mutually to determine each other.*

That activity which is to determine the *form* of the reciprocity, or the reciprocity *as* such, but is to be absolutely independent of it, is a *going over* from one of the links of the reciprocity to the other.

That activity which determines the *content* of the reciprocity is an activity which posits that into the links whereby it is made possible to go from the one to the other.

The latter activity gives the X which is in both links, and can be contained *only in both*, but not in one of them merely ; and which makes it impossible to remain content with the positing of the one link, but forces us to posit at the same time the other link, because it shows up the incompleteness of the one without the other. This X is that to which the unity of consciousness clings, and must cling if no *hiatus* is to arise in it ; it is, as it were, the *conductor* of consciousness.

The former activity is consciousness itself, in so far as it floats òver the interchanging links while clinging to X, and in so far as it is a unit; although it changes its objects, these links, and necessarily, must change them if it is to be a unit.

The former determines the latter signifies, the going from the one link to the other is the ground of the content of the reciprocity ; the latter determines the former signifies, the content of the reciprocal links is the ground of the going from the one to the other as act. Both mutually determine each other signifies, therefore : by positing the mere going over, you posit in each link that which makes this going over possible, and by positing them as reciprocal links you immediately go from the one to the other. The going from one link to the other becomes possible only by *doing* it ; and it is only possible in so far as it is actually done. It is an absolute act without any other ground. The ground of the going over from one link to the other lies in consciousness itself, not outside of it. Consciousness, because it is consciousness, must go from one link to the other, and would not be consciousness if it did not, because a *hiatus* would arise in it.

(*b.*) *The form of the reciprocity and its content are mutually to determine each other.*

The *reciprocity*, as we have said before, is distinguished from the *activity presupposed through it*, by abstracting from this presupposed activity, (for instance, by abstracting from the activity of an intelligence which observes the reciprocity.) In this view, *the interchanging links of the reciprocity are thought as interchanging through themselves ;* we transfer into the things what in truth is only in us. How far such an abstraction may be valid will appear in time.

From such a stand-point, therefore, the links interchange through themselves. And their mutual *joining* is the *form*, while the *activity and passivity*, occurring in this joining, (namely, each joins and is joined,) is the *content* of the reciprocity. We shall call this content here the mutual *Relation* of the interchanging links.

Now, that joining is to determine the relation of the links; that is, immediately and through the mere joining of the links, as *joining*, is the relation to be determined, and *vice versa*. Their joining and their relation is to be one and the same. In other words:

The relation of the links consists in this, that they interchange, and they have no other mutual relation. If they are not posited as interchanging, they are not posited at all.

Again : through this mere form of a reciprocity being posited between them, the content of the reciprocity is immediately and completely determined. The links *interchange* necessarily and only in one possible manner, which is absolutely determined by the very fact that they interchange. If *they* are posited, a determined interchange or reciprocity of them is posited ; and if a determined reciprocity of them is posited, then they are posited. The links and a determined reciprocity are one and the same.

(*c.*) *The independent activity as synthetical unity determines the reciprocity as synthetical unity, and vice versa ; that is, both of these synthetical unities mutually determine each other, and are themselves synthetically united.*

The activity and synthetical unity has been discovered as an absolute going from one link to another, the latter as an in itself absolutely determined joining. The former determines the latter signifies, by the going from one link to the other their joining is posited. The latter determines the former signifies, as the links join, the activity must neces-

sarily go from the one to the other. Both determine each other mutually signifies, the positing of
the one posits the other, from each you can and
must proceed to the other. It is all one and the
same, and the whole is absolutely posited ; rests on
itself. To make this important result clearer, we
apply it to the propositions involved in it.

The activity which determines the form of the
reciprocity determines all that occurs in the reciprocity, and *vice versa.* Determines the form: that
is, the mere reciprocity in its form, or the joining
of the links, is not possible without the act of going from the one to the other, and only through the
going from the one link to the other is their joining
posited ; and *vice versa.* No joining of the links, no
going from the one to the other ; no going from the
one to the other, no joining. Both is one and the
same, and is distinguishable only in reflection.

Determines also the content: that is, through the
necessary going from one of the links to the other
these reciprocal links are first posited *as such,* and
indeed since they are only posited *as* such, posited
at all, and *vice versa ;* through the positing of these
links as interchanging links is the activity first
posited which goes from the one to the other.

Hence, you may start from which of the moments
you will, the positing of the one always involves
the positing of the other three.*

* Four moments and their unity, that is to say, five in all. This
fivefold FICHTE has shown up in other works with particular ear-
nestness, as occurring in every synthesis of consciousness.—TRANS-
LATOR'S NOTE.

THE SCIENCE OF KNOWLEDGE. 147

The activity which determines the content of the reciprocity determines the whole reciprocity: that is, it posits that by means of which the going over is made possible, and hence necessary. It therefore posits the activity of the form, and through it all the rest.

Hence, the activity returns into itself by means of the reciprocity, and the reciprocity returns into itself by means of the activity. Every thing reproduces itself, and no *hiatus* is possible; from each link you are driven to all the others. The activity of the form determines that of the content; the activity of the content determines the content of the reciprocity; the content of the reciprocity determines its form; the form of the reciprocity the activity of the form, etc. They are all one and the same synthetical condition. The act returns into itself through its circular movement. But the whole circular movement is absolutely posited. It is because it is, and there is no higher ground for it.

And now, having shown the full significance of our proposition, let us proceed to apply it as heretofore.

APPLICATION UNDER THE CONCEPTION OF CAUSALITY.

Our proposition was : *The reciprocity and the activity independent of it are mutually to determine each other.*

According to the just established scheme this involves the following :

1st. The activity of the form determines that of the content, and *vice versa.*

2d. The form of the reciprocity determines its content, and *vice versa.*

3d. The synthetically united activity determines the synthetically united reciprocity, and *vice versa.*

I.—*The activity of the form determines that of the content, and vice versa.*

As mere form, this activity was characterized as a transferring, that is, a positing through a not-positing. This activity of the form is to determine the activity of the content of the reciprocity, which latter was found to be an independent activity in the Non-Ego, which made possible a passivity in the Ego. This latter is determined by the former, means : The activity is posited in the Non-Ego through the Ego, but only *in so far* as something is *not* posited. The activity of the Non-Ego is thus inclosed in a limited sphere, that is, *in the activity of the form.* The Non-Ego is active only in so far as it is posited active through the Ego, in virtue of a not-positing. No positing by a not-positing—no activity of the Non-Ego. But, on the other hand, the activity of the content, or the independent activity of the Non-Ego, is to determine that of the form, that is, the transferring or the positing through a not-positing.

This means, therefore : the activity of the Non-Ego is to determine the transferring *as* a transferring ; or, it is to posit the X, whereby the incompleteness of the one link is shown up, and thus the necessity of positing it, as interchanging link, or as a link in reciprocity with another link. This second link is a passivity, *as* passivity. Hence, the Non-Ego is the ground of a *not*-positing, and thus determines and conditions the activity of the form. No activity of the Non-Ego, no positing through a not-positing.

Here we have again the conflict of Realism, which says that activity can not be transferred unless an independent reality of the Non-Ego is presupposed ; and of Idealism, which says, that all reality of the Non-Ego is simply transferred to it by the Ego. This conflict is to be reconciled.

This is done in the following synthesis :

Activity in the Non-Ego is passivity in the Ego, and both are altogether one and the same. Neither is the ground of the other ; both are one and the same act. In so far as the Ego does not posit in itself, it posits in the Non-Ego, that is, in so far *it is itself Non-Ego*.

Let us explain this : When the Non-Ego is considered as limiting the Ego, it is not considered at all as *positing*, but merely as canceling ; hence, it is opposed to the Ego as *qualitatively* distinct, is *real ground* of a determination in the Ego. But when the Ego is viewed as limiting itself, it is still viewed as positing ; that is, as positing a negative ; hence, as in part positing, and in part not-positing. The Ego is, therefore, only *quantitatively* opposed to it-

self—is only the *ideal ground* of a determination
in itself ; and since it posits that which it does not
posit in itself, in the Non-Ego, it is the ideal ground
of the reality of the Non-Ego, to which that determination corresponds.   But that the ideal ground
should thus become a real ground in the Non-Ego,
this is what common sense can not comprehend.

Ideal ground and real ground are, therefore, one
and the same.   The reason why common sense
refuses to comprehend it is because it considers
the Ego as an external thing.   Just as in external things we distinguish the real ground of their
mutual relation, that is, the independent content
or quality which makes them related ; and the
ideal ground of their relation ; that is, that *we*
posit them as related ; so common consciousness
posits its Ego as an external thing, related to other
things by an inherent something ; for instance, as
the magnet is related to iron.   But in the Ego
positing itself is the same as *being*.   In it real and
ideal ground are one and the same.   Again, not
positing itself, and not being, is for the Ego the
same.   The Ego does not posit something as itself
means, the Ego is not that something.   The Non-
Ego is to influence the Ego means, it is to cancel
a positing in the Ego ; it is to cause the Ego *not* to
posit.

Again, the Ego is to recognize a Non-Ego means,
it is to posit reality in the Non-Ego ; for the Ego
recognizes no other reality but what itself posits.

Activity of the Ego and of the Non-Ego are one

and the same means : the Ego can only posit something *not* in itself, by positing it in the Non-Ego ;
and can only posit in itself by *not* positing in the
Non-Ego. The Ego must posit, however, as sure
as it is an Ego ; but it need not posit *in itself.*

Passivity of the Ego and of the Non-Ego is also
one and the same. The Ego does not posit something in itself means, that something is posited in
the Non-Ego.

Activity and passivity of the Ego are one and
the same. For what the Ego does *not* posit in
itself it posits in the Non-Ego.

Activity and passivity of the Non-Ego are one
and the same. In so far as the Non-Ego is to influence the Ego, to cancel something in the Ego,
this something has been posited in the Non-Ego
by the Ego.

Thus the synthetical solution is complete. None
of the moments are grounds of the others ; all are
one and the same.

The question, What is the ground of the passivity in the Ego ? is, therefore, not a proper one, for
there is no such passivity. But one question may
be put : What is the ground of this whole reciprocity ? To say simply it is because it is, is not
allowable, for only the Ego is absolutely posited ;
and the mere Ego does not involve this reciprocity.
Such a ground, however, if it is to be found, is not
to be found in the theoretical part of the science of
knowledge, because it is not involved in its fundamental principle, that " the Ego posits itself as

determined by the Non-Ego." On the contrary, the theoretical part presupposes such a ground.

At the same time, our expression, " limited, restricted activity of the Ego," is now perfectly clear. It is an activity which is directed upon something in the Non-Ego, hence an objective activity. The activity of the Ego generally is not at all limited, and can not be limited ; but its positing of *the Ego* is limited by this, that it must posit a Non-Ego.

II.—*The form and the content of the reciprocity determine each other mutually.*

The form of the reciprocity is the mere mutual interchange of the'links—the content is that in them, which makes them capable of this mutual interchange, and impels them to realize it. The characteristic form of the reciprocity is here (under the category of causality) a *becoming* through a *vanishing*. (From time we must abstract as yet. The X which becomes through the —X, which vanishes, must both be thought together, or, rather, not at all in time.) The characteristic of the content of this reciprocity is *essential opposition* of the two links, or the *qualitative* incompatibility of both.

The form is to determine the content means, the two links are essentially opposed, because and in so far as they cancel each other. Their actual mutual canceling determines the sphere of their opposition. If they do not cancel each other, they are not essentially opposed. (A seeming paradox, to be explained directly.)

The content determines the form means, their

essential opposition determines their mutual canceling ; only on condition that the links are opposed,
and only in so far as they are mutually opposed
can they cancel each other. Form and content
mutually determine each other signifies, the essential opposition of the links necessitates their mutual
canceling, and hence their actual connection and
influence upon each other, and *vice versa.* Both is
one and the same.

The real result of this synthesis is, that a necessary connection is posited between the links. This
synthesis denies the possibility to distinguish a
being in itself from a being in the reciprocity ; both
are posited as interchanging links, and are otherwise not posited at all. Real and ideal opposition
are one and the same. This is what appears para-
doxical, but it does not appear so when it is remembered that the one link is the Ego, to which
nothing *is* opposed, which it does not *posit* as opposed to itself, and which *is* opposed to nothing,
but to what it *posits* itself as opposed.

III. — *The synthetically united activity and the
synthetically united reciprocity mutually determine
each other, and constitute in themselves a synthetical
unity.*

The activity as synthetical unity may be called
a *mediated positing*, (a positing of reality by means
of a not-positing ;) the synthetically united reciprocity is the *identity* of *essential opposition* and *real
canceling*

The former determines the latter signifies : The

mediateness of the positing is the ground and the condition of the identity of essential opposition and real canceling. These two links are identical because of the *mediateness* of the positing.

If the interchanging links were posited *immediately*, opposition and canceling would be distinct. Call these links A and B. Let A = A and B = B; but now posit also A = —B, in some quantitative respect, and B = —A ; and, nevertheless, they do not necessarily cancel each other. For you may abstract from their characteristic as opposites, and again view them as having been posited immediately and independent of each other, (A = A and B = B,) in which case they are no longer posited as interchanging links, but also as reality in themselves. Interchanging links can only be posited mediately ; A is = —B, and nothing else ; and B = —A, and nothing else ; and from this mediateness óf the positing follows their essential opposition and their mutual canceling, and the identity of both. For if A and B are thus posited, as existing merely in essential opposition to each other, and if they can receive no other predicate (not even that of a thing)—if A can therefore not be posited as real otherwise than through not positing B, and B not except through not positing A—their common essence evidently consists in this, that the one is posited through the not-positing of the other, and hence—if we abstract from an intelligence which posits them—that they do cancel each other. Their essential opposition and mutual canceling are, therefore, identical, in so far as each link is only posited through the not-positing of another.

Now, this is the case with the Ego and the Non-Ego. The Ego can transfer reality into the Non-Ego only through *not* positing the same in itself; and into itself only through not positing the same in the Non-Ego. (We speak here of *transferred*, not of *absolute* reality.) The essence of the Ego and the Non-Ego, therefore, as interchanging links, consists only in this, that they are opposed to each other, and cancel each other. The *mediateness* of the positing (that is, the law of consciousness, " no subject no object, and *vice versa*,") is the ground of the essential opposition of the Ego and the Non-Ego, and hence of all the reality of the Non-Ego as well as of the Ego ; that is, in so far as this reality is posited simply *as* posited, or, ideal reality ; for the absolute reality remains, of course, in the *positing*. This mediateness, so far as we have now advanced in our synthesis, is not again to be grounded through that whereof it is the ground, nor can it be so in any proper application of the proposition of the ground. The ground of this mediateness, therefore, can not be contained either in the reality of the Non-Ego, or in the posited reality of the Ego. The ground must, therefore, be in the absolute Ego ; and this mediateness must be itself absolute, that is, grounded in and through itself.

This, on our present standpoint, very correct result establishes a new and still more abstract

idealism than we had before. In that former idealism, an itself posited activity was canceled through
the nature and the essence of the Ego, canceled
absolutely, without further ground ; and this absolute canceling made an object and subject, etc.,
possible. Representations developed themselves
as such, out of the Ego in a manner utterly unknown and inaccessible to us.

In the present idealism the activity has its law
immediately in itself; it is a mediate activity and
no other, simply because it is mediate. From this
its mediateness every thing else, reality of the
Non-Ego, and, in so far, negation of the Ego ; and
negation of the Non-Ego, and, in so far, reality of
the Ego, can be completely explained. Representations develop themselves out of the Ego according
to a determined and cognizable law of its nature.
It is only the ground of this law of mediation which
is here inaccessible.

This idealism necessarily abolishes the former,
since it explains what to the former was inexplain-
able from a higher ground. The fundamental principle of this latter idealism would be, *the Ego is
finite simply because it is finite.*

Now, although such an idealism rises higher, it
does not rise high enough, does not rise to the
absolutely posited and unconditioned. True, finity
is to be absolutely posited ; but all finite is, by its
very conception, limited by its opposite, and absolute finity is thus, an in itself contradictory conception.

I shall call the former idealism, which cancels something posited in itself, *qualitative idealism ;* and the latter, which originally posits itself a limited quantity, *quantitative idealism.*

2d. The latter determines the former signifies : the mediateness of the positing is determined by this, that the essence of the interchanging links consists merely in their essential opposition ; only through the latter fact is the mediateness possible. For if their essence were not thereby exhausted, the not-positing of the one would by no means necessitate the positing of the other in its complete essence ; but if their essence consists only in this, then they can only be posited *mediately.*

From this view the essential opposition is the absolute fact—not the mediateness of the positing as above—and is the ground of that mediateness.

A system which takes this view, results in a quantitative realism, well to be distinguished from our previous qualitative realism. In the system of qualitative realism an independent Non-Ego, having reality in itself, impresses the Ego and restricts the activity thereof. The quantitative realist recognizes, on the contrary, that reality is posited in the Non-Ego for the Ego only by the applying of the law of the ground, though he, also, does maintain *the real existence of a limitation of the Ego, whereof the Ego is not the cause.* The qualitative realist asserts the independent reality of a *determining ;* the quantitative realist merely the independent reality of a *determination.* The latter says, there is

14

a determination in the Ego of which the ground
can not be posited in the Ego. This to him is a
fact ; that is, that determination exists for him absolutely without any ground. True, the law of the
ground compels him to relate it to the Non-Ego as
the real ground of that determination ; but he also
knows that that law of the ground is his own, and
hence he is not deceived by it. It appears at once
that this system is the same as that of critical idealism ; and KANT, indeed, has established no other
than this, as indeed, from the standpoint of reflection he had placed himself upon, he neither could
nor wished to establish another one.

The above quantitative idealism is distinguished
from the present quantitative realism in this, that
although both assume a finity of the Ego, the
former system posits that finity as absolutely posited ; the latter system as accidental, but also as unex-
plainable. Quantitative realism abolishes quantitative idealism, because it explains without its assist-
ance, though making the same error, the existence
of an object in consciousness. I say, with the same
error, for it also can not explain, how a real determination may become an ideal one, how an in itself
existing determination may become a determination
for the positing Ego.

True, we have seen now how the essential opposition determines and grounds the mediateness of
the positing ; but through what is positing itself
grounded ? *If* a positing is to be realized, then, of

course, it can only be through mediation ; but positing in itself is an absolute act of the absolutely
undetermined and undeterminable Ego.   Hence,
this system can not explain the possibility of proceeding from the limited to the unlimited.   The
above quantitative idealism removes this difficulty
by abolishing the unlimited altogether, but this
involves it in the contradiction, that it *absolutely*
posits a *limited.*

Probably by uniting both syntheses we shall
obtain a critical quantitative idealism as the true
result.

3d. Each is to determine the other signifies : to
oppose and to be opposed, *being* and *being posited,*
ideal and real relation is to be the same.   This can
only be when the positing and the posited of the
relation is one and the same, that is, when the
posited is Ego.   The Ego is to be in relation to an
X, which, in so far, must be a Non-Ego, by which
relation the Ego is posited only through the not
positing of this Non-Ego, and *vice versa.*   The Ego,
however, is in a relation only in so far as it posits
itself in a relation.   Hence, it is the same whether
you say of the Ego it *is posited* in this relation, or
it posits itself in this relation.   Ideal and real relation are the same.

Let us develop more clearly the important result
of this synthesis, a result, however, which is only
derived from the fundamental principle of the theoretical part of our science, and has only validity so
far as that principle has it.   The Ego can only

posit through a non-positing, that is, mediately;
can only mediately posit itself as well as the Non-
Ego. It is always positing, but it is *posited* only
through positing the Non-Ego, as not posited, or
through negating it. In other words, the Ego is
only the opposite of the Non-Ego, and *vice versa.*
No Ego, no Non-Ego; no I, no Thou; no subject,
no object. Subject is that which is not object, and
has no other predicate as yet, and *vice versa.*

This result establishes the critical quantitative
idealism of which we spoke.

The *difficulty* was to assign a ground for the determination of the activity of the Ego as such.
Quantitative realism assigns this ground to the
passivity of the Ego, caused by a *real* Non-Ego.
Quantitative idealism assigns it to the positing of
the Ego, that is, posits the Ego simply as *absolutely*
limited through itself. The present system asserts
that both are wrong, that the law of that determination is neither a merely subjective and ideal, having
its ground only in the Ego, nor an objective and
real one, having its ground *not* in the Ego; but
that it must be both in the object and subject.
How? This question can not yet be answered.

APPLICATION UNDER CATEGORY OF SUBSTAN-
TIALITY.

We have the same three propositions:

1st. The activity of the form and of the content
mutually determine each other.

2d. The form and content of the reciprocity mutually determine each other.

3d. The synthetically united activity and the synthetically united reciprocity mutually determine each other.

I.

The activity of the form and of the content mutually determine each other.

While the characteristic of the category of causality was the positing through a non-positing, the characteristic of the activity of the form under the category of substantiality is the positing of something as *not posited* through the positing of another as *posited*, that is, negation through affirmation. The not-posited *is* posited *as* not posited. Hence, it is not *annihilated* as before, but merely *excluded*, excluded from a certain sphere. Hence, again, it is not negated through positing *generally*, but through a determined positing. The not-posited has, therefore, merely a negative character ; it is *not this* determined sphere. Call the posited sphere A, the excluded not-posited, B. A, by itsèlf, is posited as absolute totality ; but this can not be if B is anywise posited. A is, therefore, posited both as totality and not-totality ; totality with reference ˊto A, not-totality with reference to B. But B is merely determined negatively as not A. Hence A is posited as determined, and in so far total part of an undetermined whole, which whole embraces both spheres, the determined and the undetermined

14*

spheres. This higher sphere must be posited to make both lower ones possible, and the activity which posits it is the activity of the content we are looking for.

Example.

Let us posit iron $= A$ as absolute totality in itself. It excludes motion $= B$. Now take a piece of moving iron $= C$. By excluding motion $= B$ from the conception of iron $= A$, you do not deny the moving iron $= C$, but you place this C in an undetermined sphere, because you do not know under what condition the motion $= C$ is connected with the iron. The sphere, A, is totality of the iron, and also is it not, because it excludes $= C$ which equally belongs to iron. Hence, you posit a higher sphere, embracing both moving and not-moving iron. In so far as iron fills this higher sphere it is substance; in A it is merely a thing. Motion and not-motion are its accidences.

The activity of the form determines that of the content signifies : only by excluding from the absolute totality can you posit a higher sphere ; no exclusion, no higher sphere ; no accidence in the Ego, no Non-Ego. The absolute totality of the Ego is *positing itself.* If an object is posited by it, this objective positing is excluded from that sphere, and placed in the opposite sphere of *not-positing itself.* Not to posit itself and to posit an object is the same. It excludes simply because it excludes, and did it not exclude, the higher sphere of *general positing* would not be possible. It will be seen that the word positing itself has here a double significance, first, that of absolute totality, and secondly, that of a determined part of an undetermined whole. Also, that substance signifies the *all-embracing*, not the *permanent*, as is generally supposed. (This results again in a system of quantitative idealism.)

The activity of the content determines that of the form signifies : the higher sphere is absolutely posited, and only through it is the exclusion (as real act of the Ego) possible. This again opens a qualitative realism, which maintains that the Ego and the Non-Ego are posited as opposites, that the Ego is generally *positing;* and that, if the Ego *does not posit* the Non-Ego, it *must* certainly posit itself ; but this *must* is accidental, and determined through the ground of the positing, which ground is not contained in the Ego itself. According to this realism, the Ego is a representing being, which must be governed by the quality of the things.

Neither this result nor the previous one is to be valid ; both must, therefore, be mutually modified. Because the Ego is to exclude something from itself, a higher sphere must be, and be *posited;* and *vice versa.* Or, there is a Non-Ego because the Ego posits something as its opposite, and it posits something as its opposite because a Non-Ego is, and is posited. This will again establish the above critical idealism.

II.

*The form and the content of the reciprocity mutual-
ly determine each other.*

The form consists in the excluding of the links
through each other. If A is posited as absolute
totality, B is excluded from its sphere, and placed
in the undetermined but determinable sphere B.
Again, if B is considered as posited, A is now excluded from the absolute totality; that is, *it belongs
with B to a higher undetermined but determinable
sphere.* (Let this be well remarked.)

The content consists in this, that the totality is
determinable. In the form we had two totalities :
first A alone, and then A + B. If these two can
not be distinguished, we have no interchange, no
reciprocity. Hence, there must be a determined
character of the totality as such, whereby it can be
distinguished, whereby it can be determined, which
is the true totality.

Example.

Posit iron as isolated, in rest, in space ; and you
rightly ascribe motion, when it occurs, to an external cause. Still, you also and rightly now ascribe
motion to iron. Your former conception of iron is,
therefore, no longer sufficient, and you complete it
by adding the characteristic of attractability by the
magnet. Now, from the one view, *rest* is essential to iron, and *motion* accidental ; from the other,
both are accidental, because both are determined by
the absence or presence of the magnet. Hence,
you are in a quandary ; unless you can assign a

ground why you take the first or second view, that is, unless you can determine from what totality you must proceed, whether from the determined totality which has been absolutely posited, or from the determinable totality which has arisen from it and from the excluded sphere.

The form of the reciprocity determines its content signifies : the mutual exclusion determines which of both totalities is absolute. That which excludes another from the totality is, *in so far* as it excludes, the totality, and *vice versa*. If the absolutely posited A excludes B, then, *in so far*, A is totality ; and if B is reflected upon, and hence A not regarded as totality, *in so far* A + the undetermined B is the determinable totality. Result : There is no other ground of the totality than a relative one. You may optionally take either view. Take the absolutely posited conception of iron, and rest is essential ; take its merely determinable conception, and *rest* is accidental. Both conceptions are right, and you may take whichever you choose. The distinction is purely relative.

The content of the reciprocity determines its form signifies : the determinability of the totality, as explained by us, and *which is therefore posited,* determines the mutual exclusion ; that is, one of the totalities is the absolute one, either the determined (B) or the merely determinable, (A + B.) If B is the absolute totality, then that which it excludes is also *absolutely* excluded. Result : There is an *absolute ground* of the totality, and it

is not merely relative. It is not the same whether
you take the determined or the determinable conception of iron, and whether you posit rest as
essential or accidental to it. If from some unknown ground the determined conception of iron
must be the first conception, *only* motion and not
rest is its absolute accidence.

The form and the content mutually determine
each other signifies: absolute and relative ground
of the determination of the totality are the same ;
the relation is absolute, and the absolute nothing
but a relation.

Both the results heretofore attained were wrong.
There is an absolute law, our synthesis now says,
for the determination of the totality, but this law is
not contained in either of the above modes of determination, but in positing both as *mutually·deter-
mining* each other. Neither of the two totalities is
the desired totality ; both together, determining each
other, give the true totality. Not A is absolute totality, nor A + B, but A determined by A + B. The
determinable is determined by the determined, and
vice versa, and the thus resulting unity is the true
totality.

What does this mean : the determined and the
determinable must mutually determine each other ?
Evidently this : the determination of that which is
to be determined is determinability. It is a *determinable*, and nothing else ; therein its whole essence
is expressed. This determinability is the looked-for
totality ; that is, determinability is a fixed quantum,

has its limits, beyond which no further determination occurs, and all possible determinability lies
within these limits.

The Ego posits *itself;* this is the absolute totality of the reality of the Ego. The Ego posits *an
object.* This objective positing must be excluded
from the sphere of the self-positing of the Ego ;
and yet must also be ascribed to the Ego. Thus
we obtain the sphere A + B as (unlimited as yet)
totality of all the acts of the Ego. Now, both these
spheres, the A and the A   B, are mutually to
determine each other. A gives what it has, absolute limit ; A + B gives what it has, content.
Thus the Ego is now positing an object, and then
it is not the subject ; or the subject, and then it is
not an object ; in so far as it *posits itself*, as positing under this rule. In this manner both spheres
are united, and unitedly first form a single *limited*
sphere ; and in so far the determination of the Ego
consists in its *determinability through subject and
object.*

Determined determinability is the totality we
sought, and such a totality is called *Substance.* No
substance, unless you first proceed from the absolutely posited, (the Ego, here,) which posits
only itself ; or, unless something is first excluded
from it, (the Non-Ego, here.) But the substance
which as such is nothing but determinability, and
yet is to be *fixed* determinability, is no substance,
(not *all*-embracing,) unless again determined by
the absolutely posited, (here, by the itself-positing.)

The Ego *posits itself* as *self-positing* by excluding
the Non-Ego, or it posits *the Non-Ego* as *positing*
by excluding itself. Remark the two characters of
the *self-positing* in this sentence ; the first an *unconditional*, the second a *conditional* positing, determinable by excluding the Non-Ego.

Example.

If the determination of iron in itself be rest, then
a change of place is excluded from it, and, in so far,
iron is *not substance*, for it is *not determinable.*
Still, the change of place is to be ascribed to the
iron. This you can not do so as utterly to cancel
its rest ; for if you do, you cancel the iron itself as
posited by you. Hence, you only cancel that rest
in part, and the change of place is thus determined
and limited by the rest of the iron ; that is, the
change of place occurs only within the sphere of a
certain condition, (for instance, within the attraction
of a magnet.) Beyond this sphere the iron is again
in rest. Who does not notice here the double significance of the word rest? In the first instance,
it is *unconditioned ;* in the second, *conditioned,*
namely, by the absence of a magnet.

Again, as A + B is determined by A, so B is
determined, for it now belongs to the sphere of the
determined determinable ; and A itself is now a determinable. Hence, in so far as B itself is now determined, it also can determine A and B, and *must*
determine it in order to form an absolute relation.
Hence, if A and B is posited, and A is in so far

placed within the sphere of the determinable: A and B is again determined by B.

Let us explain this: The Ego is to exclude something from itself. This something must be in the Ego previous to the exclusion, that is, *independent* of the excluding. It must be absolutely posited in the Ego. Hence, for this something it is *accidental* that the Ego should exclude it, (should make a representation of it, as we shall see hereafter.) Even without this excluding it would exist, (not without the Ego, but *in the Ego*, of course.) The object (A + B) is the determined; its being excluded, the determinable. It may be excluded or not, and still remains object. The object is, therefore, posited here in two different ways: first, it is posited *unconditionally* and absolute; next, *under condition* of a being excluded through the Ego.

Example.

From the iron posited as in rest, motion is to be excluded. By the conception of iron, iron was not to involve motion; but now motion is to be excluded from the iron. Hence, motion must be posited independently of this excluding, and must be posited—with reference to its not being posited in iron—absolutely. In other words, if you wish to oppose motion to iron, you must first know motion; but the knowledge of motion is not given you through iron. Hence, you know it from some other source; and since here we have only iron and motion to look to, you know it absolutely.

15

Now, if we start from this conception of motion, then it is accidental to this conception that it is applied to iron among other things. It is the essential, and iron is for it the accidental.

Motion is posited absolutely. Iron is excluded from its sphere, because it is in rest. Now, you cancel rest in iron and ascribe motion to it. And, whereas, at first the conception of motion was absolute and unconditioned, it is now conditioned by the canceling of rest in iron.

The result of our synthesis was this :

The totality consists simply in the complete relation, and there is . nothing in itself determined whereby it is determined. The totality consists in the completeness of a *relation*, not of a *reality*.

The links of a relation, singly considered, are *accidences;* their totality, *substance.* Substance is nothing fixed, but a mere change. If a substance is to be determined, or, in other words, if something · determined is to be thought as substance, the change, it is true, must proceed from one of the links, which is in so far fixed as the change is to be determined. But it is not *absolutely* fixed, for I might as well proceed from its opposite link, and then the former link would be accidental, etc. In short, the accidences, synthetically united, give .the substance ; and the substance is nothing but the totality of accidences. A permanent substrate must not be entertained. Every accidence is its own substrate, and the substrate of its opposite accidences. The positing Ego, by the most marvelous of its powers, (productive imagination,) holds the vanishing accidence firmly, until it has compared it with the accidence whereby it is pushed aside. This power is it which, from perennial opposites, forms a unity which enters between moments (contradictions) that would mutually cancel each other, and thus maintains both ; this power is it which alone makes life and consciousness (and particularly consciousness as a continuing series of time-moments) possible ; and all this it achieves simply by this, that it diverts and guides along itself and in itself accidences which have no *common* bearer, and can have none, because they would mutually destroy each other.

III.—*The activity as synthetical unity, and the reciprocity as synthetical unity, mutually determine each other.*

The activity as synthetical unity can be best characterized *as an absolute gathering together and holding firmly of opposites* (subjective and objective) *in the category of determinability*, wherein they are also opposed to each other.

To make this synthesis clearer, let us compare it with the former synthesis (§ 3) of the Ego and the Non-Ego through quantity. Just as the Ego was there in its *quality*, absolutely posited as absolute reality, so here we absolutely posit *something*, that is, a *quantitatively* determined, in the Ego, or, in other words, so here we absolutely posit the Ego as *determined quantity ;* a *something* subjective is po-

sited as an absolutely subjective ; and this proceeding here is a *thesis*, and a quantitative thesis in distinction from the above qualitative thesis.   From a
thesis, however, all the modes of acting of the Ego
must proceed.

(At least it is a thesis in our theoretical part,
because we can not in it break through the limit of
its fundamental principle ; when we do so in the
practical part, we shall see that it is also a synthesis,
a synthesis which results from the highest thesis.)

Again, as in § 3, a Non-Ego was opposed to the
Ego as opposite *quality*, so here to the subjective
is opposed an objective, by the mere exclusion
thereof from the sphere of the subjective ; hence,
merely through and by means of *quantity*, (of limitation, determination,) and this proceeding is a
quantitative antithesis, as that in § 3 was a qualitative antithesis.   But now the subjective is not to
be canceled by the objective, and *vice versa*, precisely as the Ego was not to be canceled by the Non-
Ego, and *vice versa ;* both are to coexist.   They
must, therefore, be united, which is done through
that wherein they are equal, determinability.   Both,
—that is, not the subject and object in themselves,
but the subjective and objective posited through
the thesis—are mutually determinable through each
other, and only in so far as they are so determinable
can they be taken up and held together by the active power of this synthesis, (productive imagination.)

Again, as above, this antithesis is not possible

without thesis, because only to the posited can be opposited; and here also the required thesis is, in its content, not possible without the content of the antithesis; for, until something is absolutely determined, that is, until the conception of quantity can be applied to it, it must exist in its quality.

But in form, again, the antithesis is not possible without synthesis, for otherwise the antithesis would cancel the posited of the thesis, and would thus be no antithesis, but would be itself a thesis. *All the three acts are only one and the same act, and are distinguished only in reflection as moments of one act.*

The reciprocity as synthetic unity is sufficiently characterized as mere relation, as mere mutual excluding, or as determinability. This, of course, must be abstractly conceived—indeed, in our whole theoretical part, we must always abstract from *something*—must be conceived as mere relation without any thing related. A and B, for instance, are opposites; if one is posited, the other is not; nevertheless they are both to be posited, and not merely in part, (quantitatively limited,) but wholly. But they can not be thought together, except in so far. *as they mutually cancel each other.* You can not think A, nor can you think B. But you can think their *union.*

Example.

Posit in the physical time-moment light $= A$, and in the immediately succeeding moment darkness $= B$. Then they are divided. But the moments join each other. Hence, they are not divided. For, let the dividing line be D, then D is not light, which is in A ; nor darkness, which is in B. Hence it is neither. But you can also say it is both, for there is no such line. Of course, the line D is extended by imagination to a moment in the latter view, and so it is. But so are also A and B, and *imagination* is their origin. Hence, I *can* and I *must*, moreover, extend D, if I want to think the immediate junction of A and B. Productive power of imagination is indeed our most marvelous·function, and upon it the whole mechanism of human spirit may be grounded.

1. The activity as synthesis determines the reciprocity as synthesis means, the *joining* of the interchanging links as such is conditioned by an absolute activity of the Ego, by means whereof this Ego opposes an objective to a subjective, and unites both. Only in the Ego, and by virtue of this act of the Ego, are they reciprocal interchanging links, and do they join together.

It is clear that this result is idealistic. If the activity established in it is taken as exhausting the essence of the Ego, representation consists in this, that the Ego posits a subjective and posits an objective in opposition to it, etc. We discovered above a law of the mediateness of positing, according to which no objective could be posited without canceling a subjective, and *vice versa*. To this law is here added the determination that both are synthetically united, and must be posited through one and the same act of the Ego ; and by this addition the unity of that wherein the reciprocity occurs, while the reciprocal links remain opposites, is explained, which the law of mere mediation could not explain.

This result, therefore, establishes an intelligence as existing with all its possible determinations through its mere spontaneity. The Ego is constituted *as* it posits itself, and *because* it posits itself as thus constituted. Still there is here also a defect left yet. For, go back in the series as far as you will, you must always arrive finally at something already existing in the Ego, wherein a subjective and objective are already posited as opposites. The existence of the subjective may thus be explained, for it follows from the self-positing of the absolute Ego, but not that of the objective.

2. The reciprocity determines the activity signifies, not through the real existence of opposites, but through their mere joining or touching each other in consciousness is oppositing and the gathering together of the opposites through the activity of the Ego made possible ; that joining is the condition of this activity.

This sentence says, in complement of the previous result, that the excluded objective need not have this existence; it will suffice if a *check* has existence for the Ego, that is to say, if there is a ground —unknown—but not contained in this activity of the Ego—why it must limit itself, and thus oppose an objective to a subjective. In other words, the presupposition of such a system—realistic as it is, but more abstract than all previous realistic systems—is, *that the Ego is merely determinable*, (or, has in itself the problem to determine itself.) This realism, therefore, does not posit a determination (like the quantitative realism) as its presupposition, but leaves it to the active Ego to posit this determination. (The determinability which it posits in the Ego we shall hereafter learn to know as *feeling*. For, though feeling is a determination of the Ego, it is not one of the Ego as intelligence, that is, of the Ego, which posits itself as determined by the Non-Ego, of which we speak here.)

This system has the defect of every realism, that it views the Ego as a Non-Ego ; and hence does not explain the transition from the one to the other. The determinability, or the requirement that the Ego shall determine itself, is posited, that is true ; but it is posited without any activity of the Ego. Hence it is clear enough *how the Ego could be determinable for something outside of the Ego*, but not how the *Ego can be determinable through and for itself.* For the Ego is only determinable in so far as it posits itself as determinable ; and how it can posit itself as determinable, or as being required by its very nature to determine itself, this has not yet been explained.

3. Both results are to be synthetically united ; the activity and the reciprocity are mutually to determine each other.

We found that we could not assume that the mere reciprocity, or a mere check, existing with-

out any action of the positing Ego, could propose
to the Ego the task of limiting itself ; for the
ground of explanation did not contain what was to
be explained.

We shall, therefore, have to show that that
check does not exist without the action of the
Ego, but that it is, on the contrary, directed upon
the activity of the Ego in positing itself ; that this
activity, ever, as it were, proceeding outwardly,
is thereby driven back (reflected) into itself ; and
from this reflection we shall then show easily how
self-limitation, and every thing else resulting therefrom, follows naturally. This will give us a true
synthesis of the reciprocity and the activity. The
check—not posited by the positing Ego—occurs
only in so far as the Ego is active, and is therefore
only a check, in so far as the Ego is active ; the
activity of the Ego is the condition of the check.
No activity of the Ego, no check. On the other
hand, the self-determining of the Ego will be conditioned by the check. No check, no self-determination of the Ego. Again, no self-determination,
no object and subject, etc. Let us make clearer
this very important and final result.

The activity of the Ego in gathering together
opposites, and the in itself independent joining
together of these opposites are to be one and the
same. The chief distinction lies evidently in the
gathering together and the *joining together.* How
the latter is conditioned by the former is easily
seen. For joining they are only in so far as a limit

is posited between them, for they are complete opposites, and this limit is not posited by either of
them, but by an independent positing. But the
limit is only that which both have in common ; to
posit their limits, therefore, is to gather them together, and to gather them together is only possible
by positing their limits. They join only on condition of a gathering together, *for* and through that
which gathers them together.

But, again, the gathering together, or the positing
of a limit, is only to be possible on condition of a
joining together ; or—since that which is active in
this limit-positing is to be one of the joining links,
and only *as* active—on condition of a check upon
the activity of this active link. The activity must,
therefore, extend into the unlimited, infinite, undeterminable. If it did not, its limitation would not involve at all that its activity had been checked ; for
the limitation might be involved in its own conception, (as is the case in every system which holds that
the Ego is finite.) In other words, the opposites
here held together are essential opposites, without
any point of union. All finite things, however, are
not essential opposites ; they are equal in the conception of determinability. And all infinites, in so
far as there can be a plurality, are thus equal in the
conception of undeterminability. Hence, the only
two essential opposites are : the infinite and the
finite, of which we have spoken here.

Both are to be one and the same ; that is, *no infinite, no limitation, and vice versa ; both are united in*

one and the same synthetic unity. If the activity of the
Ego were not infinite, it could not limit this activity itself. The activity of the Ego consists in un-
limitedly positing itself. This activity is checked.
If the activity of the Ego were thrown back by this
check, that activity which lies beyond the line of
the check would be completely annihilated and canceled ; and the Ego in so far would not posit at all.
But it is to posit even beyond this line. It is to
limit itself, that is, it is in so far to posit itself as not
positing ; it is to place in this sphere the undetermined, unlimited, infinite limit $=$ B, and hence it
must be infinite.

Again, if the Ego did not limit itself, it would
not be infinite. The Ego is only what it posits
itself as being. It is infinite signifies : it posits
itself as infinite ; determines itself by the predicate
of the infinite ; or it limits itself as substrate of
the infinite ; or it distinguishes itself from its infinite activity, which, nevertheless, is also to be its
own activity, and must, therefore, be in one and
the same act distinguished and taken back as its
own. (A + B must be determined by A.) By
thus taking it back into itself, it determines the activity, and hence makes it not infinite ; at the same
time it is to be infinite, and hence it must be posited *outside* of the Ego.

This interchange of the Ego with itself, in positing itself at the same time as finite and infinite—an
interchange which is, as it were, a self-contradiction, and which reproduces itself constantly, since

the Ego seeks to unite what is not unitable, now trying to take the infinite into the form of the finite, and now again driven back to posit it outside of that form, but in the same moment attempting again to seize it in the form of the finite—this interchange is the power of *Imagination.*

By this power the gathering together and the joining is completely united. The joining of opposites, or the limit, is itself a production of the gathering power, for the sake of gathering it. (Absolute thesis of the imagination, which in so far is absolutely productive.) In so far as the Ego and this production of its activity are opposed, the joining members themselves are opposed, and in the limit neither of them are posited. (Antithesis of imagination.) But in so far as both are again united, as that productive activity is to be ascribed to the Ego, the *limiting* links themselves are gathered together in the limit. (Synthesis of imagination, which in this its antithetical and synthetical activity, is *reproductive*, as we shall see hereafter.)

The opposites are to be gathered together in the conception of mere *determinability*, not of determination. If the limit between the opposites (the Ego and the object) were fixed and unchangeable, then the union would be through *determination*, and the totality would not be complete ; for A + B would be determined only through the determined A, and not through the undetermined B. Hence, that limit is not fixed. The power of imagination posits, therefore, an infinite limit, the product of its

infinitely extending activity. This positing activity
it tries to ascribe to itself, (to determine A + B by
A.) If it succeeded, the activity would no longer
be infinite, but determined, because posited in a
determined subject. Hence, the imagination is
driven back into the infinite, that is, is called upon
to determine A + B by B. Hence, also, only determinability occurs here, but not determination itself.

Indeed, the imaginative power posits no fixed
limit at all, for it has no fixed stand-point ; only
reason posits something as fixed by first fixing the
power of imagination. Imagination is a power
which floats between determination and undetermi-
nation, between the finite and the infinite ; and
hence, A + B is in it always determined at the
same time by the determined A and the undetermined B, which is indeed the above synthesis of
imagination. This floating imagination character-
izes through its product ; it produces it, as it were,
while it floats, and through its floating.

This floating of imagination between irreconcilable
links, this its self-contradiction is, as we shall hereafter show, that which extends the condition of the
Ego to a *time*-moment. (For pure reason every
thing is at once ; only for imagination is there.a
time.) Imagination can not stand this floating
long, that is, not longer than a moment, (except in
the feeling of the sublime, where *astonishment*, a
halt of the interchange in time, arises.) Reason
steps in, (and thus there arises a reflection,) and

determines imagination to take B up in the determined A, the subject; but as soon as this is accomplished, the determined A must again be limited by
an infinite B, etc. etc., until it has arrived at a complete determination of the (here theoretical) reason,
which needs no other limiting B outside of reason
in imagination, that is, until it has arrived at the
representation of the representing.   In the practical
sphere the power of imagination continues in an
infinite direction to the absolutely undeterminable
idea of the highest unity, to determine which would
be possible only after a completed infinity, which is
itself impossible in time.

FINAL REMARKS.

The fundamental principle of our theoretical
part, *the Ego posits itself as determined through the
Non-Ego*, has now been exhausted.   The Ego can
not posit itself, can not be subject, without positing
itself as determined through the Non-Ego.   (No
object, no subject.)   At the same time, the Non-
Ego being its own product, it also posits itself as
determining.   (No subject, no object.)

The problem how two opposites, the Ego and
the Non-Ego, could be posited together as determining each other, is not only shown up as possible,
but it has been shown that without it the fundamental requirement, the self-positing of the Ego, is
not possible.   Hence, what was at first problematical has now apodictical certainty; and this part of

the science is exhausted, since we have returned to our first starting-point and proved it.

Again, if our result has shown itself as the truth, it must appear as an *original fact in our conscious-ness*, that is, not—like the other thoughts which arose during our investigation, (for instance, like the real-istic conception of an absolute substance of the Non-Ego)—an *artificially* created fact, not a fact of our *reflective consciousness*.

The science of knowledge shows up facts, and ^V thereby distinguishes itself from an empty formula-philosophy ; but it does not postulate facts ; it proves *that* something must be a fact,

If this fact is to be a fact in the consciousness of an Ego, the Ego must posit it *as* in its conscious-ness ; or, in other words, must try to explain it to itself. This it does, of course, according to the laws of its own being. Hereafter we shall there-fore observe how the Ego proceeds to modify, de-termine, and work out that fact which was the result of our investigation.

It is clear that thus we shall obtain a second dis-tinct series of reflection. In the first, we had a series wherein, by pure spontaneity of thought, we produced the object as well as the form of our re-flection, and finally arrived at the only possible result, as moreover a fact to be found in conscious-ness. Now, we have to reflect upon this *fact*, as a fact already in this consciousness, which, therefore, is not *produced*, but merely *raised to consciousness*. Hence, while formerly we had to wade through a number of hypotheses in order to reach the final truth, now these hypotheses vanish, and we have only to deal with realities.

Both modes of reflection take opposite directions. The first one started from the proposition: The Ego posits itself as determined through the Non-Ego, and proceeded to the fact; the second one starts from the fact and goes back to the first sentence, which it then shows up to be a fact; that is, it proceeds until it has established as a fact that the Ego posits itself, as positing itself determined through the Non-Ego.

Now, since the fact is the point of union of both reflections, and since the fact is a synthesis of two opposites, it seems that the same opposites which the fact had for the first reflection must appear to the second reflection, and that the second reflection will only be a repetition of the first. Hence, if both are, nevertheless, to be distinct, the two series of reflections must receive a distinct characteristic in this very last synthesis of the fact. What is this character?

In the first reflection both opposites are merely opposites—a mere relation; the one is what the other is not; purely negative character—nothing positive. Pure thoughts, without reality. Each annihilates the other; and as neither can appear without its opposite, which annihilates it, neither appears. Our consciousness is empty; neither can fill it.

It is true, our first series of reflection would,

therefore, have been in itself impossible, but for
a certain deception of imagination, which always
made us put a substrate under these mere opposites. This deception we did not and could not
wish to remove ; all that was necessary was to de-
duct it at the conclusion from the final result of our
calculation as we now do.

But in the second reflection, after the synthesis,
they have changed to something tangible, which consciousness can seize. *They become for the reflection.*
(Precisely as light and darkness did, which did not
annihilate each other in our illustration, but became
something tangible in the line D, through the power
of imagination.)

We have already seen how this change is effected in the synthesis by productive imagination.
Both opposites are to be thought as *one.* This they
can not be, and in the endeavor so to think them
they receive in their *mutual relation to each other* a
certain extension and content which will appear
hereafter as the manifold in time and space. The
condition of this endeavor is called contemplation.
The power active in it, productive imagination, as
we have already said.

Thus it appears how the absolute contradiction,
which threatened to destroy a theory of human
knowledge, here becomes the only condition which
makes it possible. We could not see how it would
ever be possible for us to unite absolute opposites ;
now we see that an explanation of the occurrences
in our mind would not at all be possible without
absolute opposites, since that power of imagination

16*

upon which all these occurrences are based would not be possible at all, unless absolute opposites, not unitable and completely contradictory to the Ego, did occur. And this serves at once as the clearest illustration that our system is correct, and that the explanation has been exhaustive. The presupposed can only be explained by the discovered, and *vice versa.* From the absolute opposition results the whole mechanism of the human mind ; and this whole mechanism can only be explained through an absolute opposition.

At the same time, we now see clearly how ideality and reality can be one and the same ; and lead the one to the other, and are only different when regarded as different. The absolute opposites (the finite subjective and the infinite objective) are in advance of the synthesis mere thoughts, and hence ideal, in the sense in which we have always used the word. As soon as they are to be united in thinking, but can not be so united, they receive —through the floating of thinking, which in this its function is called imagination — reality, because through this floating they become capable of being contemplated. In other words, they receive there-by reality generally, for there is and can be no other reality than by means of contemplation. Now, by abstracting again from this contemplation—as can be done for mere thinking, though not for consci-ousness generally—that reality changes again into ideality ; that is, its being is solely derived from the laws of the power of representation.

We therefore teach here that all reality—of
course, *for us*—is solely produced through imagination. One of the greatest thinkers of our age,
Kant, who otherwise teaches the same system, so
far as I have knowledge thereof, calls this a *deception* through imagination. But every deception can
be avoided. Now, if it is shown, as our system is
to show, that that so-called deception of imagination is the ground of the possibility of our consciousness, of our life, and of our being for us, that is,
of our being as Ego, then it can not be removed,
unless we desire to abstract from the Ego, which is
a contradiction, since the abstracting can not abstract from itself. Hence, the deception does not
deceive, but gives us truth, and the only possible
truth. To assume that it deceives is to establish a
skepticism which teaches to doubt one's own being.

III.

SECOND PART

OF THE

THEORETICAL PART

OF THE

SCIENCE OF KNOWLEDGE.

SCIENCE OF KNOWLEDGE.

INTRODUCTORY REMARKS.

T<small>HE</small> result of the first part of the theoretical part of the science of knowledge, and which we have postulated as necessarily occurring in consciousness, was this : By means of an as yet incomprehensible check upon the absolute activity of the Ego, the power of imagination produces out of the two directions thereby occasioned, namely, the original and the reflected directions of the activity, a composite of both directions.

We have said that this fact, since it is to be in the Ego, must be posited, that is, originally determined and grounded in and by the Ego ; and that this *positing* of it would give us a second part of the theoretical part. For, whereas the first part only proceeds to show up the fact, the second part involves a system of all the facts which occur in consciousness in its *original* explanation of that one fact. *Original* explanation, for it is not, as the links of the first part were, *created* by us, but is originally within us, and we only make ourselves conscious of its shape in us by this explanation.

KANT proceeded from the assumption of a manifold which was to be collected in the unity of consciousness ; he proceeded from the particular to the general. He thus attained a general, but only a collective general, not an *infinite* general. For finity opens no path to infinity, whereas there is a path from undetermined and undeterminable infinity to finity, by means of the determining power. (Hence, all finite is product of that power.) We, therefore, take the opposite way, and prove that there is given a *manifold* for empirical consciousness, which proof runs in this wise : the given must be *something*. As such there must be another, which is also something. When this proof shall be possible, we enter upon the sphere of the particular.

The *method* of the theoretical science of knowledge has been described before, and is simple and easy. The thread of our argument is carried along in accordance with the principle : *Nothing appertains to the Ego but what it posits in itself.* We make the deduced fact our starting-point, and see how the Ego may proceed to posit it in itself. This positing of the fact is again a fact, and must also be posited by the Ego in itself, and in this manner we continue until we have arrived at the highest theoretical fact, namely, the fact by which the Ego posits itself *consciously* as determined through the Non-Ego. Thus, the theoretical science of knowledge closes with its fundamental principle, returns into itself, and is completed through itself.

DEDUCTION OF SENSATION.

The conflict of opposite directions of the activity of the Ego, which have been described in the first part, is something distinguishable in the Ego. As sure as this conflict is in the Ego, it must be posited by the Ego in the Ego, and hence must be distinguished. The Ego posits this conflict signifies, firstly : The Ego *opposits* itself to this conflict.

Hitherto, that is, on this stand-point of reflection, nothing has been posited in the Ego ; nothing is in it but what originally pertains to it, *pure* activity. The Ego *opposits* something to itself can, therefore, here signify nothing but : it posits something as *not pure* activity.

And thus the condition of the Ego in the conflict of opposite directions is posited as the opposite of the pure activity of the Ego. Hence, it is posited as mixed, as itself resisting and self-annihilating activity. (This act of the Ego here shown up, whereby it posits that condition of a conflict as the opposite of its free activity, is purely antithetical.)

We do not investigate at all here, how, in what ↓ manner, and through what power the Ego can posit any thing ; since in this whole theory we only speak of the products of its activity. But we have sug-

17

gested already in the first part, that, if the conflict is ever to be posited in the Ego, and if ever any thing further is to result from it, then, through the mere *positing* of the conflict, the conflict as such, that is, the floating of imagination between the opposites, must stop, and only the trace of the conflict must remain as a *something*, as a possible substance. How this may be done we can see here already, although we do not yet see the power through which it is done. For :

The Ego must posit that *conflict* of opposite directions, or opposite powers ; must, therefore, posit both powers, and both *in conflict*, in opposite, but mutually each other balancing activity. But opposite activity, which balances itself, cancels itself, and nothing remains. Yet something is to remain and to be posited. Hence, there remains a *permanent substance*, a something which *has power*, but can not actively utter it on account of the opposite activity—a *substrate* of the power. Any one may convince himself of this at any moment by an experiment. And this substrate, which is the important point here, remains not as a *preposited*, but as *mere product of the union of opposite activities.* This is the ground of all substance, and of all possibly remaining substrate in the Ego, (and nothing *is* outside of the Ego,) as will be always more clearly seen.

The Ego is to posit that conflict of directions *in itself.* Hence, there must be in the Ego not only a ground of distinction, but also a ground of rela-

tion with this condition ; and since the Ego is
as yet nothing but pure activity, this ground of relation must lie in the pure activity. In other words,
the conflict of opposite directions must also contain
pure activity ; or, rather, pure activity must be
posit d—synthetically transferred into it.

The conflicting activity of the Ego has just been
posited as *not pure.* Now, it is to be posited as *pure*,
in order to be related to the Ego. It is to be pure,
and to be not pure. Hence, it is to be opposed to
itself. But this is a contradiction, and can only be
if there is a third synthetical link of union, wherein this contradiction is made possible. *This third
link must therefore be posited.* Such a third link is
an activity (of the Non-Ego) *opposed to all activity
of the Ego generally.*

For the conflict of opposite directions can now,
by means of this third link, be posited as pure activity, when the opposite activity of the Non-Ego
is abstracted from ; and is not pure activity, but
objective activity, when the activity of the Non-
Ego is placed in relation to it. Hence, it is pure,
and is not pure, under condition ; and this condition makes the contradiction possible.

The act shown up here is thetical, antithetical,
and synthetical, all at once. Thetical, in so far as
it absolutely posits an unperceivable opposite activity of the Non-Ego. (*How* this can be done will
be shown hereafter ; we only show now *that* it must
be done.) Antithetical, in so far as, by the positing
or not positing of a condition, it posits one and the

same activity of the Ego in opposition to itself.
Synthetical, in so far as it posits this activity as
one and the same, by positing the activity of the
Non-Ego as an *accidental* condition.

We now see clearly how the Ego can posit
the condition of a conflict of contradictory directions in *itself.* It can do so, because that condition
may also be considered as pure activity of the Ego,
that is, when we abstract from the influence of the
activity of the Non-Ego ; and becomes objective
activity only through that utterly foreign influence
of the Non-Ego.

It is to be remembered that this condition of
contradictory directions is posited in the Ego *together with all its synthetical content heretofore discovered ;* although the *ground* of relation is only
the pure activity of that condition.

Now, in thus relating itself to (positing within
itself) the condition of contradictory directions, by
means of an activity altogether opposed to the Ego,
the Ego invariably *excludes* that activity from itself,
no matter whether it regards its own activity as
pure or as objective. For in either case the Ego
posits that opposite activity as the condition of the
relation ; in the first case, as the condition from
which it must abstract ; in the second case, as the
condition it must reflect upon. Here we have the
highest ground of all externalization of the Ego ;
the ground why the Ego goes beyond itself and
posits something as external to itself. Here we see
for the first time clearly how something, as it were,

loosens itself from the Ego, which will probably change gradually by further determination into an external universe. It is because the Ego in either case *excludes*, posits outside, externalizes that activity of the Non-Ego.

This relation of the condition of contradictory direction to the Ego is called sensation ; a discovering, a finding of a foreign other. It is the canceled, repressed activity of the Ego which is felt in sensation. It is felt, found as something foreign, because it is canceled, limited ; whereas, the original activity of the Ego is pure and absolute. Hence, it is externalized. But it is also felt in sensation, *in* the Ego, because it is only canceled activity on condition of an opposite activity, without which it would not be canceled but pure activity.

DEDUCTION OF CONTEMPLATION.

We have deduced sensation as an act of the Ego, whereby it relates a foreign something in itself to itself, and posits it as its own. The act, sensation, we now know, and also its object, that which enters sensation. But we do not yet know the *sensating*, that is, the Ego, active in that relation ; nor do we know yet the opposite activity of the Non-Ego which was excluded in the sensation. Let us now seek to know of them.

Sensation occurs in the Ego ; hence, the Ego must posit it originally in itself. How does the Ego posit sensation in itself ; or how does it posit

17*

itself as the sensating? To do this it must first be
able to distinguish between its activity in the sensation and the object of the sensation. The object
of sensation is activity of the Ego, in so far as it is
considered as in opposition to another equal activity; as not-activity which would be activity, if the
opposite activity were removed; as *latent* activity,
substance, or substrate of power.

The activity of the Ego in sensation, to be distinguished from this latent activity, must, therefore,
be posited as not suppressed, not checked; hence,
as real activity.

Both the activity of the object of sensation and
of the sensating are to be posited in the Ego.
Hence, there must be a ground of relation, of equality, of these two opposites. This ground of relation must be both, real activity and suppressed activity. As real activity, it must be a positing of the
Ego; the Ego must be its *real ground*. As suppressed activity, it must be a *determined*, limited
positing; but the Ego can not limit itself. The
ground of limitation must, therefore, be in the Non-
Ego. The Non-Ego is its *ideal ground*, is the
ground that it has quantity at all. It is to be both
together, to be regarded in both ways. Its *limitation*
is also to have its ground in the *Ego;* and its *being*
its ground also in the Non-Ego. Ideal and real
ground are to be both one and the same. The act
is to be regarded absolutely as both; as the absolute act of the Ego in regard to both its being and
determinateness; and as the absolute act of the

Non-Ego in regard to both its being and determinateness.

Such an act is called *contemplation*.

The Ego contemplates a Non-Ego. In the contemplation the Ego posits itself as absolutely independent of the Non-Ego; contemplates it because it
does so, without outward force. It posits by its own
activity, and with the consciousness of its activity,
each of the characteristics (qualities) of the Non-
Ego. But, at the same time, it posits them as
merely reproductions of the characteristics of an
external something. This external something is to
have the same characteristics originally and independent of the Ego, and is to have them according to
its own laws, not by virtue of the laws of the consciousness of the Ego. As the Non-Ego is not the
cause that the Ego contemplates it, so the Ego is
not the cause of the determinateness of the Non-
Ego; both are to be utterly independent, and yet
in complete harmony. The truth is, if it were possible to regard the Non-Ego as in itself, and not as
in the contemplation, and the contemplating Ego
as in itself, and not as in relation to the contemplated Non-Ego, they would both be found determined in the same manner, and hence their harmony.

We have now deduced the ground of all cognition as such; we have shown why the Ego is and
must be intelligence, namely, because the Ego must
originally (that is, without consciousness and for
the very sake of making consciousness possible)

unite a contradiction existing *within itself*, between
its activity and its passivity. It is clear that we
could not have made this deduction had we not
gone beyond all consciousness.

We add the following for the purpose of throwing
a clearer light on the foregoing, and of promoting
an insight into our method. In our deductions we
always regard only the *product* of an act of the human mind, not the act itself. But in every subsequent deduction the act which gave rise to the first
product becomes itself product by a new act which
gives rise to it. Thus, whatever is established in
every preceding deduction without any further determination simply as an act of the mind, is posited
and thus further determined in every subsequent
deduction. So, also, in the present case. If we
look close, we shall find that the contemplation, just
now synthetically deduced, is to be found already
in the previous deduction as an act. That act con-
sisted in this : The Ego, we found, must posit its
conflicting activity, as pure or as not pure under
condition, in the Ego. Such an act of positing is
evidently the contemplation now deduced. In itself, *as* act, it is solely grounded in the Ego, in the
postulate that the Ego must posit in itself whatsoever is to occur in the Ego. But it also posits
something in the Ego which is absolutely not to
have its ground in the Ego, but in the Non-Ego,
namely, the impression of the act. *As* act this contemplation is completely independent of the impression and the impression of it ; both proceed in parallel.

UNION OF SENSATION AND CONTEMPLATION.

How can the Ego posit itself as the sensating? or, popularly expressed, how does the Ego manage in order to have sensation? This was the question we had to solve. The deduced contemplation would seem to preclude the possibility of such a positing. For contemplation, though as act having its ground in the Ego, posits something in the Ego which has its absolute ground in the Non-Ego.

The Ego is to posit something foreign to it in itself; this foreign something is not-activity, or passivity, and the Ego is to posit this passivity in itself through activity; the Ego is, therefore, to be active and passive together, and only on the supposition of such a union of activity and passivity is sensation possible. We must, therefore, show up a third link, wherein activity and passivity are so thoroughly united that *this* determined activity is not possible without *this* determined passivity, and *vice versa;* that one can only be explained through the other, and that each considered in itself is incomplete.

No activity in the Ego can be so related to passivity as to *produce* it; for, in that case, the Ego would both posit and annihilate something in itself at the same time, which is a contradiction. But the activity may be so related to the passivity as to *determine* it, to draw its limit. And this is indeed an activity which is not possible without a passivity. For the Ego can not cancel itself a part of

its activity; the canceling must occur through
something outside of the Ego. The Ego can, therefore, draw no limit, unless a something to be limited
has been given it externally. Determining is, therefore, an activity which necessarily relates itself to a
passivity. Likewise passivity is necessarily related
to an activity when it is considered as simply a
limitation of activity. Our third link is, therefore,
limitation.

Sensation is only possible, therefore, in so far as
the Ego and the Non-Ego mutually limit each
other, and extends no further than this common
limit. Beyond the limit the Ego is no longer sensating, but intelligence.

By means of limitation, therefore, can the Ego
be posited as the sensating. If it were not limited
by an opposite, the Ego could not be posited as the
sensating.

But the Ego is to be limited *for itself,* is to posit
itself as the limited, the sensating. In so far as the
Ego *is* limited, it only extends to the limit; but, in
so far as it *posits itself* as limited, it necessarily
goes beyond the limit. The Ego is posited as limited means, therefore: in so far as it extends merely
to the limit, the Ego is opposed to an unlimited
Ego which goes beyond the limit. Such an unlimited Ego must, therefore, be posited for the purpose of relating the limited Ego to it; and this Ego
is unlimited and unlimitable in so far as its activity
is altogether grounded in itself; or in so far as it is
ideal activity, while as limited Ego it is *real* activity.

The real activity of the Ego only goes to the
limit ; its ideal activity extends beyond that limit.
Neither activity is without the other.   Ideality and ✓
reality are synthetically united in the Ego.

The real activity can be related to the Ego, because it is also ideal ; and by reason of this, its very
ideality, (freedom, spontaneity,) it is ascribed to
the Ego as real and limited activity, or as sensation.

Now, it will be observed that the ideal activity
has no relation at all to a Non-Ego, is purely ideal.
The Non-Ego being thus invisible to that ideal
activity, so the Ego also is invisible to it.   We, ✓
looking down upon the Ego, see the Ego act, it is
true, but the Ego itself does *not* posit itself on this
stand-point as acting.   It forgets, if we may say so, ✓
itself in the object of its activity ; and thus we have
an activity which has all the appearance of a passivity.   The act is an *unconscious contemplation.*   The ✓
Ego is the *contemplated,* in so far as it has sensation ; but it is also the *contemplating,* only not conscious thereof, not positing itself as contemplating.

Here we first meet with a substrate for the Ego,
namely, the pure activity of the Ego which is posited as being, although there be no foreign influence upon it.   *The being* of this activity is *independent* of all foreign influence upon the Ego ; but,
since it can be *posited* only through its opposite,
the *positedness* of this activity is dependent upon a
foreign influence.

Sensation is to be posited.   This is our task

But sensation is only possible in so far as the sensating is directed upon an object of sensation, and
posits the same in the Ego. Hence, the object of
sensation must also be related to the Ego by the
mediating conception of limitation.

True, it has already been thus related in our first
deduction of sensation. But at present sensation
itself is to be posited. We have just thus posited
it by means of a contemplation ; but this contemplation excluded the object of sensation. Therein
it was.insufficient, for the object of sensation must
also be posited as included in and appropriated by
the contemplation.

This appropriation is to be achieved by means of
the conception of limitation, and is only possible if
the limitation is posited. The solution, therefore,
required is, how is the object of sensation limited ?

Evidently, the very fact of its being excluded in
sensation, and posited as limiting this sensation,
proves that it is posited as limited by the Ego,
or as a Non-Ego. But again, because it is thus
limited by, excluded from, the Ego, it is also posited, in a higher sense, *in the Ego.* The Ego limits
it ; hence, it must be in the Ego.

And now we see clearly how the object of sensation is placed in relation to the Ego by the conception of limitation. The limitation is the act of the
Ego, whereby the object of sensation is necessarily
placed within its sphere of action, and appropriated
by the Ego as its own.

In our deduction of sensation we already touched this point. There the object of sensation was related to the Ego, by the positing of an activity opposed to the Ego as the condition of such relation ; that is, as an activity which might or might not be posited. The Ego was, therefore, endowed with the faculty of positing or not-positing something. Mark well : not the faculty to posit, nor the faculty not to posit, but the faculty *to posit or not to posit ;* that is, the power to posit a something, and not posit this same something in one and the same synthetically united act.

Namely : Sensation, we had shown, is only possible if the Non-Ego is posited as accidental condition of the object of sensation ; *how* this positing was done we did not stop to inquire. But this positing can only be achieved if the Ego posits and not-posits at the same time ; hence, such an act of positing and not-positing must necessarily occur in sensation as a connecting link. Now let us see how such an act is accomplished.

The activity in this positing and not-positing is √ evidently ideal activity. It goes beyond the point of limitation. It has, moreover, its ground only in the Ego, since we deduced it solely from the requirement that the Ego must *posit* in itself whatever is to *be* in the Ego. But, if the activity is thus solely grounded in the Ego, it is a mere not-posit-

18

ing, and no positing whatever ; it is simply pure
activity.

But this activity is also to be a positing ; and it
is a positing, because it does not cancel or diminish
the activity of the Non-Ego, but only places it
beyond its own sphere ; and since a Non-Ego is
never beyond the sphere of the Ego, but only opposed to it, the Ego by this its activity posits the
Non-Ego—only it posits it throughout an arbitrary
infinity.

The Ego is, therefore, limited, because a Non-
Ego is posited through it ; and is, at the same time,
unlimited, because it posits the Non-Ego by its
ideal activity throughout an infinity.

The activity of the Ego, therefore, in this positing and not-positing is a *limiting* through ideal·
(that is, free and unlimited) activity.

Now let us determine this activity of positing
and not-positing by its opposite ; that is, by a *posited* and *not-posited.*

The activity of the Non-Ego is such a posited and
not-posited. That activity is posited and not-posited at the same time   It is posited, for, if it were
not posited by the Ego, there would be no limit ;
and it is at the same time not-posited, because the
Ego constantly extends the limit, and thus cancels
it.   The limit is always posited by the Ego and the
Non-Ego together, only by each in a different manner ; and therein they are opposites.   In so far as
the limit is posited by the Ego it is *ideal;* and in
so far as it is posited by the Non-Ego it is *real;*

but is both in a synthetical unity. It is real only in so far as it is ideal ; or in so far as it is posited by the Ego ; it is ideal (that is, it can be extended by the Ego) only in so far as it is real ; or in so far as it is posited by the Non-Ego.

Thus the activity of the Ego, which penetrates beyond the limit, becomes both real and ideal. It is real because it tends upon something posited by the real ; it is ideal, because it tends upon it by its own election.

Thus the perceived becomes relatable to the Ego. The activity of the Non-Ego remains excluded, for it is pushed together with the limit into the infinite ; but the product of this activity, the limitation in the Ego, as the condition of its ideal activity, becomes relatable to the Ego.

But since that, to which the product of the Non-Ego becomes related, is the *ideal activity* of the Ego—the same activity which is to posit the relation —there is no distinction between the relating and that to which something is to be related. Hence, there is no relation at all with the Ego ; and the whole deduced occurrence is a *contemplation,* in which the Ego loses itself in the object of its activity. The *contemplated* is an idealistically viewed product of the Non-Ego, which contemplation extends into the infinite. And thus we obtain a substrate for the Non-Ego, as we before obtained one for the Ego. The *contemplating* is, of course, the Ego, which, however, does not reflect upon itself.

Sensation was to be posited. We have seen both

how the sensating and the object of sensation are posited through contemplation; but, in order to have sensation posited, the sensating and the object of sensation must not be posited separately, but in synthetic unity. This is now our concluding task.

In order to posit the Ego as limited, as sensating, we required an ideal activity, opposed to the limited activity. Again, in order to posit the object of sensation, which was beyond the limit, nevertheless within the sphere of the Ego, we required an activity of the Ego, always removing the limit into an infinity. The synthetical union of both would signify: The Ego, in order to be able to limit itself, must remove (extend) the limit; and in order to remove the limit it must limit itself. Thus sensation and contemplation would be synthetically united; and in sensation, inner contemplation (the contemplation of the sensation) and outer contemplation (that of the object of sensation) would also be synthetically united; and our task would be accomplished.

1st. The limited activity of the Ego is to be determined by its opposite, the ideal activity of the Ego. In so far, therefore, the ideal activity is the presupposition, the *condition* of a relation between the two activities—by no means the sequence of such a relation. If both are to be related, then the ideal activity is presupposed.

The limited activity is limited, let us say, in C. Its opposite, therefore, the ideal activity, is characterized by this, that it is *not* limited *in* C, (whether it be limited in another point is left, and must be left, undetermined.) Hence, the determined point C is in this relation related to the ideal activity; and, since the latter is its presupposition, must be contained in it. The ideal activity is not originally directed upon C, but touches it in the relation by chance, as it were. As soon as the relation occurs, however, the point C is posited wherever it occurs; and there is no freedom in positing its place of occurrence. This place is determined; and only the express positing of the point *as* point is activity of the relation. Moreover, in the relation, this ideal activity is posited as *going beyond this point* C. This, again, is not possible, unless the point is posited *in* the ideal activity as a point, beyond which it goes. Hence, throughout all the extension of the activity, this point is carried over in it, as an idealistic point of limitation, wherewith to measure the distance, as it were, from the first fixed and immovable point. But since the activity is to *go* beyond, and never to be limited, this second ideal point is also not fixed, but always a moving one, and in such a manner that throughout the whole extension no point can (idealistically) be posited, which this point has not touched. As certain, therefore, as that ideal activity goes beyond the point of limitation, that point is carried out into the infinite, (until, perhaps, we shall touch a new limit.)

Now, what activity carries the point thus beyond the ideal activity, or that of the relation? Evi-

dently, since for the ideal activity no such point exists previous to the relation ; and since, on the other
hand, the relation itself presupposes that carrying
beyond, it must be thus : that in the very relation
and through it the point of limitation as well as its
carrying beyond are posited synthetically in it ;
and since all relation is grounded in the Ego, this
must also be done through ideal activity, but
/ through another ideal activity than that which we
know. We have thus the following three acts of
the Ego : one, which has the ideal activity as its
object ; another, which has the real and limited
activity as its object ; and these two must be one
and the same, though as yet we do not see how this
can be ; and thirdly, an activity which carries the
limit from the real into the ideal activity. By
means of this latter, the ideal activity itself is distinguished : firstly, as going merely to C, and thus
far remaining altogether pure ; and, secondly, as
going beyond C, and carrying forward the limit.

2d. But this solving the difficulty of positing the
Ego as limited and unlimited together, by calling
its limited activity real and the other ideal, will not
suffice. For if you ask, again, what is its real activity, all you can say is, its limited activity, etc.,
and the explanation is a circle. We must have a
different ground of distinction than that of limitation, or we have no explanation at all.

Before finding this ground, let us premise what
we shall discover as the final result ; that is, the
Ego cannot posit itself *for itself* at all, unless it

limits itself, and hence unless it goes beyond it-self.

Originally the Ego is posited through itself; or, it is what it is, for any outside intelligence; it is its own ground; that is, thus it must be thought, if the Ego is thought. Moreover, it has a tendency (see the " Practical Part ") to *fill up* and *encircle* the infinity; or, to reflect upon itself as an infinite. But this mere tendency produces no act of the Ego.

Now, posit it thus, tending toward C, and at that point checked—of course, for any possible outside intelligence, which observes the Ego, and which has posited that tendency in its own consciousness. What will thereby arise in the Ego? Evidently a tendency to reflect upon itself, which it could not 'do before, since all reflected must be limited, and the Ego before was not limited.

In C the Ego is limited; hence, in C there arises in the Ego, together with the limitation, the reflection upon itself; it returns into itself, finds itself, feels *itself*, but clearly nothing outside of itself.

This reflection of the Ego upon itself is, as we clearly see from our stand-point of an outside intel-ligence, an act of the Ego, grounded in the neces-sary tendency and the added condition. But what is this reflection for the Ego itself? Clearly: In this reflection it first finds itself; arises first *for it-self*. It can not accept itself as the ground of something before it ever was! Hence, that self-feeling, self-finding is for the Ego a mere passivity;

it *reflects* not for itself, but is *reflected* by an outside
something. We, the outside intelligence, saw it
act, it is true ; but the *Ego itself* does not see itself
act ; is purely passive.

The Ego *is* now for itself, because, and in so far
as it is limited, and being an Ego, it must posit itself
as limited ; that is, must oppose to itself a limiting
something. This is done by an activity, which goes
beyond the limit C, and views the limit as an opposite to the Ego. This activity is altogether grounded in the Ego. The Ego *posits* a limiting something,
because it *is* limited, and because it must posit whatever it is. It posits it *as* a limiting something, and
hence as an opposite and Non-Ego, because it is to
explain its own *limitation*. Let no one, therefore,
believe that we open here a way to penetrate into
the thing *per se ;* that is, the thing without reference to an Ego. Our presupposition was : the
Ego is limited. You ask : Has this limitation in
itself, that is, without reference to a possible intelligence, a ground, and how is this ground constituted ? But how can you ask so ? And how can
I answer you rationally when you require me to
abstract from all reason ? For the Ego, (for reason,) *that limitation has a ground*, since all limitation presupposes a limiting ; and for the Ego
this ground is also *not* in the Ego, for then the Ego
would be contradictory, but in an opposite ; and
such an opposite is, therefore, posited as such by
the Ego, according to those laws of reason, and is
its product.

Let us repeat this : We say the Ego must be limited if it is to be an Ego ; and must, by the laws of its being, posit this limitation and its ground in a limiting something ; the latter is, therefore, its product.

Now, if any body should be so thoroughly penetrated with transcendent dogmatism that he can not yet tear himself from it, he might probably argue thus against us : " I admit all this ; but this merely explains the representation of the thing in the Ego, which certainly is its product, but not the thing itself which I want to know about. You say the Ego is limited. Very well. But this *limitation, considered in itself,* and abstracting altogether from its reflection through the Ego, *must have a ground,* and this ground is the thing in itself." To this argument we reply : You explain just like the Ego which we are considering ; and you are that Ego just as surely as you follow the laws of reason in your argument. If you will but reflect maturely upon this fact, you will see that you with your argument remain, though unconsciously, in the same circle which we have just pointed out. You will never escape that circle, unless you can get beyond those laws of thinking. But when you do get beyond them, you will cease to urge such objections

The Ego is, therefore, in this whole act utterly passive and unconscious of its activity ; wherefore, the product thereof, if it should appear to the Ego, will necessarily appear to it as existing independently of it.

3d. The Ego has gone, for an outside observer, beyond C with the tendency to reflect upon itself. But as it can not reflect without being limited, it is clear that it must be again limited beyond C, say in the point D. The Ego also produced, for an outside observer, a Non-Ego, but unconscious of its activity. Now, it reflects upon its product, and posits it *as* a Non-Ego, of course without further determination and without consciousness, contradictory as it may sound, since the Ego has not yet been reflected upon.

This second product, a *posited* Non-Ego, must again be reflected upon. The Ego in sensating is posited as passive; the opposite Non-Ego must be posited as active.

This Non-Ego, posited as active, must again be reflected upon; and now we enter the field of our investigation.

Through the Ego and in the Ego, though without consciousness, as we have repeatedly said, an active Non-Ego is posited. This is reflected upon, or a new activity of the Ego is directed upon it. Reflection only tends upon a limited; hence, the activity of the Non-Ego is necessarily limited, limited *as* activity, not in its extent, as might be supposed, for as yet we have no space. The Non-Ego, therefore, is checked in its activity, becomes passive; the manifestation of its power is checked, and only a *substrate* of the power remains. In so far as the Ego reflects, it does not reflect upon this reflection itself; hence, it does not become conscious of

its activity therein, and we thus again obtain the
above external (though not yet posited *as* external)
first original contemplation, which has neither consciousness, self-consciousness, nor even consciousness of the object.

We are now at the same point from which we
started in our second part of the theoretical part
of the science of knowledge, that is, at the contradictory opposite activities of the Ego and the
Non-Ego. We have seen that no activity of the
Ego can be annihilated by the Non-Ego, unless the
Ego proceeds from what we may describe as its
original sphere, that is, the sphere between A and
C, into the sphere of the Non-Ego, which extends
from C into infinity. We have also seen that no
activity of the Non-Ego is possible unless the Ego
first posits the Non-Ego and its activity ; both are
products of the Ego. But we have only seen this
from the stand-point of an outside observer ; it remains that the Ego should see this *for itself*.
How ?

The observer discovered an Ego as a something,
and a Non-Ego also as a something, and a point of
union between these two. The limitation of the
Ego, however, did not appear until the observer
began to reflect upon the latter two ; by reflection
he discovered this limitation and all the acts resulting therefrom in the Ego. By virtue of these acts
the Ego has now attained the same stand-point of
reflection which the observer occupied. For it has
been shown now that within the Ego itself, within

its own sphere of action, as heretofore posited *for the observer*—and as the product of the Ego itself there is another Ego, so to speak—an Ego perceptible because limited, and besides this Ego a Non-Ego, and a point of union between both. Hence, the Ego need only undertake the same reflection which the observer undertook, to discover the same.

It is true the Ego has already reflected at the very commencement of its action.   But that reflection was necessary.   The Ego had a tendency to reflect ; the limitation of the Ego came as the condition of the possibility of such reflecting, and hence the Ego reflected necessarily.   From this necessary reflection arose sensation feeling, and all we have deduced.   The tendency to reflect, however, still continuing in the Ego—because it extends into the infinite—the Ego can now reflect upon its first reflecting, and all the consequences of that reflecting, since the condition of all reflection, limitation through something which may be regarded as a Non-Ego, exists.

If the original reflection of the Ego, therefore, was necessary, its present reflecting is *not* so.   For the condition of this present reflecting is not unconditionally a Non-Ego, but may also be regarded as contained in the Ego.   It is not limited by an absolute Non-Ego in this reflection, but by a Non-Ego which is its own production, and which hence may be regarded as such ; and thus the limitation, the condition of the reflection, may be taken away.

But if what we have posited in the Ego really is

in the *Ego, then* the Ego must reflect. Hence, we postulate the reflection. For example, many impressions may be made upon the Ego; unless it reflects upon them, no impressions have been made upon the *Ego.* It may, and it may not, so reflect. At present we postulate it.

Hence, the demanded reflection occurs now with absolute spontaneity; the Ego reflects because it reflects. Thus, not only the tendency to reflect has its ground in the Ego, but even the *act of reflection;* to be sure, it is *conditioned* by a Non-Ego, by a received impression, but it is not *necessitated* thereby

In this self-reflection of the Ego there are two links, the reflected Ego and the reflecting Ego. Both will probably be united in a third, according to our synthetical method.

1st. The Ego we have hitherto been able only to characterize as feeling, as a feeling Ego and nothing else. The reflected Ego *is* limited means, therefore, it feels itself limited, feels an outside compulsion. Again, in so far as the Ego posits itself as limited, it goes beyond the limit, that is, it posits, at the same time, a Non-Ego, but without consciousness of its action.

The feeling of compulsion is, therefore, united with a contemplation, but an unconscious contemplation, of the Non-Ego.

Both the itself-feeling Ego and the contemplated Non-Ego must be synthetically united; this is done by the limit. The Ego, because it feels itself limited, posits the contemplated *Non-Ego* as the *cause* of its limitation, as the explanation of the feeling of compulsion.

But the difficulty is, where does the original feeling of compulsion arise from? To be sure, I explain it by the Non-Ego, but the feeling *precedes* the contemplation of the Non-Ego. Hence, it must be explained independently of the Non-Ego. This question leads to our second, the antithesis.

2d. The act of the reflecting Ego we have characterized as absolutely spontaneous, ideal activity of the Ego. As such it must be posited, that is, as going beyond the limit into the infinite. But to be reflected upon, it can not go into the infinite; hence, in its going beyond the limit, it must nevertheless be limited. There must be a limitation conjointly with the unlimitedness. How?

The activity can not be reflected as activity, (the Ego can never become immediately conscious of its activity,) but as *substrate*, that is, as product of an absolute activity of the Ego, a product contemplated by the Ego without consciousness of the contemplation. Hence, in so far as the Ego reflects upon the absolute spontaneity of its reflection in the first act, an unlimited product of the activity of the Ego, as such, is posited. This product, posited as product of the Ego, must be placed in relation to the Ego. It can not be related to the contemplating Ego, for this Ego has not yet been posited; it must be related to the Ego which feels itself limited. But this latter Ego is opposed to that

Ego which produces through freedom an unlimited ; the Ego which feels itself limited is not free, but is under compulsion ; and the producing Ego is not compelled, but produces spontaneously.

Thus, indeed, it must be, if relation and synthetical union is to be possible and necessary ; and we have only to find the ground of the relation.

This ground must be activity with freedom, or absolute activity. But such an activity can not be predicated of the limited Ego ; hence, a union of both seems impossible.

One step more, and we shall find the surprising result, putting an end to all old errors, and reinstating reason for evermore in her eternal rights.

The Ego is to be the relating. Hence, the Ego necessarily, absolutely of itself, and against the outward ground of limitation, proceeds beyond itself, and thus appropriates the product which, through freedom, it makes its own product ; ground of relation and the relating link are the same.

Of this act the Ego never becomes conscious, and never can become conscious ; its essence consists in absolute spontaneity, and, as soon as you reflect upon it, it ceases to be spontaneity. The Ego is only free in acting ; as soon as it reflects upon this act, it ceases to be free, and the act becomes product.

From the impossibility of the consciousness of a free act arises the whole distinction between ideality and reality, between representation and the thing in itself.

Freedom, or, which is the same, the immediate acting of the Ego, is the uniting link of ideality and reality. The Ego *is* free in positing itself as free, in liberating itself; and it posits itself as free, or liberates itself in being free. Determinateness and being are one; acting and product are one; in determining itself to act, the Ego acts; and in acting it determines itself.

The Ego can not posit itself in reflection as free, for this would be a contradiction which could never lead to freedom. But it appropriates something as product of its own free activity, and thus mediately posits itself free.

3d. The Ego is limited in feeling itself, and posits itself in so far as limited. This was our first statement. The Ego is free, and posits itself at least mediately as free, because it posits the limitation as product of its free activity. This was our second statement. Both statements, limitation in feeling and freedom in producing, are utterly opposites. They might be united by showing that the Ego could posit itself in different respects as free and limited. But our statements have distinctly asserted that the Ego is to posit itself as limited, because and in so far as it posits itself free, and *vice versa*. The Ego is to be free and limited in one and the same respect, and this is the contradiction which is to be solved in a third statement. Let us look at the two statements a little closer.

THESIS.

1st. The Ego is to posit itself as limited because and in so far as it posits itself as free ; or, the Ego *is* free only in so far as it *acts.* Now, What is acting ? What its distinction from not-acting ? All acting presupposes power. Absolute acting means, a power determining itself solely through and in itself, that is, giving itself a direction. Before, the power had no direction, was latent power, a mere tendency to apply power. The Ego, to posit itself as absolutely acting, must, therefore, in reflection, also be able to posit itself as not-acting. To determine itself as acting presupposes rest.

Again, the power gives itself a direction, that is, an object. Gives itself an object ; hence, it must have had the object before ; must have received the object passively. Hence, a self-determining to act on the part of the Ego presupposes passivity.

New difficulties everywhere ! But from them the clearest light will be thrown upon a subject.

ANTITHESIS.

2d. The Ego is to posit itself as free because and in so far as it posits itself as limited. The Ego posits itself as limited means, it posits a limit to its activity, (it does not produce this limit, but posits it as posited by an opposite power, a Non-Ego.) Hence, in order to be limited passively, the Ego must previously have acted ; its power must have

19*

had a direction, and a self-determined direction. All limitation presupposes free activity.

3d. The Ego is as yet for itself limited, necessitated, in so far as it goes beyond the limitation and posits a Non-Ego which it contemplates without self-consciousness. Now, this Non-Ego is, as we have seen from our higher stand-point, a product of the Ego, and the Ego must reflect upon it as its product. This reflection necessarily occurs through absolute self-activity.

But the Ego, this very same activity, can not, at the same time, produce a Non-Ego and reflect upon it as its production.

Hence, it must interrupt its first activity; and must so interrupt it through absolute spontaneity. Only thus, indeed, is absolute spontaneity possible. For the Ego is to determine itself. But the Ego is in essence nothing but activity. Hence, it must limit one of its acts; and, because it is nothing but activity, it must limit the act by another opposite act.

Again, the Ego is to posit its product, the opposite Non-Ego *as* its product. Through the same act which interrupts the first one it thus posits the Non-Ego, and elevates it to a higher degree of reflection. The lower, first region of reflection is thus broken off; and all we have to do now is to seek the point of union of both forms of reflection.

But since the Ego is never immediately conscious of its acting, it can posit the product as its product only through a new reflection by mediation.

Through this new reflection the product must be posited as product of absolute freedom, the distinctive characteristic whereof is, that it might be otherwise, or might be posited otherwise. Contemplation floats between several determinations, and posits amongst all possible determinations only one, whereby the product receives the peculiar character of an *image.**

In so far as the Ego posits this image as product of its activity, it necessarily opposes to it something which is not its product, which is no longer determinable, but perfectly determined, and thus determined through itself, not through the Ego. This is the *real thing* by which the Ego is guided in

* Let us exemplify this by an object with various characteristics. In the first contemplation, the productive contemplation, I am lost in an object. I reflect upon myself at first, find myself, and distinguish myself from the object. But as yet all is mixed and confused in the object, and it is nothing further than an object. I then begin to reflect upon its several characteristics, for instance, its figure, color, etc., and posit them in my consciousness. At each separate characteristic of this kind, I am at first in doubt and hesitating. I then make some arbitrary scheme of a figure, color, etc., the basis of my observation, and now observe closer. And now I first begin to determine my scheme of the figure, perhaps as a cube, and my scheme of a color, perhaps as dark green. By this process of going from an undetermined product of free imagination to its complete determinateness in one and the same act, that which occurs in my consciousness becomes an image, and is posited as an image. It becomes *my* product, because I must posit it as determined through absolute self-activity.

sketching its image, and which must, therefore, necessarily appear to it in its imaging, (in its representation.)   This *real thing* is the product of the
interrupted act, but which can not now be possibly
posited as such product.

The Ego images after this thing.   Hence, the
thing must be entertained in the Ego and accessible to its activity ; or, in other words, we must be
able to show a ground of relation between the thing
and the image of the thing.   Such a ground of relation is the perfectly determined but unconscious
contemplation of the thing.   For and in this contemplation all the characteristics of the thing are
perfectly determined, and in so far it is related to
the thing, and the Ego is passive in the contemplation.   Still, it is also an act of the Ego, and, hence,
relatable to the Ego, active in the imaging of this
thing.   The Ego has access to this contemplation,
and determines the image in accordance with the
characteristics furnished in the contemplation.   In
other words, the Ego reviews spontaneously the
several characteristics of the thing, enumerates
them, and gives its attention to them.   Or, this unconscious contemplation is the ground of all harmony we assume between our representations and
the things, and explains the whole difficulty.

In imaging, the Ego is perfectly free.   The
image is determined thus, because the Ego freely
so determines it ; and this freedom makes the image
relatable to the Ego, and capable of being posited
in the Ego as its product.   But the image is to be

not empty, but corresponding to a thing outside of the Ego ; hence, it must be relatable to this thing. The thing has become relatable to the Ego, as we have seen, by means of a presupposed immediate unconscious contemplation thereof. The image, to be related to the Ego, must be determined by the thing so as to be an exact counterpart of it, and this complete and same determination of image and thing is their ground of relation. There is no distinction now at all between the image and the unconscious contemplation of the thing.

But this result is a contradiction of our former statement, that nothing which is necessarily determined as such or such can be a product of the Ego.

What in our former statement was a representation, now becomes a thing *per se*, and the question still remains, whether there are only things and no representations, as the last result would imply, or representations and no real things, as our former statement asserted.

A synthetic solution of these conflicting statements would assert : an image is not at all possible without a thing ; and a thing—at least *for* the Ego —is not possible without an image.

The Ego is to relate the image to the thing. This relation, we must show, is not possible without presupposing the image *as such*, that is, as free product of the Ego. In other words, the thing is not possible without the image.

Again, the Ego is to construct the image with

freedom. It must be shown that this is not possible without presupposing the thing; or, that the image is not possible without the thing, of course, for the Ego.

1st. The Ego is to relate the image to the thing. As this act of the Ego does not occur in immediate consciousness, it is difficult to see how a distinction can be posited between the image and the thing, unless the Ego occurs *mediately* in consciousness, that is, unless the object (or unconscious production) of the activity of the Ego (the thing) is posited as product of freedom, that is, as accidental, as a thus which could be otherwise.

The thing is thus posited as accidental, in so far as the perfectly determined image is related to it. The perfectly determined image, for instance, or quality, is the red color. This is to be related to a thing by an absolute act of the Ego. The thing is to be determined by the image. Hence, the thing must be posited before this relation, and independently of it, as such, which may be, or may not be, thus determined; and is only thus posited as accidentally determined in consequence of the act of relation. Hence, the thing discovers itself, since its quality is altogether accidental, as presupposed product of the Ego, which has no predicate but that of being. The free act, and the necessity that such a free act should occur, is the only ground for proceeding from the undetermined to the determined, and *vice versa.*

ANOTHER ILLUSTRATION OF THIS POINT.

You say A is red. A, the first posited, is posited as, firstly, completely determined by itself. A is A, and nothing else. Now, you add and say, A is *red.* Red is also completely determined, it is what it is, and nothing else. Now, you join both together. What was A, as far as *redness* is concerned, before this joining? Evidently altogether undetermined. You might have predicated any color of it. It is the joining, expressed by the copula *is*, which makes the undetermined determined, which negates all other determinations but the one stated. If A had been previously determined, you could not have made an assertion of it.

Result : *If the reality of the thing (as substance) is presupposed, the quality thereof is posited as accidental, and hence the thing is mediately posited as product of the Ego.*

It is the quality of the thing to which we relate the Ego.

2d. The Ego is to construct the image with perfect freedom. In so far as it does this, floating between many possible determinations of the thing and choosing one, the Ego mediately posits itself as Ego, and limits itself. The image is not yet determined, but it is being determined ; the Ego is in the act of determining. We will call this its condition, A. (It is the inner contemplation of the Ego in constructing.)

In so far as the Ego acts, it posits over and

against this free floating image, and mediately against itself, the imaging, the perfectly determined quality, of which we have said above that it is taken up and seized by the Ego, by means of the immediate but unconscious contemplation of the thing. This determined quality is posited as opposite, hence as excluded from the Ego. We will call it B.

If A is totality, B is excluded from it ; but, if B is posited, A is excluded from the totality. For the Ego posits the quality as determined, and must do so if it is to posit itself as free in the imaging. The Ego must, therefore, reflect on this determination of the quality ; and by this the Ego is excluded from the totality ; that is, it is no longer self-sufficient, no longer through itself, but through another and an opposite ; that is, its condition, its reflection, the image within it, can no longer be explained altogether out of itself, but only by an external other. Hence, we have A + B, or A determined by B as totality. (External, determined, *pure* contemplation.)

The reflection must turn upon A + B in this their connection, that is, it must turn upon the quality, *as a determined*, particular quality, if the quality is to be in the Ego, or in consciousness. This reflection occurs, of course, like every reflection, through absolute spontaneity ; the Ego reflects because it is Ego. It does not become conscious of this spontaneity ; but the object of its reflection, *as such*, becomes product of this spontaneity, and must, therefore, bear the character of a product of a free act, that is, *accidentalness.* But it can not be accidental in the same manner in which it is posited as *determined,* hence it must be so in another respect. We shall soon see how.

This accidental character makes it a product of the Ego ; the Ego, therefore, determines itself again, and this it can not do without opposing to itself something, that is, a Non-Ego.

REMARK.

(The Ego reflects with freedom, an act of determining which, by its very nature, becomes itself determined ; but it can not reflect or posit a limit without, at the same time, absolutely producing something as that which forms the limit. *Determining* and *producing,* therefore, always go together ; and it is this which keeps up the identity of consciousness.)

This something, opposed to the Ego, is *necessary* in relation to the determined quality ; and this quality is *accidental* in relation to the something. Again, this something, like the quality, is opposed to the Ego, and hence, like it, is a Non-Ego, but a *necessary* Non-Ego.

But the quality, as determined, as something against which the Ego is merely passive, we have seen, must be excluded from the Ego ; and the Ego, when reflecting upon it as so determined, must thus exclude it.

20

Now, we have just found another Non-Ego, which the Ego, in reflecting, excludes as determined and necessary. Both, therefore, must be placed in relation to each other and be synthetically united. Their ground of union is that both are Non-Ego, and hence, in relation to the Ego, both are one and the same ; their ground of distinction is, that the quality is accidental, might be otherwise ; but the *substrate*, as such, is necessary in relation to the quality. The quality *must* have a *substrate*, but the substrate must not necessarily have this particular quality. Such a relation of the accidental to the necessary in their synthetical union is called the relation of *substantiality*.

The reflection must turn upon the excluded B, the *necessary* Non-Ego. From this reflection it follows that A + B, which was heretofore posited as totality, can no longer be totality, that is, can no longer be the only contents of the Ego, and hence accidental. It must be determined by the necessary B. The formula now is, A + B determined by B.

First of all, the quality, the image, or whatever you choose to call it, must be thus determined by the necessary Non-Ego. This quality was posited as accidental, the thing as necessary ; both, therefore, as opposites. Now, in the reflection of the Ego, they must be united in the same Ego. This is done by absolute spontaneity. The union is altogether product of the Ego. The union is posited means, a product is posited through the Ego. The Ego, however, is never immediately conscious of its

acting, but only in and by means of the product.
The union of both must, therefore, be posited as accidental ; and since all accidental is posited as arising
through acting, it follows that the union itself must
be posited as having arisen through acting.   But
that which, in its existence, is itself accidental and
dependent, can not be posited as acting ; hence,
only the necessary can be thus posited.   Hence, in
the reflection, and by means of it, the conception
of acting is transferred to the necessary, though in
reality this conception lies only in the reflecting,
and the accidental is posited as product thereof, as
expression of the free activity of the necessary.
Such a synthetical relation is called the relation of
causality, and the thing, viewed in this synthetic
union of the necessary and the accidental in it, is
the *real thing*.*

* We append at this important point the following remarks :

1. The just discovered act of the Ego is evidently an act through
the power of imagination in contemplation ; for, firstly, the Ego
unites opposites in it, which is the business of imagination ; and,
secondly, it loses itself in this act, and transfers what is in it upon
the object of its activity, which is the characteristic of contemplation.

2. The so-called category of causality shows itself here, therefore,
as having its origin only in the power of imagination, and thus it is
indeed ; nothing can get into the understanding except through the
power of imagination.   What alteration the understanding may
make of this product of the imagination can here already be fore-
seen.   We have posited the thing as acting *free* without any rule,
(and until the understanding comprehends its own manner of acting
it is thus posited in consciousness as *fate*,) because the power of
imagination transfers to it its own *free* acting.   The sequence of a
law is wanting.   Whenever understanding shall be directed upon

That which we have called expression of the activity of the thing, and which we found perfectly
determined, is posited in the Ego, and is determined

the thing so as to comprehend it according to law, then the thing
will also appear as working in obedience to those laws.

3. KANT, who causes the categories to be originally generated as
forms of thinking, and who, from his point of view, is very correct
in this, stands in need of the schemes sketched by the understanding in order to make possible their application to the objects; hence,
he does as we do, and makes them accessible to the working of the
imagination. In the science of knowledge these categories arise in
imagination itself, *at the same time and together with the objects,*
and in order to make these first possible.

4. MAIMON views the category of causality in the same manner
as the science of knowledge; only he calls this procedure of the
human mind a deception. But we have seen that that can not be
called deception which is proper and necessary by virtue of the
laws of a rational being, and which can not be avoided unless we wish
to cease being rational beings. But the real point of dispute lies here.
MAIMON would say: "Supposing, as I admit, that your laws of
thinking are *à priori*, then you can certainly apply them to objects
only by the power of imagination; and hence, in applying them,
object and law must be, at the same time, in imagination. But how
do you get the object?" The answer is, Imagination itself must produce the object. If you assert the object to be produced in any
other manner, you become a transcendent dogmatist, and utterly
removed from critical philosophy.

5. MAIMON has only doubted the applicability of the law of
causality, but he might as well have doubted all *à priori* laws.
This HUME does. He says: "It is your self who transfer the conception of causality which you have in you to the external things,
and hence your knowledge has no objective validity." KANT admits
the first part of the sentence not only with respect to the law of
causality, but for all *à priori* laws; but he rejects the conclusion by
proving that an object is only possible for a subject. MAIMON
says, it is only by imagination that you apply the law of causality to
objects; hence your knowledge has no objective validity, and it is a
mere deception if you apply your laws of thinking to objects. The
science of knowledge admits the premise not only for the law of

for the Ego, as we have also seen. Hence, the Ego mediately is determined by the thing, and thus, ceasing to be Ego, becomes itself product of the Non-Ego, because that which fills it is product of the Non-Ego or of the thing. The thing, by means of this its expression, works even upon the Ego, and the Ego is no longer posited through itself, but posited in this its determination through the thing. (This is the famous influence of the thing upon the Ego, or the physical influence of the LOCKE school and of the new eclecticians, who, from the utterly heterogeneous components of the LEIBNITZ and the LOCKE systems, have composed an unconnected whole, the true statement of which we have just now attempted, but which has truth also only in this transitory connection.)

But the Ego can not be Ego and product of the Non-Ego. Such, however, was the result of our formula: A + B determined by B. Hence, this formula must be again posited in the Ego, or must be again determined by A.

A, that is, the effect which was said to have been produced in the Ego by the thing, is posited with respect to the Ego as accidental. Hence, there is necessarily opposed to this effect and to the Ego, in so far as it is determined thereby, an independent in itself and through itself existing Ego. Just as we opposed to the accidental in the Non-Ego

causality, but for all *à priori* laws, but shows by a closer determination of the object that our knowledge has objective validity for that very reason, and can only have it on that condition.

the necessary thing, so we now oppose to the accidental in the Ego the necessary or the Ego *per se;*
and this latter, like the necessary Non-Ego, is product of the Ego itself. The necessary is substance ;
the accidental an accidence of it. Both must be
synthetically united as one and the same Ego.
But since they are absolute opposites, they can
only be united by absolute activity of the Ego,
whereof the Ego never becomes immediately conscious, but rather applies it to the objects of the
reflection, thus positing the relation of causality
between the two. In the reflection the accidental
becomes effect of the activity of the absolute Ego
and hence something real for the Ego, its utterance. That it is effect of the Non-Ego is altogether
lost sight of in this reflection, since it can not be
posited at the same time as effect of the Ego and
of the Non-Ego. Thus, the thing and its utterance are completely excluded from the Ego and
opposed to it.

Both the Ego and the Non-Ego exist in themselves necessary, and both completely independent
of each other ; both utter themselves in this independence, each by its own activity and power,
which power, however, is as yet perfectly free.

We have now shown how we came to oppose an
acting Ego and an acting Non-Ego, and to consider
both as completely independent of each other. In our
present view the Non-Ego exists because it exists,
and is altogether determined through itself; but
that it is imaged, represented by the Ego, is acci-

dental for the Non-Ego. Again, the Ego acts absolutely through itself; but that it images the Non-Ego is accidental for it. The utterance of the thing in its appearance is product of the thing; but the appearance, in so far as it exists *for* the Ego, is again product of the Ego.

The Ego can not act without having an object; hence, the acting of the Ego posits that of the Non-Ego. Again, the Non-Ego can not act, that is, *for the Ego*, unless the acting of the Ego is preposited. The utterance of both powers is, therefore, necessarily synthetically united, and we must now show the ground of their union, their harmony.

This union occurs through absolute spontaneity. But what is posited through freedom has the character of the accidental; hence, the present synthetical union must have this character. It is, therefore, the accidental unity of the acting we have to examine, or the accidental junction of the acting of the Ego, and of the acting of the Non-Ego *in a third, which is and can be nothing but their junction*, and which we shall call for the present *a point*.

TIME AND SPACE.

Contemplation is determined in time, and the contemplated in space.

We have determined contemplation, in our last paragraph, as the synthetical union of the acting of the Ego and of the acting of the Non-Ego through their accidental junction in a point. This contemplation occurs in the Ego means, it is posited as *accidental.* The contemplation X is posited *as contemplation* accidental means, another contemplation—not another object, determination, or any such thing, but—another *contemplation,* which we shall call Y, is opposed to it. Y is necessary when opposed to X, and X is accidental in opposition to Y. Y is, therefore, completely excluded from the Ego, which rests in the contemplation of X.

X, as contemplation, necessarily rests in a point. So does Y, but in an opposite, distinct point. One point is not the other.

The question is now, What necessity is it which Y has in relation to X, and what accidentalness which X has in relation to Y? Clearly, the contemplation Y and its point are necessarily synthetically united if X is to be united with its point, or the union of X and its point presupposes that of Y and its point, but not *vice versa.* In that point wherein X is posited *another* contemplation *might* be posited; at least, so the Ego judges; but in the point of Y none but Y can be posited, if X is to be posited as contemplation of the Ego. Only in so far as the accidentalness of this synthesis is posited, is X to be posited as contemplation of the Ego; and only in so far as to this accidentalness is opposed the necessity of the same synthesis is the accidentalness itself to be posited.

The much more difficult question remains, how the points X and Y are to be otherwise determined

than through the respective contemplations X and
Y. As yet they are only points wherein a causality of the Ego and the Non-Ego meet. It is, however, clear that, if X is to be posited as the point
wherein another contemplation *may* be posited, and
Y as its opposite in which no other can be posited,
both points dirempt from their contemplations, and
must be distinguishable from each other. We can
not yet see *how* this is possible, but we can see *that*
it must be possible if ever a contemplation is to be
ascribed to the Ego.

1st. We have shown before that, if A is posited as
totality, B is excluded. If A signifies the image to
be determined spontaneously, B signifies the independent and necessary quality of the image. We
now apply this here.—From the contemplation X,
as such, the determined object X is excluded ; and
the same in the contemplation Y. Both objects, as
such, are determined ; that is, the Ego in contemplation must posit them exactly *as* it posits them.
This, their determinateness, is to remain, of course.

But the same relation which exists between the
contemplations must exist between the objects.
Hence, the object X is *accidental* in reference to Y,
but Y necessary in reference to X. The determination of X necessarily presupposes that of the
Y, but not *vice versa*.

But since both objects, *as objects of contemplation*,
are perfectly determined, their postulated relation
can have no reference to this determinateness, but
must refer to another as yet unknown determinate-

ness, one through which something does not become an object generally, but an object of a contemplation distinguishable from another contemplation.   The required determination does not belong
to the *inner* determinations of the object, (in so far
as it is $A = A$,) but is an external one.   Unless
we have the required distinction, a contemplation
can not be posited in the Ego.   The distinction,
however, is not possible without this external determinateness of the object, and the object can not
be an object of contemplation without this determinateness.   It is, therefore, the exclusive condition
of all contemplation.   We call this unknown somewhat through which the object is to be determined
O ; the way in which Y is determined through it,
we call Z ; and the way in which X is determined
through it, V.

The mutual relation is, therefore, as follows : X
must be posited as to be or *not* to be synthetically
united with V, and hence V also as to be united
thus with X or with any other object ; but Y must
be posited as necessarily in synthetical union with
Z, if X is to be united with V.

If V is posited as to be united with X, or as not
to be united with X, Y is posited necessarily as
united with Z.   From this it results that every possible object may be united with V except Y, for Y
is already inseparably united.   Thus, also, may X
be united with every possible O, except with Z, for
this is inseparably united with Y.

X and Y are both completely excluded from the

Ego ; the Ego loses and forgets itself completely in their contemplation. The relation we have here shown up is, therefore, *to be ascribed to the things themselves ;* the relation appears to the Ego as not dependent upon its freedom, but as determined through the things.

The relation was: because Z is united with Y, X is excluded from it. It must, therefore, applied to the things, be expressed thus : Y excludes X from Z ; Y determines X negatively. If Y extends to the point d, X goes to this point ; if it only extends to c, X goes to c. But since the only ground why X can not be united to Z is this, that Y excludes it, X certainly begins where Y ceases to exclude it ; hence, continuity belongs to both.

This exclusion, this continuity is not possible unless X and Y are both in a common sphere, (which we do not know as yet,) and meet in *one* point in this sphere. The positing of this sphere constitutes the synthetic union of both as required. Hence, such a common sphere is produced by the absolute spontaneity of the power of imagination.

2d. We have shown before that, if the excluded B is reflected upon, A is thereby excluded from the to-tality, from the Ego. But since B has been posited in the Ego by reflection, and is, therefore, itself posited in union with A as totality, (as accidental,) it follows that another B, in reference to which it is accidental, must be excluded or posited as a neces-sary opposite. We now apply this here.

Y is now, with reference to its synthetical union

with an unknown O, determined ; and X in respect
to, and by means of, Y, is also at least *negavtiely*
determined.

But if they are to be united with A, or to be posited in the Ego, they must be posited *as accidental
also in this respect*, that is, a necessary X and Y
must be opposed to them, in regard to which they
are accidental : substances whereof they are accidences.

This necessary X and Y, whereof the accidental
X and Y in the Ego are the utterances, are their
presupposed powers, *free* powers.   The same relation which exists between X and Y as utterances
exists, therefore, between these powers.   The utterance of power Y is utterly independent of that
of power X ; but the latter in its utterance is dependent upon and conditioned by Y.   Conditioned,
that is, the utterance of Y does not determine the
utterance X *positively*, but *negatively ;* not the qualitativeness of X, but in this that X can *not* utter
itself in a certain manner.

But it has been expressly stated that X as well
as Y are to utter themselves through free, unlimited
causality.   How, then, can X be conditioned by Y ?
Evidently X has causality as well as Y, and the
causality of the latfer is not the condition of that
of the former ; Y does not compel or urge X to
utter itself.   Nor does it determine the character
of this, the utterance or causality of X.   But how,
then, does it condition it ?

X and Y are to be in a synthetical relation to an

unknown O. For in and only through their relation to O are they mutually related. Each must,
therefore, have an independent relation to O.

O must be a something which leaves to both perfect freedom of causality, for in this, their free causality, are they to be united with O. And since
the resistance of every power to a causality limits
that causality, O can have no power, no activity,
no intension. It can, therefore, have no reality at
all, and is nothing.

We have seen how Y and Z being synthetically
united, X is excluded from Z. We have also seen,
now, that this synthetical union of Y and Z is effected through the own free causality of the inner
power Y. Not that Z is product of the power Y,
but, being necessarily united with Y, it must also
have a distinctive feature. Now, this union of Y
and Z *excludes* the causality of X and its product
from Z; hence, Z is the *sphere of causality* of Y,
and is *nothing but this sphere;* it is nothing in itself, has no reality, and can have no predicate but
the one just shown up.

Again, Z is sphere of causality *only* of Y ; for, by
being posited as such a sphere of Y, X and all other
possible object is excluded from it. The " sphere
of the causality of Y " means the same as " Z;"
both · are in all respects the same. The causality
of Y *fills up* Z, that is, excludes all other but the
causality of Y.

If Z goes to c, d, or e, the causality of X is thus
far excluded. But, since the latter is only excluded

because Y excludes it, there is necessarily continuity between the spheres of causality of both, and
both meet or join in a point. The power of imagination unites both and posits Z and −Z, or, as we
determined it above, V = O.

But the causality of X is to remain free *although*
excluded from Z. This exclusion would not leave
X free, if the causality of Y in Z negated or canceled something in X, or made any in itself possible
utterance of X impossible. Hence, it must be that
no possible utterance of X does ever come in conflict
with the causality of Y and Z; there must not be
any such tendency of filling up Z in X. There
must be in X itself a ground by virtue of which Z
is not its sphere of causality; there must not be in
X any ground of a possibility that Y could be its
sphere of causality.

Y and X, therefore, unite accidentally in a point,
in the absolute synthetical union of absolute opposites, without any mutual influence or action upon
each other.

3d. We have shown before that A + B must be
determined through B. Hitherto only B has been
thus determined; but mediately A also is determined
through it. This formula we interpreted : that which
is in the Ego—that is, contemplation—is determined
through the Non-Ego, and is mediately a product
thereof. We now apply this here.

X is product of the Non-Ego, and is, in regard
to its sphere of action, determined in the Ego; Y
is the same, both through themselves in their abso-

lute freedom. Both through their accidental junction determine also the point of this junction ; and the Ego is only passive in regard to it.

But this can not be. The Ego, as sure as it is an Ego, must produce this determination with freedom.

We have solved this same problem before in this way : The whole reflection of substantiality is dependent upon the absolute freedom of the Ego. We now solve the problem in the same way. The Ego is absolutely free to reflect or not reflect upon Y and X as an *abiding*, as a *simple*. If it does so reflect, it must, by the law of that reflection, undoubtedly place Y in the sphere of action Z, and posit C as a limit between the spheres of action of Y and X ; but it also *may not* so reflect, and may posit, instead of X and Y, every possible object as substance through its absolute freedom.

Suppose the spheres Z and V as connecting in the point C. In the sphere Z, the Ego can posit an a or a b instead of Y ; it can make Z the sphere of action of *both*, and their limit, the dividing line, G. Let us now call the sphere of action of a, H. Then the Ego can now again proceed to take this H, and, instead of positing a in it as indivisible substance, it can posit E and D in it, and so on *ad infinitum*. But, if an a and a b have once been posited, the Ego must assign to them a sphere of action connecting in one point.

This accidentalness of Y and its sphere of action for the Ego the Ego must *now posit as real through*

its power of imagination.   O is thus posited as an
extended, continuous, infinitely indivisible, and is
SPACE.

REMARKS.

1st. The power of imagination, by positing the
possibility of other substances with other spheres
of action in the space Z, *first dirempts space from the
thing which actually fills it,* and sketches an empty
space ; of course, only as an attempt, and transitively
in order to fill it immediately again with any
desired substances and their spheres of action.
Hence, there is no empty space but in this transition from the filling up of space by A to its being
filled up by B, C, D, etc.

2d. The infinitely smallest part of space is always
a space, a continuity, but not a mere point, or
the limit between places in space.   It is thus a
continuity, because in it *can* be posited, and is posited in so far as itself is posited, a power which
necessarily utters itself, and which can not be posited except as uttering itself.   But it can not utter
itself unless it has a sphere of its utterance, which
is nothing but such a sphere.

3d. Hence, intensity and extensity are necessarily
synthetically united, and one can not be deduced
without the other.   Every power fills up (not through
itself, *for the power is not in space,* and is, in fact,
nothing at all without utterance, but through its
necessary product, which is this same synthetical
ground of union of intensity and extensity) a place

in space ; and space is nothing but this sphere, filled or to be filled by these products.

4th. Apart from the inner determinations of the things, (their qualitativeness,) which only refer to feeling, (more or less pleasure or disgust,) and which are not at all accessible to the theoretical faculty· of the Ego, as, for instance, that the things are red or smooth, bitter or sweet, heavy or light, etc., these things are only distinguishable· from each other by the space they occupy. Hence, that which pertains to these things in such a manner that it is only ascribed to them and not to the Ego, though it does not belong to their inner essence, is the space which they occupy.

5th. But all space is equal, and through it, therefore, no distinction and determination is possible, except in so far as one thing $= Y$ has been posited in a certain space, and thus determined and characterized space. In that case you can say of X, it is in another space than Y. All determination of space presupposes a space filled up, and determined by that filling up. Posit A in the infinite empty space, it remains as undetermined as it was before, and you can not answer my question, *Where* is it? for you have no fixed point from which you can measure it. The place which it occupies is only determined through A, and A is only determined through that place. Hence, there is in reality no determination except in so far as you posit one; it is a synthesis through absolute spontaneity. To express this sensuously, A might move continuously

from one point to another in space, and you would
not observe the movement, because for you there
would be no points, but only the limitless, endless
spaces. For you it would always remain where it
is, because it would always remain in space. But
if you put B aside of it, then B is determined;
and if I ask you where it is, you reply, By the side
of A. This satisfies me, unless I ask again, But
where is A ? If you posit C, D, E, etc., aside of B,
then you have for all of them *relative* determinations of place; but you may fill up space as far as
you like, and you will always have in the filled up
space only a finite space which can have no relation
to the infinite space. This finite space is only determined in so far as you have determined it by
virtue of an absolute synthesis. An evident truth,
it seems to me, which ought long since to have
proven the ideality of space.

6th. The object of the *present* contemplation is
characterized as such by this, that we posit it through
the power of imagination in a space as *empty* space.
But this, as we have shown, is not possible, unless
a filled up space is presupposed. A dependent
succession of the filling up of space, but in which,
from reasons we shall show up hereafter, one can
always go further back infinitely.

To restore the freedom of the Ego, and to posit
the Non-Ego as accidental, we posited the Ego as
free to connect Z with Y, or a, b, c, etc.; and
through positing this freedom we first discovered
O as space. This sort of accidentalness remains;

but the question is, whether it has solved the problem.

True, the Ego is generally free to posit in space
Y, X, or a, b, c, etc.; but, *if* it is to reflect upon
X as substance, from which presupposition we
started, it must *necessarily*, as we have shown, posit
Y as determined substance, and as determined by
the space Z; hence, in that condition it is not free.
Nor is it then free in determining the place of X is
space, for it must place X aside of Y. Hence, the
Ego, under this condition, remains always determined by another. But it *shall* be free; and the
contradiction must be solved. This is done as follows

Y and X must both be determined and opposed
to each other in another manner than through their
determinedness and determinability in space; for
both have been posited above independent of their
space, and as distinct from each other. They must
have other characteristics, in virtue of which the
sentence A = A is applied to them; for instance,
that X is red, Y yellow, etc. Their place in
space has no reference to these determinations,
does not make Y, *as yellow*, the determined in
space, or X *as red*, the determinable in space. It
only posits one of both as determined, and the other as determinable, without any reference to any
inherent characteristics they may possess. Thus
freedom attains its sphere again. Freedom must
oppose a determined and a determinable; but it
can make either opposite the determined or the de-

terminable. Whether X be determined through
Y, or *vice versa*, depends only upon the spontaneity
of the Ego. In other words, it is the same what
series you describe in space, whether from A to B,
or *vice versa ;* whether you place B on the side of
A, or A on the side of B, for the things *mutually*
exclude each other in space.

This, its freedom of making either determined or
determinable, the Ego posits through the power of
imagination. It floats between determinedness and
determinability, ascribes to both both, or, which is
the same, to neither neither. But if a contemplation and object of a contemplation is to be, then the
Ego must make *one* of the in themselves determined
two a *determinable in space.*

Why it posits X or Y, or a, b, c, d, etc., as determinable admits of no ground, and can not admit
of a ground, for it is an act of absolute spontaneity.
This shows itself as accidentalness. But it must
be well observed wherein this accidentalness consists, namely, in the *being posited*, or in the *existence*
of the determinable. The positing of this determinable becomes an accidence of the Ego, to which
the Ego itself, as shown before, must be opposited
as its substance.

Ego and Non-Ego are now again complete opposites, and independent of each other. Inner powers
of the Non-Ego work with absolute freedom, fill up
their spheres of action, accidentally meet in a point,
and thus mutually exclude each other, without limiting their respective freedom, from their spheres of

action, or from their places in space. The Ego, again, posits as substance whatsoever it chooses, divides space, as it were, amongst substances, spontaneously decides which shall be the determined and which the determinable in space, or in what direction it will course through space.

Thus, all connection between the Ego and the Non-Ego is broken off; both are only connected by empty space, which, being empty, and only the sphere wherein the Non-Ego, *realiter* with freedom, posits its products, and the Ego, *idealiter*, posits also with freedom its products, as imaginary products of a Non-Ego, does limit neither nor connect one with the other. The opposition of both and the independent existence of the Ego and the Non-Ego is explained; but not the required harmony between both. Space is justly called the form, that is, the subjective condition of the possibility of the external contemplation. Unless there is another form of contemplation, the required harmony between representation of a thing and a thing itself and their mutual relation; hence, also, their opposition through the Ego, is impossible. Let us find this form.

TIME.

1. Y and X, in all their possible and mutual relations, are products of the free causality of the independent Non-Ego. But this they are not *for the Ego*, nor are they indeed at all *for the Ego* without a free causality of the Ego itself.

2. This causality of Ego and Non-Ego, therefore, must be reciprocal causality, that is, the utterances of both must meet in a point, in the absolute
synthesis of both through imagination. This point
of union the Ego *posits* by its absolute power, and
it posits this point *as accidental,* that is, *the connecting of the causality of both opposites is accidental.*

, 3. If Y or X is to be posited, such a point of
union must be posited ; or, in other words, the
positing of an object involves such a union with the
causality of the Ego.

4. The Ego is perfectly free in regard to the
determinateness. or undeterminateness of the X or
Y means, therefore, the Ego is perfectly free to
connect Y or X with the point (*and thus with the
Ego*) or not.

5. This thus determined freedom of the Ego
must be posited through the power of imagination,
that is, *the mere possibility* of a synthesis of the
point with a causality of the Non-Ego must be
posited. This is only possible if the *point* can be
posited apart from the *causality of the Non-Ego.*

6. But such a point is nothing but a synthesis of
the causality of the Ego and of the Non-Ego.
Hence, by altogether removing it from the causality
of the Non-Ego, you destroy the point. Hence, we
only remove the determined X from the point, and
unite the point instead with an undetermined product (a, b, c, or d, etc., a *Non-Ego*) so as to have
it retain its determined character as synthetical
point.

7. The Ego is really synthetically to unite the point with X. This is our whole presupposition, for we require a contemplation of X, which, even as contemplation, is not possible without such a synthesis. This synthesis, as we have also shown, occurs through absolute spontaneity. But, by uniting X with the point, all other possible powers are excluded from the point.

8. This synthetical connection of X with the point is to be a real *connecting*, and to be posited as such, that is, it is to bear the characteristic of absolute spontaneity, namely, *accidentalness*, and this not merely in the respect heretofore mentioned, but in its very characteristic as a connecting of a synthesis. But such accidentalness of its character *as synthesis* is only possible through opposition with another necessary synthesis of a determined Y with a point ; of course, not with the point of X, for from that point all other is excluded, but with *another opposite point*. Let us call this point c, and the point with which X is connected d.

9. This point c, like d, is synthetical point of union of the causality of the Ego and of the Non-Ego But it is opposed to d in this, that with d the synthetical union is considered as dependent upon freedom, as that which might be otherwise, while with c the union is considered as necessary.

10. This accidentalness of the synthetical union with d must be posited ; hence, also, must the necessity of the union with c be posited. Both must, therefore, be posited in this respect as necessary

and accidental in regard to each other. If the synthetical union with d is to be posited, that with c must have been posited before, but not *vice versa.*

11. Now, this synthesis with d is really to be posited ; hence, it is posited as *dependent*, as conditioned by the synthesis with c. But c is *not, vice versa*, conditioned by d.

12. Again, the synthesis with c is to be exactly as the synthesis with d, that is, an arbitrary, accidental synthesis. If it is posited as such, another synthesis with *b* must again be opposed to it as necessary, as the synthesis of which it is dependent and by which it is conditioned. The synthesis with c, if posited accidental, must thus be posited as preceded by a synthesis with b, and dependent upon that, but not *vice versa.* The synthesis with b, again, must be posited as accidental, and hence, as preceded by another synthesis, and so on *ad infinitum.* Thus, we attain a series of points as points of synthetical union between a causality of the Ego and of the Non-Ego in contemplation, wherein each point depends upon a determined other which does not depend upon it, and wherein each *has* a determined other which is dependent upon it while itself does not depend upon this other ; in short, we obtain a *time series.*

13. The Ego posited itself as perfectly free to unite with the point whatever it might choose, hence the whole infinite Non-Ego. The thus determined point is only accidental and not necessary ; is only dependent without having another which is

dependent upon it, and is called the *present* point, the present moment.

14. Hence, if we abstract from the synthetical union of a determined point with the object—and thus from the whole causality of the Ego, which is only connected with the Non-Ego through this point—*all things*, considered in themselves, and independent from the Ego, *are at the same time in space*, that is, are synthetically unitable with one and the same point. But they can be posited in perception only *after each other* in a successive series, wherein each link depends upon another which does not depend upon it.

CONCLUDING REMARKS.

a. There is for us no *past* except in so far as it is thought in the *present*. Whatsoever was yesterday *is not;* it is only in so far as I think in the present moment *that it was*. The question, Has not really a time passed away? is just of the same nature as the question, Is there a thing in itself? Of course, a time has past if you posit one as past, and, if you ask that question, you do posit a past time; if you do not posit it, you will not ask that question, and then no time has past for you. A very evident observation, which ought long ago to have led to the correct conception of the ideality of time.

b. But a past is necessary for us; for only on condition of a past is a present, and only on condition of a present is consciousness possible. This proof we recapitulate as follows : Consciousness is only possible on condition that the Ego posit a Non-Ego as its opposite, and this oppositing de-mands that the ideal activity of the Ego should be directed upon the Non-Ego. This activity belongs to the Ego only in so far as it is free ; hence, in so far as it may be directed upon any of all possible objects. In this, its freedom, it must be posited and is posited, and it is the character of the present moment that any other possible perception might fill it. This, again, is only possible if another mo-ment is posited wherein no other perception can be posited than that which is posited therein ; and this is the character of the past moment. Con-sciousness, therefore, is necessarily consciousness of freedom and of identity ; of freedom, as we have shown ; of identity, because every moment, to be a moment, must be connected with another.

The perception, B, is no perception, unless an-other perception, A, is presupposed. You may posit C now, and then A may vanish, but you will now have to posit B as the condition of C, and so on *ad infinitum.* This is the law of the identity of consciousness, for which we only need, strictly speaking, two moments. There is no *first* moment of consciousness, only a *second.*

c. True, the past moment can again be posited in consciousness, can be represented or reproduced in the present, can be posited as having occurred in the *same* subject, if you reflect that another perception *might have* filled him. In that case, you again oppose to it a preceding moment, in which, if you posit in the latter a *determined* perception, no other perception could occur but that which did occur in it. Hence, we can always go back in this series of moments so far as we please into the infinite.

d. A determined quantity of space is always *at the same time;* a quantity of time always in a succession, one moment after another. Hence, we can only measure the one through the other : space through the time we need to pass over it ; time through the space we, or any other regular moving body, (the sun, the pendulum, etc.,) can pass through in it.

IV.

PRACTICAL PART

OF THE

SCIENCE OF KNOWLEDGE.

22*

SCIENCE OF KNOWLEDGE.

FUNDAMENTAL PRINCIPLE.

The Ego posits itself as determining the Non-Ego.

We might proceed to evolve this principle in the same manner as we did the fundamental principle of the theoretical part ; but a shorter way is possible. For there is one chief antithesis in this principle which embraces the whole conflict between the Ego as intelligence, and in so far limited, and the Ego as absolutely posited, and hence unlimited being, and which compels us to assume as connecting link a practical power of the Ego. We shall first look up this antithesis.

The Ego is Ego ; it is absolutely one and the same Ego by virtue of its being posited through itself, (§ 1.)

Now, in so far as the Ego is particularly *representing*, or an *intelligence*, it is *as such* also one, true enough ; is one power of representation under necessary laws, but it is not in so far one and the same with the absolute through itself posited Ego.

For, although the Ego, *in so far as it is already intelligence*, is in its particular determinations within this sphere of the intelligence determined through itself, and although also in so far nothing ever occurs in the Ego which it has not posited within itself, yet *this sphere itself*, considered generally and in itself, is not posited by the Ego for itself, but is posited for it through an external something. True, the *mode* and *manner* of representing objects is determined through the Ego itself; but *that* the Ego is at all representing, is an intelligence, is not determined through the Ego, as we have seen. For we could only think representation on the presupposition that the undetermined and infinite activity of the Ego receives a check. Hence, the Ego, *as intelligence generally*, is *dependent* upon an undetermined and as yet altogether undeterminable Non-Ego; and only by means of such a Non-Ego is the Ego intelligence.*

But the Ego is to be in all its determinations absolutely posited through itself, and, hence, perfectly independent of any possible Non-Ego.

Hence, the absolute Ego and the intelligent Ego (if it is permissible to express myself thus) are not

---

* Whosoever may conjecture a profound significance and vast consequences in this expression is a welcome reader to me. A finite being is finite only as intelligence; the practical (moral) legislation which he is to have in common with the infinite can not depend upon any thing external.

one and the same, but opposed to each other, which contradicts the absolute identity of the Ego.

This contradiction must be solved, and that can only be done as follows : Since it is the *dependence* of the Ego, as intelligence, which is to be removed, *the Ego must determine through itself that same unknown Non-Ego*, to which the check has been ascribed, which makes the Ego intelligence. Thus, the absolute Ego would determine the Non-Ego of the representation *immediately*, and the representing Ego *mediately*, by means of that determination of the Non-Ego, and the Ego would become completely independent, that is, self-determined.

The Ego, as intelligence, stood in the relation of causality to the Non-Ego to which it ascribed the check. The Non-Ego was the cause ; it the effect. For the causality relation consists in this, that, by restricting activity in the one, the same quantity of activity which is restricted is posited in the opposite of the one, according to the law of mutual determination. Now, if the Ego is to be intelligence, part of its infinitely extending activity must be canceled, and thus posited in its opposite, the Non-Ego. But since the absolute Ego can not be restricted at all, being absolute activity and nothing but absolute activity, it must be assumed, as we have shown, that the postulated Non-Ego is also determined, that is, passive, and hence the quantity of activity which is opposed to this passivity of the Non-Ego must be posited in the opposite of the Non-Ego, that is, in the Ego ; not in the

Ego as intelligence, however, since as such it is determined by the Non-Ego, but in the absolute Ego.
And such a relation being a relation of causality,
it follows that the absolute Ego is to be *cause* of
the Non-Ego, in so far as the Non-Ego is last
ground of all representation.

The absolute Ego is only active and thus determines the Non-Ego, which is now passive, in so far
as this Non-Ego is to determine the Ego as intelligence. The activity opposed to this passivity of
the Non-Ego is now posited in the absolute Ego
as a *determined* activity; and thus the Ego, as intelligence, and as absolute, is placed in a state of
self-relation. The grounds of this circuitous way
of the Ego to influence itself are as yet unknown,
but may, perhaps, appear in the future.

The absolute Ego is, therefore, cause of that in
the Non-Ego which remains, when we abstract
from all forms of representation; for those forms result, as we have shown, from the laws of representation in the Ego as intelligence. That is, the absolute Ego is to be the cause of the mysterious thing
in itself, the hidden substance, the check; all the
rest follow necessarily in the manner shown.

But, whereas it was easy enough to show how—
after once assuming the check—the Ego as intelligence is cause of all the necessary laws of representation, it is a far different question, How can the
Ego be *cause* of the Non-Ego? Surely not through
absolute positing.

For the Ego can certainly posit itself without

any further ground, and *must* posit itself if it is to posit any thing else; for that which *is* not can not posit, and the Ego *is* (for itself) only by virtue of its positing itself.

The Ego can not posit the Non-Ego without limiting itself. For the Non-Ego is the complete opposite to the Ego, and whatsoever the Non-Ego is, that the Ego is not; hence, in so far as the Non-Ego is posited, the Ego is not posited. If the Non-Ego were posited without quantity, that is, unlimited and infinite, then the Ego would not be posited at all, which is a contradiction. Hence, the Non-Ego must be posited in a determined quantity, and the Ego must be restricted by the posited quantity of reality of the Non-Ego.

The Ego is, therefore, in our presupposition to posit a Non-Ego absolutely and without any ground, or to limit itself without any ground. The ground thus to limit itself must, therefore, be in the Ego itself; it must have the principle in itself to posit itself, and also the principle not to posit itself. Hence, the Ego in its essence must be contradictory and self-annihilating, and cancels itself.

We stand here at a point from which the true significance of our second fundamental principle, *a Non-Ego is opposed to the Ego*, and thus the true significance of our whole science of knowledge, can be more clearly explained than was heretofore possible.

Of that second fundamental principle of the whole science of knowledge only part is absolute; but part of it presupposes a fact, which *à priori* can not be shown up at all, but only in the experience of each individual.

Namely, besides the self-positing of the Ego there is to be another positing. This is *à priori* a mere hypothesis ; that there is such another positing (or, that there is any thing at all) can not be proven, but can only be shown up by a fact of consciousness ; and every one must prove it to himself by this fact, but no one can prove it to another by demonstrations.

(True, he might reduce any admitted fact, through thinking, to that highest fact ; but such a fact would only show to the other, that by admitting any fact he has also confessed that highest fact.) But it is absolutely certain and grounded in the essence of the Ego that, if there is such another positing, then it must be an *oppositing*, and that which is thus posited must be a *Non-Ego*. In other words, how the Ego can distinguish something from itself can not be proven by any higher ground of possibility ; on the contrary, the fact that the Ego thus does distinguish (separate or dirempt) is itself the ground of all deduction and all grounding. But it is absolutely certain that all positing, which is not a positing of the Ego, must be an oppositing. Hence, the argumentation of the science of knowledge is *à priori* valid, that is, it establishes only propositions which are *à priori* certain ; but reality it obtains only in experience. If any one could not become conscious of the postulated fact—it can be certainly known that this can not be the case with any finite rational being—then the whole science of knowledge has no content for him ; and yet its formal correctness he also must acknowledge. Let me illustrate this :

For a Godhead, that is, for a consciousness (to us unthinkable) for which the self-positing of the Ego is the positing of all, our science of knowledge would have no content ; for its consciousness would embrace no other positing than the self-positing of the Ego ; but the *form* of our system would be valid ✓ even for God, since it is the form of pure reason itself.

The contradiction existing between the independence of the Ego as absolute being, and the dependence thereof as intelligence, we sought to remove by postulating the absolute Ego as cause of the Non-Ego. But this postulate we also discovered ᵔ to be a contradiction ; for if the Ego has causality upon the Non-Ego, then the Non-Ego ceases to be Non-Ego, ceases to be the opposite of the Ego, and becomes itself Ego. But the Ego has itself posited the Non-Ego as its opposite, and, if that positing is canceled, then the Ego itself ceases to be Ego. The contradiction lies, therefore, in this, that although the Ego is to be the cause of the Non-Ego, the Non-Ego is to remain opposed to the Ego. We must solve this contradiction.

In so far as the Ego is absolute, it is *infinite* and *unlimited.* Every thing that is the Ego posits, and what it does not posit is not ; and whatever it posits it posits as Ego, and it posits the Ego as every thing it posits. Hence, as absolute Ego the Ego contains in itself all reality, that is, an infinite, unlimited reality.

But in so far as the Ego opposits a Non-Ego, it necessarily posits *limits*, and posits itself in these limits. It divides the totality of posited reality between the Ego and Non-Ego, and hence posits itself necessarily in so far as *finite*.

Here we have, therefore, a still higher contradiction : The Ego posits itself one time as infinite, and then again as finite. How can this contradiction be reunited ?

The Ego posits itself as infinite in so far as its activity is directed upon itself, or *returns in itself;* for then the product of this activity, being the Ego again, is infinite. (Infinite product—infinite activity, and *vice versa.*)

The Ego posits itself as finite in so far as its activity is directed upon a Non-Ego which it opposes to itself. This is no longer *pure* (infinite) but *objective*, limited activity.

Both activities are to be one and the same. Let us find their synthetical connection, and then we shall doubtless see how the *required causality* is possible ; for such a connection would be this very relation of causality, since it would make the in itself returning activity the cause of the objective activity ; and through the former the Ego would determine itself to the latter ; the pure activity would return into the Ego, but in so returning determine the Ego *as* determining the Non-Ego, and, hence, *mediately* it would be directed upon the Non-Ego, while *immediately* it would be directed upon the Ego.

The self-positing of the Ego is, therefore, now to be the *cause* of its positing the Non-Ego. But if this were so, then the Ego would posit the Non-Ego by positing itself, and thus would cancel itself. Moreover: the second fundamental principle from which we started ($-A$ not $= A$) resulted in this, that the Ego opposits a Non-Ego to itself absolutely, and without any ground. The present result, therefore, unqualified, would overthrow § 2, and hence our whole system. That second fundamental principle, however, showed itself—though absolute in form—to be conditioned in *content;* the opposite was to be an opposite of the Ego. Let us examine this.

THESIS.

The Ego opposes *absolutely* to itself an object, an opposite Non-Ego. In the positing thereof the Ego is utterly independent. That is, the Ego may posit the object where it chooses, but is conditioned in this, that by positing the object it limits itself. The Ego is finite, because by positing the Non-Ego it limits itself; it is also infinite, because it may posit the Non-Ego infinitely. It is finite in its infinity; infinite in its finity. It is utterly independent, absolute in positing an object; it limits itself simply because it does. But this absolute self-limitation is opposed to § 1, to the absolute self-positing the Ego, and hence impossible.

The Ego posits an *object*, and thus posits an activity independent of its own, opposed to its own.
This activity of the object must be, in one sense, in
the Ego, (since the Ego posits it,) but in another
sense in the Non-Ego, in the object. In the latter
sense it must be opposed to that activity of the
Ego which posits it, (since to this it is related,) and
hence, if there is to be an object, *the possibility of
positing it presupposes an activity in the Ego different from the activity which posits the object.* Let us
call this unknown activity X.

X *will not be canceled* by the object, since both
are opposites. Both are to be posited ; each must
be independent of the other. X must be absolutely
grounded in the Ego, since it depends not upon the
positing of the object, but rather the object depends
upon it. X is, therefore, posited by the absolute
self-positing of the Ego. Again, X must be infinite, since it is opposed to the object which can be
extended into the infinite. X *is, therefore, the infinite activity*, posited by the Ego in itself, *and which
is related to the objective activity of the Ego* as the
ground of possibility to the grounded ; that is, the
object is posited only in so far as an activity of the
Ego meets resistance ; no such activity of the Ego,
no object. Again, it is related as the determining to

the determined ; that is, only in so far as that activity is resisted can an object be posited ; no resistance, no object.

Now, consider this infinite activity in relation to
the activity of the object. Both are utterly independent of each other ; there is no relation between
them. And yet, when an object is posited, they
must be so related by means of the objective activity of the Ego, of which X is the ground. That
is, they are related in so far as an object is posited ;
not, not. Again, as the object is absolutely posited,
so the relation must be absolute, without ground.
They are absolutely related means, they are posited
as equals. At the same time, as sure as an object is
posited, they are not equal. They *shall* be equal,
but are not. (Kant's Categorical Imperative.)

The question remains, In which of both is the
ground of relation to be posited ? Which is to
rule ? The Ego is the totality of all reality ; it is
to be absolutely independent ; all else dependent
upon it. The object is, therefore, to be equal to
the Ego ; and it is the absolute Ego which demands
this for the very sake of its absolute being.

For instance : let the activity Y be given, (in what
will hereafter appear as object,) and place an activity of the Ego in relation to it. Thereby you think
an activity outside of the Ego, (= —Y,) which is
equal to that activity of the Ego. Wherein now
lies the equality ground of this relation ? Of course,
in the thesis that *all* activity is to be equal to that
of the Ego. —Y lies, therefore, in a *world* wherein

23*

all activity would *really* be equal to that of the Ego,
and is an ideal. Now, since Y is not equal to —Y,
but is opposed to it, we ascribe Y to an object.
Without this relation and the absolute thesis which
is the ground of it, there would be no object for the
Ego ; and the Ego would be every thing, and for
that very reason nothing.

The absolute Ego, therefore, relates itself absolutely to a Non-Ego (—Y) which it appears is to be
a Non-Ego in its form, (that is, in so far as it is to
be any thing outside of the Ego, a thing in itself,)
but not in its content, since it is to be perfectly
equal to the Ego. But it can not be thus perfectly
equal so long as it is, though but in form, a Non-Ego ;
and, hence, the activity of the Ego related to it can
not be a determining, but merely a *tendency* toward
determination.

RESULT.

The pure, self-returning activity of the Ego is,
in its relation to a possible object, a *tendency ;* and,
according to the above, an *infinite tendency.* This
tendency is the *condition of the possibility of all
object ;* no tendency, no object.

The pure activity of the Ego is, therefore, now,
as was required, the cause of the objective activity
of the Ego, since no object can be posited without
it. But in so far as this pure activity originally is
directed upon no object—both, therefore, being
mutually independent of the other—it is not its
cause, but related to it by an absolute act of the

Ego. This absolute act of the Ego, *as* act, is in its *form* (in its realization) *absolute*, (and this, its absoluteness, is the ground of the absolute spontaneity of reflection in the theoretical part, and of the will in the practical part of the science of knowledge, as we shall see ;) but in its *content* (in this, that it is a *relation*) it is conditioned by the absolute self-positing of the Ego as totality of all reality. In other words, that the pure activity is placed in relation to an object, has not its ground in the pure activity as such ; but that, if it is so posited, it must be posited as a *tendency ;* of this itself is the ground.

A system which would assert that the pure activity, *as such*, is directed upon an object, would be a system of *intelligible fatalism.* As applied to finite beings, the argument would be : Since no pure activity is posited unless it manifests itself, and since in finite beings it can not manifest itself, it must be posited by something outside. This system would be valid for a Godhead, that is, a being, with whose pure activity its objective activity were also posited. But such a being is not conceivable.

The thesis, that all reality must be absolutely posited through the Ego, is the thesis of what has been called *practical* reason. We have now shown that practical and theoretical reason are inseparable. Theoretical intelligence is impossible without the practical power, since an object is impossible without a tendency.

FURTHER DIFFICULTY.

But how can the tendency of the pure activity be placed in relation to the activity of the object, unless the latter is first given to the Ego? To explain the latter activity from the former would involve a circle and explain nothing. There must be an absolute first ground of the relation.

The Ego is only = Ego, it has no other determination; it is all, and it is nothing, because it is nothing for itself. An inequality, an Other appears in it. *That* this Other appears is a fact, and can not be proven *à priori;* every one must find it so. This Other can not be deduced from the conception of the absolute Ego as simply a positing of itself.

If we imagine an intelligence outside of the Ego, to that intelligence the Other would appear as limiting the Ego; but the Ego itself is to be that intelligence and to posit that limit.

If the Ego is equal to itself, it must strive to cancel this limit, to restore the activity, not interrupted by itself, and then it can compare and relate its condition of limitation to its condition of restored activity, and thus establish a mere self-relation.

Let us suppose the activity of the Ego to tend from A to C without check. Between A and C there is nothing to distinguish, nothing of which the Ego can become conscious. In C this activity —the ground of all consciousness, but never itself made conscious—is checked. But by its nature it

can not be checked. Hence, it continues beyond
C, but as an activity which has been checked, and
now maintains itself only through its own power.
But as such it continues only to that point where
the check ceases = D. *Beyond* D it is again *not*
an object of consciousness.

Limited and restored activity are, therefore, synthetically united in the Ego, and mutually condition
each other. Neither can be posited without the
other. This synthesis of limited and restored activity in the mere subject is, therefore, the condition
of all positing of the Ego. As such purely subjective relation it is called feeling.

Now, since the ground of this feeling is posited
in an activity of the object, and since this activity
of the object is thus given, as was required, to the
relating subject through feeling, we have shown
how the activity of the object can be related to the
pure activity of the Ego.

Let us now return to our stand-point. Its result
was, no infinite tendency of the Ego, no finite object in the Ego. By this result we thought to
have solved the contradiction. We said, the *infinite*
activity is not objective, but only *returning into itself*, whereas the *finite* activity is *objective.* But,
since we have now placed this infinite activity, as
tendency, in relation to the object, we have made it
also in so far objective activity ; and thus we have
now one infinite objective, and one finite objective
activity of the Ego, which is a contradiction, to be
solved only by showing that the infinite activity is

objective in another manner than the objective activity.

The infinite activity (tendency) of the Ego, in so
far as it is objective, must be finite, (determined.)
Now, since the objective activity is posited as its
opposite, it must be posited in a different manner.
If both were finite in the same manner, they could
not be distinguished. This finite objective activity,
presupposing, as we have shown, the activity of an
object, and thus having its ground not in itself, but
outside of itself, goes upon an object not grounded
in itself, that is, a *real* object.

Now, the infinite activity can, therefore, not be
finite in this manner. It can not depend upon and
determine the *real* world, which presupposes an activity of the Non-Ego reciprocally related to the
objective activity of the Ego. The infinite activity
determines, on the contrary, a world wherein through
the Ego is posited all reality, wherein no activity
of the Non-Ego is presupposed, an ideal world, absolutely posited through the Ego.

How, then, is it also finite? In so far as it tends
upon an object at all, and as it hence must determine that object. When the *real* object was placed
in relation to the objective activity of the Ego, not
the *act* of determining it, as such, depended upon
the Non-Ego, but the limit of the determination.
But in regard to the *ideal* object, both the act of
determining it, and the limit of the determination,
is to be dependent upon the Ego; and the Ego is

conditioned only in that it must posit limits at all, which, however, it can infinitely extend.

The ideal is absolute product of the Ego ; it may \ be extended infinitely, but in every determined moment it has its limit. The undetermined tendency ˅ generally—which, however, can not properly be called tendency, since it has no object, and can, indeed, have no name—is infinite, but, as such, it can not enter consciousness, since consciousness is only possible through reflection, and, hence, through determination.

But as soon as you reflect upon it, you necessarily posit it as finite. And as soon as you become conscious that it is finite, you extend it again and make it infinite. Then, when you ask once more, Is it *now* infinite ? you make it again, by that very question, finite ; and so on *ad infinitum.*

Infinite and *objective* is, therefore, contradictory. ˈ This contradiction could only be solved by altogether removing the object. But it is removed only in a finished *infinity,* that is, never. The Ego ˅ can infinitely extend the object of its tendency ; but, if it had extended it in any one moment to an infinity, the object, as such, would have vanished, and the idea of infinity would have been realized. But this is a contradiction.

In this contradiction lies the certitude of immor- ˅ tality. The very conception of the Ego involves this, that it ever infinitely extends its object, but never completes it. It always posits the absolute

✓Ego as totality of reality, but because this, its positing, is directed upon objects, (a world,) it never completes the positing. The moral world (the only
real world) is always complete, and is always realized in every act; but is, at the same time, never
realized in the actual objective world, for the very
reason that, being objective, it extends into the infinite.

Were the Ego more than a tendency, that is, if
it had infinite causality, it would not be an Ego,
would not posit itself, and hence be nothing. If,
again, it had not this infinite tendency, it could also
not posit itself, for it could not posit its opposite;
hence, it would again be no Ego, be nothing.

OTHER STATEMENT OF THE SAME RESULT.

Our RESULT was, that the pure, self-returning
activity, in its relation to a possible object, is àn
infinite *tendency*. A tendency, that is, an activity
which meets resistance, has, therefore, no causality
as such, and is in so far partly conditioned by a
Non-Ego, which has as such *no* causality. Such a
causality is, therefore, required. *That* the requirement of such an absolute causality must be originally contained in the Ego, we have proven by
showing that the contradiction between the Ego as
intelligence and as absolute Ego could not be otherwise solved; and hence our proof was only apogo-
gical; but *how* this requirement originated in the
Ego we have not yet shown. This direct and gene-

tic proof or deduction must, however, be possible. It must be possible to show up in the Ego not only a tendency to have a determined causality, (determined through a Non-Ego,) but a tendency to have causality in general—the latter to be the ground of the former.

An activity which goes beyond the object becomes a tendency only because it goes beyond the object, and hence only on condition of an object. But we must now show up a ground in the Ego for its going out of itself at all, and show how this going beyond itself of the Ego is solely grounded in the Ego itself, and how it precedes all resisted activity, and first makes it at all possible.

In other words, we must show up *in the absolute Ego the ground of the possibility of the influence of an Other* (of a foreign Non-Ego) *upon itself.* We must show how, although it only posits itself, it remains susceptible to the positing of another.

The Ego is, therefore, to find originally in itself an heterogeneous, foreign, distinguishable Other.

In itself, not outside of itself. If the latter were true, the Other would not be *for* the Ego. Hence, in some respect, the Other must be *equal*, relatable, to the Ego, must belong to it.

The Ego is = absolute activity, (self-positing ;) if the heterogeneous Other is, therefore, any ways to be ascribed to the Ego, it must be an activity of the Ego, which as such can not be foreign, but the *direction* of which may perhaps be foreign, that is, may not be grounded in the Ego. If the activity

24

of the Ego extends into the infinite and is thrown back into itself, the activity, as such, always remains activity of the Ego; only its direction, its *return*, is foreign to the Ego. Now, here arise these important questions :

How does the Ego get to distinguish between the direction of its activity *outward* into the infinite, and *inward* back into itself, and why does it ascribe the latter to a foreign Other ?

The absolute essence of the Ego is self-positing, as we know. As such it has, doubtless, a *self-returning* direction, (if we can speak of *directions* as yet, though we touch here upon the *source* of all directions, centripetal and centrifugal,) that is to say, a *centripetal* direction. But since all determination involves negation, or the positing of another, *centripetal* direction involves the silent presupposition of the centrifugal. Rightly taken, the true scheme of the above absolute Ego would be the mathematical *point*, which is content and form together, that is, which is *all that it is, where* it is. But the absolute Ego is not simply a self-positing, (which would make it an objective thing,) but it is a positing of itself *for itself.* Through this *for* the above centripetal direction at once receives its complement in the centrifugal. The direction of the activity of the Ego is centripetal in so far as it is *reflecting*, and centrifugal in so far as it is that which is reflected upon, and this centrifugality is infinite. Both the centripetal and the centrifugal directions are equally grounded in the Ego, are both one and the same, and are only different when reflected upon as different.

REMARK.

All centripetal power in the world of nature is purely product of the power of imagination of the Ego, in virtue of a law of reason to gather the manifold into unity.

But both directions can not be distinguished, unless a third link is found whereby they can be related to each other. As yet this third link has not been found; both directions are as yet undistinguishable, and consciousness, therefore, impossible.

SECOND REMARK.

God's self-consciousness could only be explained by the presupposition that God thinks his own being. But since in God *the reflected* would be all in one and one in all, and the *reflecting* would be also one in all and all in one, God could not distinguish between reflecting and reflected, between consciousness and the object thereof; and hence his self-consciousness could not be explained. Indeed, the self-consciousness of God can be explained or comprehended by no thinking which is subject to the law, that all *determination* is a negation.

The infinitely *extending* activity of the Ego is to be somewhere checked and repelled; and the Ego is not to fill up infinity. That this is so can not be *shown,* but can only be known as *fact;* but it can be shown that this must be so *if* consciousness is to be realized. But still the requirement that the Ego should fill up the infinity remains, and when taken up in reflection it is found that the requirement has not been satisfied, that the activity has been checked, repelled ; and only through this third link of the requirement is a distinction possible and a centripetal direction established, which is as such distinguishable from the first centrifugal direction of the Ego whereby it sought to fill up infinity. The centrifugal direction is the original direction of the absolute Ego, the centripetal direction the reflected direction of the *checked* Ego.

RESULTS.

1st. Because the Ego is a *for-itself* positing, a reflecting, of itself, *does it go beyond itself;* and because in thus positing itself it must posit itself as the totality of all reality has it a *tendency* to *causality.*

2d. In so far as the Ego simply posits itself it is complete in itself, and posits no other. But since it must posit itself *as* self-posited, (that is, *for* itself,) it thus, by this second (as it were) positing, posits the possibility that something could be *in* itself not posited through *itself,* and thus externalizes itself.

The first positing gives the activity of the Ego which is to be checked ; the second positing makes it possible that the first activity can be checked *for* the Ego, or that the Ego can posit itself as determined. And thus we have discovered an original self-relation of the Ego, through which alone an external influence upon the Ego is made possible.

3d. The absolute Ego posits itself as the totality of all reality. In applying this positing to the infinite objective world, the Ego becomes a *practical* or moral Ego. In this, its morality, it is not absolute, since it goes beyond itself by the tendency of its reflection ; nor is it theoretical, since its reflection tends upon the absolute Ego alone, and does not take the *check* into account at all. It is simply moral—and gives the moral, the ideal world, the world to be posited.

But if the reflection takes the check into account and thus considers its externalization limited, we obtain the *real* world determined by the Non-Ego. In doing this the Ego is theoretical, or intelligence.

Without the practical, moral faculty of the Ego the intelligence is not possible ; for, unless the Ego goes beyond the check, there is no check, no Non-Ego for and in the Ego. Again, unless the Ego is intelligence, it can not be practical or self-conscious, since only the foreign check makes possible a distinction of the directions of the Ego's activity.

ADDENDA.

We have thus obtained as the last ground of all reality for the Ego an original reciprocal causality between the Ego and an external Other, of which only this can be predicted, that it must be the *opposite* of the Ego. By this reciprocity nothing new or foreign is posited in the Ego ; it is only the ground of all motion and activity of the Ego ; and, since the Ego is nothing but activity, the ground of the existence of the Ego. The Ego is, therefore, dependent, so far as its existence is concerned. But in regard to the determinations of this existence, it is utterly independent. In other words : That the Ego must be determined, in order to be, is an absolute first fact ; but that its determinations are all its own has been clearly developed. Or : The point wherein we first attain consciousness does not depend upon us ; but all the infinite determinations of our course from this point depend wholly upon us. Our theory is, therefore, realistic, in so far as it absolutely posits an Other, a foreign check or power ; but all possible determinations of this Other it undertakes to deduce from the determining faculty of the Ego.

Our science is also idealistic. For by explaining consciousness, from an independent Other, it remembers that this very explanation necessarily takes already the stand-point of consciousness, and follows its laws ; whereas, the moment you seize the Other in thought, it ceases to be an independent Other, and becomes the production of thinking. But the possibility of this thinking again presupposes real consciousness, and hence that independent Other which makes consciousness only possible.

In short : Every thing in its *ideality* is dependent
upon the Ego ; but in its *reality* even the Ego is
dependent. But in the Ego ideal and real ground
are one and the same, and hence the reciprocity
between the Ego and the Non-Ego is at the same
time a reciprocity of the Ego with itself, a self-
relation. The Ego can posit itself as limited by
the Non-Ego, if it does not reflect that itself posits
this Non-Ego ; it can posit itself as limiting the
Non-Ego by so reflecting.

This, that the finite spirit must posit for itself an
absolute somewhat outside of itself, (the thing *per
se,*) and at the same time knows that it exists only
for it, (is a necessary *noumen,*) is the circle, which
we may infinitely extend, but can never break
through. A system which does not take account
of this circle is a dogmatic idealism ; a system
which believes to have gone beyond it is a transcendent realistic dogmatism.

We have said the consciousness of finite beings
can only be explained by presupposing an independent power. Can only be explained *for* whom ?
Who are they that want explanation ? The finite
beings themselves. As soon as we speak of " explaining," we are already in the field of finiteness ;
for all explanation, that is, not a gathering of all
determinations at once, but a gradual rise from one
determination to another, is finite ; and this very
determining or limiting is the bridge which carries
the explanation, and which the Ego has in itself.
The opposite power is independent of the Ego in

regard to its being and determination, which seeks
to modify the practical activity of the Ego, or the
tendency of the Ego, to posit itself as the totality
of all reality ; but it is dependent upon the ideal
activity, the theoretical power of the Ego. It is
for the Ego only, in so far as it is posited *through*
the Ego, and otherwise it is not for the Ego. Independent reality the other has only in so far as it
is related to the practical (moral) activity of the
Ego ; in so far as it is related to the theoretical
activity of the Ego, (the intelligence,) it is utterly
dependent, and subject to its laws. But, again, how
can it be in relation to the theoretical except
through the practical Ego, and *vice versa?* Here
we have, again, no ideality, no reality, and *vice
versa.* Hence, we can also say : The final ground
of all consciousness is a reciprocal causality, self-
relation, in the Ego, by means of a Non-Ego, an
Other, which may be viewed in various ways.

All seeming objections to the science of knowledge can be traced to an inability to hold this final
result. This may be manifested in two ways. You
may either reflect that, since this result is an idea,
it must also be in the Ego, and then you become
a dogmatic idealist, and must deny dogmatically all
external reality ; or you cling to the sayings of
your *feeling*, and of your common sense, (with
which our science, rightly understood, perfectly
agrees,) and then you deny what is clearly put before you, or accuse our science of dogmatic ideal-

ism, because you do not gather its meaning. Neither should be done ; but you should float between
the two opposite determinations of this idea. This
is the business of *creative power of imagination*,
with which surely all human beings are gifted, but
which not all have under their complete control.

V

SECOND PART

OF THE

PRACTICAL PART

OF THE

SCIENCE OF KNOWLEDGE.

SECOND PART

PRACTICAL PART

SCIENCE OF KNOWLEDGE.

———•••———

INTRODUCTORY.

THE result we have attained now as our final one is this: In positing the tendency of the Ego, a counter tendency of the Non-Ego is posited at the same time which holds it in balance.

With this result we shall have to do as we did with the result of the theoretical part of our science, that is to say, the Ego must posit it now in itself. It must become *for* the Ego ; the Ego must realize ✓✓ it. The realization of the theoretical result has shown itself up as the quantitative side of the construction of the universe, contemplation, sensation, time, and space, etc. ; the realization for the Ego of the practical result will, therefore, undoubtedly give its qualitative side, impulse, feeling, qualities of things, etc.

25

1. To clear the way, let us first state more precisely the contents of our result:

The conception of a tendency is the conception of a cause which is not cause. But every cause presupposes *activity*. Every tendency has power; if it had no power, it could not be cause.

2. The tendency, as such, has necessarily its determined quantity as activity. It wants to be cause. But it does not become cause, does not attain its end, and hence is *checked*. If it were not checked, it would be cause, and not tendency.

3. The tendency is not checked, limited by itself, for the conception of tendency involves that it should seek to be causality. If it limited itself, it would not be tendency. Hence, every tendency must be limited by another power opposed to it.

4. This opposing power must also be a tendency, that is, strive to be causality; for, if it did not so strive, it would have no relation to the first tendency. Moreover, it must not have any causality; for, if it had causality, it would annihilate the tendency of its opposite by annihilating its power.

5. Neither of the two opposite tendencies can have causality. If one of them had it, the power of the opposite would thereby be annihilated, and they would cease to be opposite tendencies. Hence, they must hold each other in balance.

THE TENDENCY OF THE EGO IS POSITED AS IMPULSE,
THE COUNTER TENDENCY OF THE NON-EGO AS
CHECK, AND THE BALANCE OF BOTH AS FEELING.

The tendency of the Ego, the opposing tendency
of the Non-Ego, and their mutual balance is now
to be posited, that is, to become *for* the Ego.

A. The tendency of the Ego is posited as such.

1. It is posited generally as *something* after the
general law of reflection ; hence, not as *activity*, as
something in motion, but as a fixed, permanent
something.

2. It is posited as a *tendency*. Tendency is a
desire to have causality ; it must, therefore, in this,
its character, be posited *as* causality. Now, this
causality can not be posited as directed upon the
Non-Ego, for then it would be posited as real effective causality, and not as tendency. Hence, it can
only return into itself, only produce itself. But an
itself-producing tendency, which is also something
fixed, permanent, decided, is called an *impulse*.

(The conception of an impulse involves, 1st. That
it should be grounded in the inner essence of that
whereunto it is ascribed, hence, that it should be
produced by the causality of that essence upon itself by its self-positing ; 2d. That it should be for
that very reason something fixed and enduring ; 3d.
That it should seek to have causality outside of itself, but should have none in so far as it is merely
impulse. Hence, the impulse is purely in the sub-

ject, and never goes beyond the sphere of the subject.)

B. The tendency of the Ego can not be posited
without the positing of a counter tendency of the
Non-Ego ; for the tendency of the former desires to
have causality and has none ; and that it has not
causality can not be grounded in itself, for the very
conception of a tendency is the desire to have causality. Hence, the ground of its not having causality must be posited outside of the Ego, and again
only as a tendency, otherwise the tendency of the
Ego, or the impulse, as we now call it, would be
suppressed.

C. The balance between both must be posited.

The question here is not that this balance must
be posited, for this has been shown before, but :
What is posited in and through the Ego by positing this balance ? The Ego tends to fill up the infinite ; it also tends to reflect upon itself, which it
can not do without being limited ; and in regard to
the *impulse,* without being limited *through a relation to the impulse.*

Let us suppose the impulse to be limited in the
point C ; then in C the *tendency to reflection is satisfied, but the impulse to have real causality is limited.*
The Ego, then, limits itself in C, and is placed in
self-relation ; the impulse urges it further on, the
reflection holds it still, and through the reflection
it holds itself still.

Both united is the expression of a *compulsion ;*
of an *I can not.* An *I can not* involves, first, a fur-

ther onward tendency, for else that which I can not would not be *for* me ; second, limitation of real activity ; and, thirdly, that the limiting should not be *in me*, but *outside of me*, or else there would be no tendency, and instead of an *I can not* we should have an I will not.

This utterance or expression of the *I can not* in the Ego is called *feeling*. In feeling is intimately united, first, *activity—I* feel, I am the feeling, (and this activity is that of the reflection ;) and, secondly, *limitation*—I *feel*, am passive, not active, there is a compulsion. This limitation necessarily presupposes a tendency to go beyond. For else it would not be limited, *for itself*, of course. Feeling is altogether *subjective*. To *explain* it we require, it is true, an objective, a *limiting*, which is the business of the theoretical part of the science of knowledge, but not to deduce it as occurring in the Ego, as being posited in the Ego.

Here we see sun clear what so many philoso-phers, who can not get rid of transcendent dogmatism, can not comprehend, that is, *that* and *how* the Ego develops out of itself whatsoever occurs in it, without ever going beyond itself or breaking through its own circles. And how else could an Ego indeed be an Ego ? There is a feeling in the Ego ; this is a limitation of the impulse ; and if it is a *determined* feeling, (distinguished from other feelings,) the possibility whereof is as yet not visible, then it is the limitation of a determined impulse, distinguished from other impulses. The Ego must posit a ground of this limitation, and must posit it outside of itself. It can posit the impulse as limited only by an opposite, and hence the impulse evidently determines *what* is to be posited as object. If the impulse is posited as Y, the object must, therefore, necessarily be not-Y. But as all this occurs in consciousness *necessarily*, a consciousness of this act never occurs, and each one assumes that he has received externally what nevertheless he has only produced by his own power in accordance with his own laws. Still, such a proceeding has also objective validity, for it is the universal procedure of all finite reason, and there is and can be no other objective validity than the one shown up.

It is true, we in our investigation appear to have broken through this circle, for we have assumed as explanation of a tendency in the Ego an independent and opposite Non-Ego. But the ground of the possibility and correctness of such a proceeding on our part is this : Every one who enters into this investigation with us is himself an Ego—an Ego, however, which long ago has passed through all the acts we have here deduced, that is, which long ago has posited a Non-Ego ; and our present investigation intends merely to show to him that this Non-Ego is his own product. He has long since *necessarily* completed the whole business of

Reason ; and now merely determines himself to take a second look at this transaction, to go over the whole account anew, as it were ; and hence he posits arbitrarily with us an Ego, which he places on the stand-point from which he originally started, and makes his experiment upon this Ego. Whenever this Ego, now investigated, shall arrive at the same point which the investigator now occupies, both Egos will be united, and the circle will be closed.

FEELING ITSELF IS POSITED AND DETERMINED.

PRELIMINARY.

The Ego is originally a tendency to fill up the infinite. This tendency is opposed to all object. The Ego also has a law in itself to reflect upon itself, as thus filling up the infinite. But it can not thus reflect, unless it is limited. Hence, the satisfaction of this tendency to reflect itself is *conditioned* by an object. The reflection-tendency may also be ✓ described as a tendency *toward the object.*

This limitation occurs through feeling, and by it the tendency is *satisfied*, so far as its *form* is concerned—the Ego *does* now reflect with absolute spontaneity ; *not satisfied*, so far as its content is concerned ; for the Ego is posited as limited, whereas it should be posited as unlimited. But this dissatisfaction is again not for the Ego, unless the Ego goes beyond the limit posited by itself.

How can this be ?   How can this dissatisfaction or feeling be posited for the Ego ?

As sure as the Ego reflects upon itself, it *is* limited.   Limited, that is, for a possible outside observer, not yet *for* itself.   Let us at present be these outside observers, or, which is the same, let us posit in place of the Ego something which is only observed, a lifeless body, to which, however, we shall ascribe what we have presupposed as pertaining to the Ego.   Let us, therefore, suppose an elastic ball, = A, and assume that it is pressed in by another body.   In this case :

A.   You posit in A a power, which, as soon as the opposite power gives way, will manifest itself without any further external influence, which, therefore, has in itself the ground of its causality. The power is in A, and tends in and upon itself to find expression ; it is a power which is directed in and upon itself, hence an internal power.   It is an immediate tendency to have causality upon itself, but which has no causality by reason of the external resistance.   It is a balance of the immediate tendency, and of the mediated counter-impression in the body itself ; hence, what above we called *impulse.*   In the elastic body A an impulse is therefore posited.

B.   In the other body, which presses A in, and which we shall call B, the same internal power which resists the reaction and the resistance of A, and which, therefore, is also itself restricted by A, but which has its ground solely in itself, is also posited ; that is, power and impulse is posited in B precisely as in A.

C. If one of both powers is increased, then the opposite is weakened, and *vice versa ;* and, if the stronger power manifested itself fully, then the weaker one would be driven completely out from its sphere of action. As it is, both completely balance each other, and the point of their junction is the point of this balance. If that point is moved in the least, the whole relation is destroyed.

This is the case with an object having a tendency, but not reflection ; (we call such an object *elastic.*) Let us now see how this will apply to our object of investigation, which is an *Ego*, and which therefore has *reflection and tendency*.

The impulse is an inner power, determining itself to manifest causality. But the lifeless body has no causality at all, except outside of itself ; and hence, since the inner power is held back by the external other body, its self-determination, its desire to manifest causality, results in nothing.

This is the case precisely with the Ego, in so far as it desires to have *external* causality ; and, if it *only* had a desire for *external* causality, the case of the elastic body would be altogether applicable.

But the Ego, precisely because it is an Ego, has also a causality upon itself, that is, a causality to posit itself, or to reflect upon itself. Now, the impulse is to determine *the power of that which has the tendency*, and hence, in so far as this power is to manifest itself *in that which has the tendency*, as is

the case with reflection, it follows that from the determining of the impulse a manifestation of such a
determining must necessarily result.   Or, in other
words, *the impulse necessarily results in the self-
reflection of the Ego.*   (An important point.)

Hence, all reflection is grounded upon the tendency ; and, again, there is no tendency, that is,
for the Ego, and hence no tendency *of the* Ego, and
indeed no Ego at all unless there is reflection.
Both tendency and reflection are synthetically
united.   Hence, also, the limitation of the Ego.
For no limitation no tendency, no tendency no reflection, etc.

Hence, also, the distinction and union of ideal
and real activity.   The original tendency of the
Ego as such is both ideal and real, both external
and internal, because neither is distinguishable.
By the limitation the *external* direction of the tendency is cut off, but not the *internal*, the self-returning, which is therefore the *ideal.*   This ideal
activity will soon appear to be the activity of representation, and hence the relation of the impulse
to it may be called the *impulse of representation ;*
which is, therefore, the first and highest manifestation of the impulse, whereby the Ego first becomes
intelligence.

Hence, finally, the subordination of the theoretical to the practical part ; and why all theoretical
laws are grounded upon practical laws, or rather
upon *one* practical law.   From this result, moreover, the absolute freedom of reflection and abstrac-

tion, and the possibility to direct your attention
upon a subject and to avert it from another subject
for moral reasons, without which indeed no morality
were possible. Fatalism is rooted out thoroughly,
and its doctrine that an acting and willing is dependent upon the system of our representations is
destroyed by the proof that this system is again
dependent upon our impulse and our *will*.

Now, in this self-reflection, the Ego as such,
which is never immediately conscious of its acting,
can not be self-conscious. And yet it is now an
Ego, a *for*—of course, for an outside observer ; and
here is the limit, where the Ego as a living essence
is distinguished from a lifeless body, in which there
also may be an impulse, as we have shown, but no
reflection. The Ego is posited now as something
for which something might be, though it is not yet
for *itself*. But it is posited as something, for which
there is an inner impelling power, which, however,
is only *felt*, since there is as yet no consciousness
of it.

(A state of the Ego which every one can experience for himself. The philosopher may thus refer every one to experience for the *what*, not for the
that. To postulate *that* a certain feeling must be
is to proceed improperly. But its content, the
what, each one must discover in himself.)

We now have a living distinct from the lifeless.
Feeling of power is the principle of all life, is the
transition from death to life.

This power is felt as *impelling;* the Ego feels impelled *to go out of itself.*

This impulse can and does not determine the *real* activity, does not produce a causality upon the Non-Ego. But it can and must determine the ideal activity, which depends altogether upon the Ego. The ideal activity, therefore, goes beyond and posits something as object of the impulse, as what the impulse would produce if it had causality. But neither this production nor the producing occurs as yet in consciousness, and we only show here how the Ego can *feel impelled toward an unknown something.*

The impulse is to be *felt* as impulse, that is, as something which has not causality. But in so far as it impels, at least to a production of its object through ideal activity, it has most assuredly causality, and in so far is not felt as *impulse.*

Again: in so far as the impulse tends toward real activity, it is also not to be felt, for as such it has not causality.

Uniting both we say: an impulse can not be felt unless the ideal activity tends upon the object of the impulse; and this can not be unless the real activity is limited.

And thus there results the reflection of the Ego upon itself as a *limited.* But since the Ego in this reflection is never conscious, this reflection is a mere *feeling.*

And thus feeling is completely deduced. It involves a feeling of power, which does not manifest itself ; an object of this power, which also does not manifest itself : and a feeling of compulsion of the I can not, which is the manifestation of feeling.

FURTHER DETERMINATION AND LIMITATION OF FEELING.

The Ego now feels itself limited, that is, is no longer limited like a lifeless, elastic body, for an outside observer, but is limited *for itself.* Its activity is canceled *for it ;* for, though we have seen that the Ego has produced the object of its impulse by absolute activity, the Ego itself has not yet seen that it has so produced it.

But the Ego can not tolerate the total canceling of its activity, and hence, to be an Ego, must restore it, and must thus restore it *for itself ;* that is, it must, at least, posit itself in a manner so as to be able to posit itself as free and unlimited, though only in a future reflection. This is done, of course, through absolute spontaneity. The Ego turns from one reflection to another simply because it does so.

Here is the boundary between life and intelligence, as above we had the boundary between death and life. This self-consciousness of the Ego occurs through absolute spontaneity. Not by virtue of a law of nature, but through absolute freedom do we attain reason ; not through a transition, but by a *leap.* Hence, all philosophy must necessarily start from an Ego, because the Ego

can not be deduced ; and hence the undertaking
of the materialists to explain the manifestations of
reason from laws of nature must always remain an
impossiЬility.

The act whereby the canceled activity is to be
restored must, of course, be one of ideal activity ;
and since it is to be altogether grounded in the .
Ego, its object must be a something in the Ego.
And since in the Ego there is nothing but feeling,
this activity must have feeling for its object.

The act occurs with absolute spontaneity, and is
in so far act of the Ego. It has *feeling* for its
object, that is, firstly, the *reflecting* of the previous
reflection, which constituted feeling. Activity thus
has activity for an object ; that which reflects or
feels is, therefore, *posited as Ego.* Or, in other
words, the Ego, which restores its canceled activity, in this act transfers its own Ego-ness to the
reflecting, since itself does not become conscious
in this act as Ego. Not being conscious that itself
is the Ego, it makes the reflecting the Ego.

But the Ego is the self-determined. Hence, the
reflecting, or that which feels, can only be posited
as Ego, in so far as it is only determined by the
impulse, (that is, by the Ego or by itself,) to reflect,
to feel ; or, in other words, in so far as it *feels itself, and its own power in itself.* (Only that which
feels is the Ego, and only the impulse, as producing feeling or reflection, belongs to the Ego. Whatsoever is beyond this limit, that is, the impulse,
which impels the Ego to go beyond, to externalize

itself, is excluded from the Ego ; which should be carefully noted, for we shall return to this excluded.)

Hence, the *felt* becomes also Ego, in and for the present reflection, because that which feels is only in so far Ego as it is self-determined, that is, as it feels itself.

The Ego can, therefore, be posited as Ego only in so far as it is both the *felt* and the *feeling;* that is, as it is self-related. It is to be so posited, and we must, therefore, posit it thus. But how ? That which feels is posited as active in feeling, in so far as it is that which reflects, and in so far the *felt* in the same reflection is *passive*, for it is the object of the reflection.

Again : that which feels is posited as passive in feeling, in so far as it feels itself impelled, and in so far the *felt* or the impulse is active.

This contradiction must be united :

That which feels is active, and only active in its relation to the *felt.* (Its passiveness, that is, that it is *impelled* to reflect, does not arise here in consciousness, where the relation is only posited to the felt, and where the reflection and impulse is, therefore, altogether lost sight of.)

That which feels is passive in relation to an impulse ; to the impulse to go out of itself, whereby the Ego is driven to produce a Non-Ego through ideal activity. (And here the activity of that which feels is lost sight of in consciousness. Hence, *for itself,* in the self-reflection of the Ego, the Ego appears to act under compulsion.)

Again : the *felt* is active through the impulse, which impels the reflecting to reflect; but it is also passive in the same relation, since it is object of the reflection. But this latter does not occur in consciousness, since the Ego is posited as *feeling itself,* and not, therefore, as reflecting again upon the reflection. Hence, this latter passiveness, which relates to the reflecting, is not posited, and the Ego is posited passive in another relation, that is, in so far as it is *limited* by a Non-Ego. In other words : every object of reflection is necessarily limited—has a fixed quantity. But in reflecting this limitation is never deduced from the reflection itself, because the reflecting goes only upon the object, not upon the reflection itself.

Both the feeling and the felt are to be one and the same Ego, and are to be posited as such. And yet the one is viewed as active in relation to the Non-Ego, and the other as passive in the same relation ; the one as producing through ideal activity a Non-Ego, the other as limited by this Non-Ego.

SOLUTION.

Both the producing Ego and the felt Ego in the reflection were posited as *passive.* Hence, *the Ego is always for itself passive* in relation to the Non-Ego, never becomes conscious of its activity in producing it, and never reflects upon this activity.

This explains why the reality of the THING appears to be felt, when only the Ego is felt.

REMARK.

And here we have the ground of all reality. Only by the relation of feeling to the Ego does reality become possible for the Ego—reality of the Ego as well as of the Non-Ego.

Something which is possible only through the *relation of a feeling*, without the Ego *becoming conscious of its contemplation thereof*, and which *appears, therefore, to be felt*, is *believed. Reality*—reality of the *Ego* as well as of the *Non-Ego*—is only a matter of *belief.*

THE IMPULSE ITSELF IS POSITED AND DETERMINED.

As we have posited and determined feeling, so now the impulse. But to posit means: the Ego reflects upon it. The Ego, however, can only reflect upon itself or upon its content. Hence, the impulse must be already manifested in the Ego, if the Ego is to reflect upon it.

That which feels is posited as Ego. This was determined by the felt original impulse to go beyond itself, and to produce something at least through ideal activity. But the original impulse does not tend upon mere ideal activity, but upon *reality*. Hence, the Ego is determined by it to produce *a reality outside of itself*. But since the tendency of the Ego is always to be counterbalanced by the tendency of the Non-Ego, it can not have this external causality, and is, therefore, in so far as it is impelled by the impulse, *limited* by the Non-Ego.

The Ego has the tendency always to reflect upon itself, whenever the condition of all reflection, limitation, occurs. It occurs here. The Ego, therefore, reflects, and, as in all reflection, the Ego forgets itself, that is, the *reflecting* Ego does not become visible. Again : this reflection occurs in consequence of a mere impulse ; hence, there is no freedom manifested in it, and it becomes, as above, a mere *feeling.* But what sort of feeling ?

The object of this reflection is the impelled, hence the *idealiter, in itself*, active Ego ; impelled by an inner impulse, hence without spontaneity. This activity has an object, which it can not *realize* as thing, nor *represent* through ideal activity. Hence, it is an activity which has *no object at all*, but which is *irresistibly impelled to produce an object*, and which is merely *felt*. Such an activity is called a *yearning* — an impulse toward a completely unknown which manifests itself solely as a *requirement*, as *dissatisfaction ;* as an *emptiness* which seeks to be *filled*, but does not signify whence. The Ego feels a yearning—a want.

Both feelings, that of yearning and the above feeling of limitation and compulsion, must be distinguished and related to each other. (For the impulse is to be determined. Now, the impulse manifests itself through a certain *feeling*. Hence, this feeling is to be determined. But it can thus be determined only through another feeling.)

Unless the first feeling of the Ego were a limitation, the second would not be a yearning, but would be *causality;* for the Ego might then produce externally, and its impulse would not be restricted to determine the Ego only *internally.*

Again : if the Ego did not feel itself as *yearning,* it could not feel itself *limited,* for only through yearning does the Ego go beyond itself, only through yearning is something posited in and for the Ego, which shall be external.

REMARK.

This yearning is an important determination. ✓ Only through it is the Ego impelled *in itself* to go ✓ *out of itself;* only through it does an *external world* reveal itself *in the Ego.*

Both feelings, yearning and limitation, are therefore synthetically united. Neither is possible without the other. Both are also complete opposites. In limitation the Ego is felt as *passive,* in yearning as *active.*

Both feelings are grounded in the *same* impulse of the Ego. The impulse of the limited Ego, which only through this limitation obtains an impulse, determines the *reflection* of the Ego, and hence arises the feeling of a compulsion. The same impulse determines the Ego to go beyond it·

self to produce an external ; and since in this respect the Ego is limited, there arises in the Ego a
yearning, which being reflected upon results in a
feeling of yearning. How does the *same* impulse
result in different feelings ? By appealing to different powers. In the first instance, it appeals to the
power of reflection ; in the second, to the absolute,
free tendency of the Ego to produce. (The production, of course, we do not yet know, nor can know.)

Hence, yearning is the *original and absolute independent expression* of the tendency in the Ego.
Independent because it pays no regard to limitation, and transcends all limitation. (This remark
is important, because it will appear hereafter that
this yearning is the vehicle of all practical, that is,
moral laws, (or conscience,) which laws are to be
recognized by the test, whether they can be deduced from this yearning or not.)

Through the limitation there arises in the yearning also a feeling of compulsion, which must have
its ground in the Non-Ego. The object of the
yearning (we will call this object the *ideal;* it is
the object which the Ego as determined by the impulse would realize, *if it had causality*) is perfectly
congruent to the tendency of the Ego ; but that
object, which may be (or is) posited by the feeling
of limitation, is opposed to this tendency. Both
objects are, therefore, opposites.

Nevertheless, since in the Ego there can be no
yearning without compulsion, and *vice versa*, the
Ego is synthetically united in both. And yet it is

also opposed to itself in both these determinations. The Ego is both : *limited* and *unlimited, finite* and *infinite.* Let us now solve this contradiction satisfactorily.

The yearning wants to realize something outside of the Ego. But this it can not. Yet it must effect what it can. It can determine the ideal activity of the Ego to go beyond itself, and produce an external. How and what can this activity so produce? There is in the Ego a determined feeling of limitation, $= X$. Again, there is in the Ego a yearning desirous of positing reality. But reality manifests itself for the Ego only through feeling, hence the yearning yearns for a feeling. Now, the feeling X can not be the yearned for feeling, for then the Ego would neither feel itself limited nor yearning, and would indeed not feel itself at all. The yearned for feeling must, therefore, be its opposite $-X$. The object which would produce this feeling in the Ego must, therefore, be produced. We will call this object also $-X$. $-X$ would be the ideal.

Now, if the first object, X, could be felt, this opposite object, $-X$, might be easily enough posited. But X can not be felt because the Ego never feels an object, only feels itself, and produces an object only through ideal activity.

Again, if the Ego could produce in itself the feeling $-X$, both feelings could also easily enough be placed in relation ; but this the Ego can not do because it has no causality. (The Ego can not

limit itself. *Vide* " Theoretical Part.") The problem is, therefore, no less than this : To make appear from the feeling of limitation, not determined
in any further way, the object of the opposite feeling of yearning, or to have the Ego produce the
latter by ideal activity after the mere suggestion of
the former feeling of lin itation.

REMARK.

(The object of the feeling of limitation is something real ; that of yearning *has* no reality, but *is
to* (*shall*) have reality. Both are opposed to each
other, because through the one the Ego feels limited, and through the other it strives to get beyond
the limitation. What the one is the other is not.)
We now proceed :

In its free reflection of feeling above, the Ego
has posited itself as Ego by virtue of the principle,
that the self-positing, or that which is both determining and determined, is Ego. Hence, in that reflection which was manifested as self-feeling, the
Ego *determined* itself, completely described and
limited itself. In that reflection the Ego was *absolutely determining.*

It is *this* activity upon which the external impulse is directed, and thus becomes an impulse to
determine, to *modify*, a something outside of the
Ego, that is, the reality given by feeling. This reality is the determinable matter, which the impelled
Ego is to determine, to modify.

The balance between the Ego and this external reality must be kept up ; hence, the reality always remains the same, that is, reality. As such, as matter, it can undergo no modification, for a modification would be in its case annihilation. Hence, the impulse of the Ego does not affect the reality as such, but effects a certain determination, modification of the reality of the matter. (It is wrong to say : different matter. Matter as such, materiality, is absolutely simple. One can only say : matter with different determinations.)

Now, it is *this* determination of the external reality through the impulse which is felt as a *yearning*. Hence, yearning does not at all tend to produce matter as such, but merely to modify it.

The *feeling* of yearning was not possible without reflection upon the determination of the Ego through the impulse. This reflection, again, was not possible without *limitation* of the impulse to determine, which alone is manifested in yearning. Limitation of the Ego, however, is only felt. What feeling is it, then, whereby the *impulse to determine* is felt as limited ?

All determining occurs through ideal activity. Hence, if the presupposed feeling is to be possible, ideal activity must have determined already an object, and this act of determining must now be related to feeling. Here occur these questions : How is the ideal activity to arrive at the possibility and reality of this determining ? How can this determining be related to feeling ?

We have shown heretofore already how the ideal activity of the Ego is determined in a certain way by the impulse. This determination forced the Ego to *posit the ground of the limitation,* as an in itself determined object which, because it is thus posited, never enters consciousness. We have just now shown up another impulse in the Ego, an impulse to merely determine, to merely modify ; and by virtue of this impulse the ideal activity must at least strive for the present to determine, modify, the posited object. We can not say *how* the Ego is to determine the object, but we know, at least, that it is to be the determining, the purely and absolutely *active* in the determining. Now, can this impulse to determine the object have causality or not ? I reply, as sure as the Ego is to be Ego, it can have no causality ; for, unless this impulse is limited, yearning is not possible ; without yearning no feeling ; without feeling no life, consciousness, etc. Hence, that impulse can not have causality. But of this the ground can not be in the impulse itself, for then it would be no impulse ; and, hence, it is in an opposite impulse of the Non-Ego, *to determine itself,* in a causality of the Non-Ego, which proceeds its own way and follows its own laws, as the impulse follows *its* own.

Hence, if there is an object, and independent determinations of this object, (that is, determinations produced by the own inner causality of nature,) and if, moreover, the ideal (contemplating) activity of the Ego is driven out, is externalized, then the

Ego must and will determine the object. In this determining the Ego is guided by the impulse, and is impelled to determine the object according to the impulse; but, at the same time, it stands under the influence of the Non-Ego, and is limited by it, that is, by the real qualitativeness of the thing, limited in the higher or lower degree, in which it can determine the object by the impulse. Through this limitation of the impulse the Ego becomes limited, and hence there arises a feeling, which is here a feeling of limitation of the Ego, not through *matter*, but through the *qualitativeness of the matter.* And thus we have answered also the second question, how the limitation of determining might be related to feeling.

Let us further illustrate this important result: The Ego, as we found above, in its free reflection of feeling determined itself through absolute spontaneity. Its activity in this determining was altogether of a *reflective* character, that is, the determining was not a modification of the Ego, but merely a *reproduction in reflection*, an imaging of itself.

With this activity the impulse is now connected, and impels it to go out of the Ego. Of course, the character of the activity does not change thereby, only its direction changes; instead of internal it is now external, but it is still the same, *merely reproducing*, imaging activity. Only, whereas, at first it imaged the Ego, it now images the Non-Ego.

But further, in the above instance the Ego determined itself through absolute spontaneity as Ego, because it posited itself as the *determined* and *determining* together in that reflection. *It posited that which is both determined* and *determining as Ego*, for the very reason that it was both *the determining and determined itself in that reflection which it produced by absolute spontaneity.* This law of determination was, therefore, in the Ego conjointly with its application.

Now, the impulse connects with the reflecting Ego, does not modify it, but merely impels it outward. It does not, therefore, modify either that law of determination in the Ego, whereby whatsoever the Ego is to reflect upon, to determine, (*idealiter*,) must be (*realiter*) "determined and determining together." Hence, also, the Non-Ego, which the Ego is to determine, must be both determined and determining, or must be *determined through itself*. Only if the Non-Ego is self-determined can the *impulse to determine* be related to it, be satisfied. That impulse demands determinedness, perfect totality and wholeness. That which is determined, and not in the same respect determining, is, in so far, *effect*, and is excluded in reflection as something *foreign* from the thing. That which is not also the determined in so far as it is *determining*, is, in so far, *cause*, and the *determining* is applied in reflection to *another* somewhat, and thus excluded from the thing. Only in so far as the thing is in causality with itself is it a thing. This characteristic is applied to the things by virtue of the law of determination, which is transferred from the Ego to the things. An important remark.

Why is sweet, bitter, red, or yellow, etc., a *simple* sensation which can not be divided into many; or, why is it an independent sensation, and not merely a component of another one? Evidently, because *in the Ego* there is this law of determination *à priori*, and it is *for* the Ego that the sensation is a simple one.

The distinction of the Ego and Non-Ego, however, remains in spite of the sameness of their law of determination. For in the Ego the *reflecting* and the *reflected* is also one and the same; but the Non-Ego is only the *reflected*.

The question remains, How is the determinable given to the Ego? How is the Ego connected with the determinable?

The Ego reflects upon itself as the determined and determining together, and is in so far limited, that is, goes only so far as the determined and determining goes. But a *limited* has a *limiting*. This limiting, opposed to the Ego, can not here be produced by its ideal activity as was presupposed in the theoretical part of our science, but must be *given* to the Ego. This given opposite we have already as that which was above *excluded* in this reflection of the Ego. In other words, the Ego posits itself as Ego only in so far as it is the determined and the deter-

mining, but it is both only ideally. Its tendency to
have *real* activity is, however, limited, that is, is in
so far posited as internal, inclosed, self-determining
power, (that is, power which is both determined and
determining,) or, since it is without manifestation,
as intensive matter. And now, in so far as this
internal power or intensive matter is reflected upon,
it is by opposition *externalized*, and thus the in
itself and original *subjective* is changed into an
objective.

REMARKS.

Here we see plainly how the Ego can not posit
itself as determined without opposing a Non-
Ego. It is the impulse—the impulse to go outward, which, since it can not connect with real
activity, connects at least with ideal activity, and
drives it outward. Through the impulse, therefore,
all determinations of consciousness are connected,
particularly the consciousness of the Ego and the
Non-Ego.

The subjective is changed into an objective, and
vice versa ; all objective is originally a subjective.
Since we speak here of a general *determined,* and
since no general determined ever arises in consciousness, we can only illustrate this by a *particular* determined. But this we can do clearly enough.
For instance : something is sweet or sour, red or
yellow, etc. Such a determinedness is evidently
altogether subjective. You positively can not describe what this is : sweetness, red, yellow, etc. ;

you can only feel it. You can only say : in me is
the feeling of bitter, sour, etc. The whole matter
is utterly subjective, not at all objective. From
such subjective feelings all our knowledge starts.
Without feeling no representation of an external
thing is possible.

Now, the subjective determination of *yourself*
you apply to an *external;* the accidence of your
Ego you change into an accidence of the thing,
which is to be external, *of a substance which is to be
extended in and to fill up space.* Now, you ought
long ago to have had some suspicion that this substance itself is something purely subjective, since
you found yourself able to apply something con-
fessedly subjective to it, without any new feeling
of a substance having entered you ; and since,
moreover, such a substance would not at all be for
you without your having applied the subjective feeling to it. Only thus is the substance in and for
you. If it had got into you originally, as a necessary means wherewith to connect the subjective
feeling, it must have gotten into you, perhaps,
through the senses. But the senses only furnish
us subjective determinations ; the substance is not
a matter of sensuous sensation, but is purely product of imagination. Or do you see the substance,
hear it, smell it ? Somebody might say : I feel it.
But the sense of feeling manifests itself only by the
perception of a resistance, of an I can not ; and I
hope you do not *feel*, but merely draw a conclusion
as to that which resists. The feeling only goes to

27*

the surface and manifests itself as, for instance, roughness, coldness, warmth, hardness, etc. ; but does not go into the interior of the body. Why, then, do you extend this warmth or coldness over a whole plane, instead of positing it in a single point ? And, moreover, how do you come to assume an interior of the body between the planes, since you do not feel that interior ? Evidently, through imagination. Still you consider this substance something objective ; and very justly, since you all have agreed and must agree as to its existence, because its production is grounded upon a universal law of reason.

The impulse is directed upon the self-reflecting activity of the Ego as such. The Ego is, therefore, to determine the thing, and hence to posit itself as the determining, or to reflect upon itself as the determining.

This activity of the Ego is one, and can not be directed upon many objects. It is to determine the Non-Ego, which we will call X. Now, we have said it is also to reflect upon itself as thus determining. The act of determining X must, therefore, be canceled, broken off, and this through absolute spontaneity, since the reflection occurs through absolute spontaneity.

The Ego in determining is, therefore, limited, and from this arises a feeling. Originally, the impulse to determine went outward, without any determination, that is, into the infinite. At present it is canceled in a point we will call C. We have thus a limitation of the determining impulse, and a re-flection of it, as the conditions of a feeling. It is a feeling of a limitation of the Ego by the *deter-minedness* of the thing, or a feeling of a *determined*, of a simple.

In the reflection, which takes the place of the broken off or canceled determining impulse, the Ego is to posit itself as Ego, that is, as the self-determining in this act. It is evident that the posited product of the Ego can only be a contem-plation of X, an image of X, not X itself. This is posited as product of the Ego in its freedom signi-fies : it is posited as *accidental*, as that which might also be otherwise ; or as accidental, not in relation to the Ego, (for the Ego does not become conscious of its freedom in imagining here—does not reflect upon its own reflection,) but in relation to another Non-Ego.

EXPLANATION.

X, in accordance with the law of determination, was to be self-determined. But by virtue of the ex-isting feeling it is also to extend to C ; no further, but also precisely so far. Of this its limitation the ground lies not in the *idealiter* determining and contemplating Ego. The Ego has no law for it. Does the self-determining X go only so far ? It will appear hereafter that, considered in itself, it extends into infinity ; but even if there should be a distinction in the thing, how is that distinction to get within the sphere of action of the ideal Ego ? For the ideal Ego has no point of connection with the Non-Ego, and is *idealiter* active only in so far as it has no such connection, as it is not limited by the Non-Ego. In popular language : why is something *sweet* and something *else* sour, opposed to the sweet ? To be sure, each is a determined something. But, besides this general character, what is their ground of distinction ? It can only exist in the ideal activity, and must, hence, be contained, at least in part, in the Ego, since it is to be a distinction *for* the Ego.

Hence, the ideal Ego floats with absolute freedom over and within the limit ; its limit is altogether undetermined. But since it is to reflect upon itself in this contemplation, it must posit itself as *determined* in it ; for all reflection presupposes determination. Now, the law of determination is, that something is determined only in so far as it is determined through itself. Hence, the Ego in the contemplation of that X must posit the limit of its contemplation for itself ; or, in other words, the Ego must determine itself to posit the very point C as its point of limitation ; and then X would be determined through the absolute spontaneity of the Ego.

But X is also an X, which, in accordance with the general law of determination, determines itself, and is only as such object of reflection. Now, X as X, that is, as both determined and determining, extends to C. Hence, the Ego *must* limit X in C, if it is to limit it correctly ; and thus X is *not* determined through the absolute spontaneity of the Ego.

The limitation of X in C is only *felt*, not *contemplated*. The *spontaneously posited limitation* of X in C, through the Ego, is to be merely *contemplated, not felt*. But both feeling and contemplation have no connection. Contemplation *sees*, but it is *empty ;* feeling relates to *reality*, but it is blind. A synthetical union of feeling and contemplation is, therefore, necessary to limit X in C as demanded. The contemplation is to limit X through absolute spontaneity, and yet so as to make X appear altogether self-limited. This is done if the ideal activity by its absolute power of production proceeds beyond X and posits a Y, (in the point B, C, D, etc., for the ideal activity can neither posit itself the fixed point of limitation, nor receive it as immediately given.) This Y, opposed to a determined somewhat, must, firstly, be also somewhat, that is, self-determined ; secondly, opposed to X, or limiting X, that is, neither determining X, as far as X is determined, nor being determined by X as far as X determines, and *vice versa ;* or it must be impossible to reflect upon X and Y as one. (Each is a somewhat ; but each is *another* somewhat. Without opposition the whole Non-Ego is a somewhat, but not a determined, particular somewhat.) The law is, therefore, that Y and Y shall mutually exclude each other. And it is to posit this opposition that the impulse determines the ideal activity. The impulse in this tendency may be called an impulse of *reciprocal determination.*

The limitation-point C is altogether posited through feeling ; hence the Y beyond C, in so far as it is to begin in C, can only be given through a relation to feeling. Feeling alone unites both in the limit. The impulse of *reciprocal determination*, therefore, also relates to a feeling ; and in this impulse, indeed, *ideal activity and feeling* are intimately united ; in it the whole Ego is one. It is this impulse which manifests itself through yearning, a yearning for *another, opposed* to the previous.

REMARK.

In yearning ideality and impulse to produce reality are closely united. Yearning longs for *another ;* this is only possible under presupposition of a previous determination through ideal activity. Again : yearning is not thought or represented, but *felt*, as the *limited* impulse to produce reality. And thus it appears how in feeling an impulse *to go outward*, hence the presentiment of an external world, may manifest itself ; for feeling is modified by ideal activity, which is free from all limitation. Here it also appears how a theoretical function of the Ego can relate back to its practical power, which had to be shown as possible if a rational being was ever to become a complete whole.

The feeling does not depend upon us, because it depends upon a limitation, and the Ego can not

limit itself. Now, an opposite feeling is to arise.
The question is : will the external condition, under
which alone such a feeling is possible, arise also ?
It must arise ; for, if it does not, the Ego has no
determined feeling, hence feels *nothing at all*, and
hence, does not live, and is no Ego.

The feeling of an *opposite* is the condition of a
satisfaction of the impulse, hence yearning is the
impulse for a change of feelings. The yearned for
object is now determined, but merely as this, that
it is to be *another* feeling.

Now, the Ego can not feel two feelings together,
can not be *limited in C* and *not limited in C* at the
same time. The *other* condition can, therefore, not
be *felt as* another. It can, therefore, only be *contemplated* as another feeling, an opposite to the
previous one. Hence, in the Ego contemplation
and feeling are always together, and both are synthetically united in one and the same point.

Again : the ideal activity can not replace or create a feeling ; it can, therefore, determine its object
only by this, that it is *not* the felt object, that all
determinations *except those of feeling* may be predicated of it. Thus the thing always remains only
negatively determined for the ideal activity, and the
felt also undetermined. It is an infinitely continued negative determining.

ILLUSTRATION.

What is *sweet ?* You determine it, it is something not related to seeing, hearing, etc., but to

taste. But what is taste? That you can only know by experience, and can recall it by imagination only *negatively*, that is, in a *synthesis of all that is not taste.* Again, sweet is not sour, not bitter; and thus you can go on and count up all the known determinations of taste. But, however many you may count, an infinite variety of possible new determinations which are *not sweet* remain.

The only remaining question is, How does the ideal activity ascertain that the feeling has changed for another? Evidently, through the satisfaction of yearning, through a feeling of satisfaction. But let us examine this closer.

THE FEELINGS THEMSELVES MUST BE POSITED AS OPPOSITES.

Through ideal activity the Ego is to oppose an object Y to the object X ; it is to posit itself as changed. But it posits Y only by virtue of a feeling, and of *another* feeling than that which posited X.

The ideal activity is altogether self-dependent, not dependent upon feeling. But if only the feeling, X, is in the Ego, then the ideal activity can not limit the object, X, can not say *what* it is, can not characterize. Hence, another feeling, =Y, must arise in the Ego, whereby the ideal activity can now characterize X, that is, oppose X to a determined Y. The change of feeling must, therefore, have an influence upon the ideal activity. How can this be?

The feelings themselves are *different* feelings for an outside observer, but they are to be different for the Ego itself; that is, they are to be posited as different. Positing is done by ideal activity. *Both* feelings must, therefore, be posited to make the positing of each possible; they must be synthetically united, but also opposed.

How, then, is a feeling posited? How are feelings synthetically united through positing? How are they posited as opposites?

A feeling is posited through ideal activity. The Ego, without self-consciousness, reflects upon a limitation of its impulse. From this arises a self-feeling. It again reflects upon this reflection, or posits itself in it as the determining and determined together. Thus, feeling itself becomes an ideal act, since ideal activity is transferred into feeling. The Ego feels, or, more correctly, has a *sensation of something*, that is, of matter. Through this reflection upon *feeling*, feeling changes into *sensation*.

Feelings are synthetically united *through ideal positing*. And their synthetical ground of union is this, that, without reflecting upon *both*, *neither* can be reflected upon as a feeling. When two feelings are related so as to limit and determine each other mutually, you can not reflect upon one without reflecting upon the other.

But if they are to be thus related, there must be, in each feeling, something suggestive of the other. And such a relation we have already indeed discovered, namely, a feeling connected with a yearn-

ing, that is, with a desire for a *change.* If this
yearning is to be fully determined, the *other,* the
yearned for feeling, must be shown up. Such another feeling we have also already postulated. The
same may determine in itself the Ego in whatever
manner; but, in so far as it is the *yearned for* feeling, it must be related to the former feeling, to the
yearning, and must, in so far, be accompanied by a
feeling of *satisfaction.* The feeling of yearning can
not be posited without a satisfaction for which it
yearns; and the satisfaction can not be posited
without presupposing a yearning which is being
satisfied. The limit is where yearning ceases and
satisfaction commences.

How does this satisfaction manifest itself in feeling? Yearning arose from an impossibility of determining, because the limitation was lacking.
Hence, in yearning, ideal activity and impulse to
produce reality were synthetically united. Now, as
soon as another feeling arises:

1st. The required determining becomes possible,
and hence, occurs really; and,

2d. From its actual occurrence follows another
feeling. (In feeling itself, as limitation, there is
and can be no distinction. But from the fact that
something becomes possible, which was not possible
without a change of feeling, it follows that the condition of the feeling has undergone a change.)

3d. By its actual occurrence *impulse* and *act* are
one and the same; the determination which the
impulse requires is now possible, and really occurs.

The Ego reflects *upon this feeling*, and upon *itself in this* feeling, as the determining and determined together, as completely united with itself, and such a determination of feeling may be called *approval.* The feeling is accompanied by approval.

But the Ego can not posit this harmony of impulse and act without positing their distinction, or something wherein they are opposites. Such is the previous feeling, which is, therefore, necessarily accompanied by *disapproval,* (by a manifestation of disharmony between the impulse and the act.) Not every yearning is necessarily accompanied by disapproval ; but, when it has been satisfied, disapproval of the previous feeling necessarily arises, and that previous feeling now appears insipid, absurd.

The objects X and Y, which are posited through ideal activity, are now determined not merely as opposites, but also by the predicates of approval and disapproval. And thus you can go on and determine infinitely ; and all the internal determinations of things, (determinations related to feeling,) are nothing but degrees of approval and disapproval.

But this harmony or disharmony, approval or disapproval, which consists as yet only for an outside observer, must become *for* the Ego itself, must be posited by it. Whatsoever is to be ideally posited, or to be felt, must be connected with an impulse ; nothing is in the Ego without impulse.

We must show up, therefore, an impulse in the Ego which tends to produce that harmony.

Harmonious is that which may be regarded reciprocally as the determined and determining. But here the harmonious is not to be a unit, but a twofold ; and hence the relation must be thus : A must be in itself both the determined and determining ; and so likewise must B. But both must have still another determination, (the determination of *how far,*) in regard to which A is posited as the determining, if B is posited as the determined, and *vice versa.*

An impulse to produce such a harmony lies in the impulse of *reciprocal determination.* The Ego determines X through Y, and *vice versa.* Examine this act of the Ego, and you will find that in both determinations each act is determined through the other, for the object of each is determined through the other.

This impulse may be called the impulse of reciprocal determination of the Ego through itself ; or the impulse to produce absolute unity and completion of the Ego in itself.

REMARK.

(We have now completed the whole circle. Firstly, Impulse to determine the Ego. Secondly, Impulse through it to determine the Non-Ego ; and— since the Non-Ego is a manifold, and since, therefore, no particular of the manifold can be in itself completely determined—impulse to determine the

Non-Ego through reciprocity or change; finally, impulse of the Ego to determine itself through itself by means of that change. This is, therefore, a reciprocal determination of the Ego and Non-Ego, which, by virtue of the unity of the subject, must change into a reciprocal determination of the Ego through itself. And thus the completeness of our deduction of the chief impulses of the Ego is attested by the return into itself of the circle.)

The harmonious, the reciprocally through itself determined, is to be impulse and act. Each is to be viewed as determined and determining together.

An impulse of this character (that is, determined and determining) would be an impulse which absolutely produced itself, an absolute impulse, an impulse for the sake of the impulse. (This is conscience, the absolute circle, impelling without higher ground. Expressed as a law, it is the absolute law, or categorical imperative, *thou shalt!*) The *undeterminedness* of this impulse is clearly visible ; for it impels without object, is merely formal. *An act* of this character (that is, determined and determining) would be an act which is done simply because it is done, with absolute self-determination and freedom. The whole ground, and all the conditions of acting, are in the acting. The undetermined here is also clear enough ; for there is no act possible without object, and the act can not give its own object.

The relation between both impulse and act is to

be that of reciprocal determination. Such a relation requires, first of all, that the act *may be regarded as produced by the impulse.*

The act is to be absolutely free, hence not at all
irresistibly determined, even not through the impulse. But this does not prevent the act from
having a characteristic, by virtue of which it may
be recognized as determined or not determined
through the impulse. The relation also requires
that the *impulse* may be posited as determined
through the act.

In the Ego there can be no opposites together.
But impulse and act are here opposites. As sure,
therefore, as the act arises, the impulse is broken
off or limited. And thus arises a *feeling.* The
act takes the possible ground of this feeling, and
posits or realizes it.

Now, if the *act* is determined through the *impulse,* then it follows that *the object* is also determined through the impulse. The impulse is now
(idealiter) determinable through the act ; that is,
it may be characterized as having been directed
upon this act.

Hence results harmony, and there arises a feeling of *approval,* which is here a feeling of *satisfaction,* of complete fulfillment. (But this satisfaction
lasts only a moment, since yearning returns.) But
if the act is not determined through the impulse,
then the object is in opposition to the impulse, and
there arises a feeling of *disapproval,* of dissatisfaction, of self-diremption of the subject. The impulse

in this case is also determinable through the act, but negatively ; it was not an impulse directed upon this act.

The act whereof we speak here is, as ever, a mere ideal act, through representation. All our sensuous causality in the sensuous world, which we *believe* in, also only appertains to us mediately through representation.

THE DIGNITY OF MAN.

Speech delivered by Fichte at the close of the foregoing Series of Lectures on the Science of Knowledge.

We have completed the survey of the human mind ; we have created a foundation, upon which a scientific system, as the correct representation of the original system in man, may be built. In conclusion, let us take a glance at the whole.

Philosophy teaches us to look for every thing in knowledge—in the Ego. Only through it is order and harmony brought into the dead, formless matter. From man alone does regularity proceed, and extend around him to the boundary of his perception ; and in proportion as he extends this boundary are order and harmony also extended. His observation marks out for each object of the infinite diversity its proper place, so that no one may crowd out the other, and brings unity into this infinite

variety. By his observations are the heavenly bodies kept together, and form but one organized
body; by it the suns move in their appointed
courses. Through reason there arises the immense
gradation from the worm to the seraph; in it is
hidden the system of the whole spirit-world; and
man expects justly that the law, which he gives it
and himself, shall be applicable to it; expects justly
the future universal acknowledgment of that law.
In reason we have the sure guarantee that from it
there will proceed, in infinite development, order and
harmony, where at present none yet exists; that
the culture of the universe will progress simulta-
neously with the advancing culture of mankind.
All that is still unshaped and orderless will, through
man, develop into the most beautiful order, and
that which is already harmonious will become ever
more harmonious, according to laws not yet developed. Man will extend order into the shapeless
mass, and a plan into universal chaos; through him
will corruption form a new creation, and death call
to another glorious life.

Such is man, if we merely view him as an observing intelligence; how much greater if we think
him as a practical, active faculty? Not only does
he apply the necessary order to existing things.
He gives them also that order which he selected
voluntarily, wherever his footsteps led him. Nature awakens wherever his eyes are cast; she pre-
pares herself to receive from him the new, brighter
creation. Even his body is the most spiritualized

that could be formed from the matter surrounding
him. In his atmosphere the air becomes softer, the
climate milder, and nature assumes a brighter smile
from the expectation to be changed by him into a
dwelling-place and a nurse of living beings. Man
commands coarse matter to organize itself according to his ideal, and to furnish him the substance
which he needs. What was formerly dead and
cold arises at his command from the earth into the
nourishing corn, the refreshing fruit, and the ani-
mating grape, and will arise into other things as
soon as he shall command otherwise. In his sphere
the animals become ennobled, cast aside under his
intelligent eye their primitive wildness, and receive
healthier nourishment from the hand of their mas-
ter, which they repay by willing obedience. ·

Still more : around man souls become ennobled ;
the more a man is a man the more deeply and ex-
tensively does he influence men ; whatsoever carries the stamp of pure humanity will never be misapprehended by mankind ; every human mind,
every human heart opens to each pure outflow of
humanity. Around the nobler man his fellow-
beings form a circle, in which he approaches near-
est to the centre who has the greatest humanity.
Their souls strive and labor to unite with each
other to form but one soul in many bodies. All
are one reason and one will, and appear as co-labor-
ers in the great, only possible destination of mankind. The higher man draws by force his age
upon a higher step of humanity ; the age looks

back and is astonished at the gap over which it has leaped ; the higher man tears with giant arms whatever he can seize from the year-book of the human race.

Break the hut of clay in which he lives ! In his being he is independent of all that is outward ; he is simply through himself ; and even in that hut of clay he is occasionally, in the hours of his exalta-tion, seized with a knowledge of this his real exist-ence ; in those hours, when time and space and every thing that is not himself vanish, when his soul tears itself by force from his body—returning to it afterward voluntarily in order to carry out those designs, which it would like to carry out yet by means of that body. Separate the two last neighboring atoms, which at present surround him, and he will still be ; and he will be, because it will be his will to be. He is eternal through himself, and by his own power.

Oppose, frustrate his plans ! You may delay them ; but what are thousand and thousand times thousand years in the year-book of mankind ?—a light morning dream when we awake. He conti-nues and he continues to act, and that which ap-pears to you as his disappearance is but an exten-sion of his sphere ; what you look upon as death is but ripening for a higher life. The colors of his plans, and the outward forms of them may vanish to him, but his plan remains the same, and in every moment of his existence he tears something from the outward into his own circle ; and he will con-

tinue thus to tear unto himself until he has devour-
ed every thing ; until all matter shall bear the impress of his influence, and all spirits shall form one
spirit with his spirit.

Such is man ; such is every one who can say to
himself : I am man. Should he not then carry
within him a holy self-reverence, and shudder and
tremble at his own majesty ? Such is every one
who can say to me : I am. Wherever thou mayest
live, thou, who carryest but a human face ; whether
thou plantest sugar-cane under the rod of the over-
seer, as yet scarcely distinguishable from the brute
creation ; or whether thou warmest thyself on the
shores of the Fireland at the flame, which thou
didst not kindle, until it expires, and weepest bit-
terly because it will not keep burning by itself ; or
whether thou appearest to me the most miserable
and degraded villain, thou art, nevertheless, what I
am ; for thou canst say to me : I am. Thou art,
nevertheless, my comrade and my brother. Ah !
at one time surely I also stood on that step of
humanity on which thou now standest—for it is a
step of humanity, and there is no gap in the development of its members — perhaps without the
faculty of clear consciousness, perhaps hurrying
over it so quickly that I had not time to become
conscious of my condition ; but I certainly stood
there also at one time—and thou wilt also stand
certainly at some time, even though it lasted million
and million times million years—for what is time ?
—upon the same step on which I now stand ; and

thou wilt surely at some time stand upon a step, where I can influence thee and thou me. Thou also wilt at some time be drawn into my circle, and wilt draw me into thine. Thee also will I recognize at some time as my co-laborer in my great plan. Such is to me, who am I, every one, who is I. Should I not tremble at the majesty in the form of man, and at the divinity which resides in the temple that bears his impress, though perhaps concealed in mysterious darkness?

Earth and heaven and time and space, and all the limits of materiality, vanish in my sight at this thought, and should not the individual vanish? I shall not conduct you back to him.

All individuals are included in the one great unity of pure spirit. Let this be the last word with which I recommend myself to your remembrance, and the remembrance to which I recommend myself to you.

RELIGIOUS SIGNIFICANCE

OF THE

SCIENCE OF KNOWLEDGE.

29

TRANSLATOR'S NOTE.

THE following fragments have been appended to this work in the hope that they might make more clear certain of its results.

They were occasioned by charges preferred against FICHTE accusing him of teaching atheism. The clear manner in which these fragments set forth the religious significance of the science of knowledge, determined us to give them this place in the present work.

THE RELIGIOUS SIGNIFICANCE

OF THE

SCIENCE OF KNOWLEDGE.

HE who wishes to understand my doctrine of religion sufficiently to have a competent judgment respecting it, must accurately know, and, as I believe, *possess* the system of transcendental idealism, and the pure moralism inseparably united therewith.

I say, must *possess* it, that is, must occupy the transcendental stand-point. For, so far as I have been able to observe in my experience, though I would not definitely decide upon it, the mere *historical* knowledge of that system is not sufficient. For, whenever it is to be concretely applied, it is often forgotten, and those who talk about it as the only truth, suddenly let go their hold of it, and fall back upon the stand-point of realism.

I also say, he who wishes to understand it so as to have a competent judgment respecting it. Students may exercise themselves upon all parts of transcendental idealism, and seek to penetrate it from every side; but unless they have comprehended the complete series of grounds, and finished the whole extent of that system, they only understand it halfways, or historically. Perhaps they may be attracted by the system, may not find it so very uneven; but they have no decisive judgment respecting it, unless they have fully comprehended it in *all* its parts.

Add to this the many philosophical presuppositions from which critics start. Unless the critics first agree with us concerning the fundamental principles, we can not dispute with each other. It is only concerning the deductions that discussions may be entered into.

Was it necessary to remark this with reference to a discussion which has arisen concerning a part of a system which can not be understood except as part of a whole? It seems to me this ought to have occurred naturally to all critics. Or is it reasonable to pass judgment upon this one part, picked up out of the whole, without the least knowledge of the premises of that one part, or of the terminology used in its representation, or of the object which is determined by the whole only? Is it fair to place this isolated part into another utterly opposite system, to interpret its language by the meaning of that opposite system, and then—to pass sentence upon it? Or is it fair to complain about indefiniteness, when the simple meaning of the part can not be found, solely because the whole is unknown?

Is it true or not, that the first originators of this discussion had never read any thing from my pen but that single article; much less studied my system? Nay, did they not, in passing judgment upon my system, connect it with utterly different systems? Is it, therefore, to be wondered at, that my system has been so vastly misrepresented? But whose fault is it?

What none of my opponents evidently possesses, and yet what alone is decisive in this matter, is a knowledge of the true essence and tendency of critical or transcendental philosophy. (Both expressions here mean the same; for on this point KANT and the better Kantians surely agree with me.) I must again call to mind this tendency of transcendental philosophy, and would request the philosophical public to give me no occasion to do so again.

There are two very different stand-points of thinking, that of natural and ordinary thinking, from which *objects* are *immediately thought*, and that of so-called artificial thinking, from which *thinking itself is thought*, consciously and purposely. The former stand-point is occupied by ordinary life and science, (*materialiter sic dicta;*) the latter by transcendental philosophy, which, for that very reason, I have called science of knowledge.

The philosophical systems before Kant did not generally recognize their stand-point truly, and thus wavered between the two. The system of Wolf and Baumgarten, which immediately preceded Kant, placed itself with consciousness, on the stand-point of ordinary thinking, and had no less an object in view than to extend the sphere thereof, and to produce new objects of their ordinary thinking by the power of their syllogisms.

Now, to this system ours is absolutely opposed in this very matter, that ours utterly denies the possibility of producing, by mere thinking, an object valid for life and for (material) science ; and that ours permits nothing to pass for real *which is not grounded in an internal or external perception.* And in this respect, that is, in so far as metaphysics are to be the system of some real knowledge produced by mere thinking, Kant and I utterly deny the possibility of a science of metaphysics. Kant boasts of having utterly eradicated metaphysics ; and since as yet not one sensible and comprehensible word has been uttered to save that science, it doubtless has been annihilated for all times to come.

Our system is equally explicit in repudiating all extension of knowledge through mere thinking ; and for its part merely proposes to exhaustively represent and comprehend that thinking. In thus thinking that ordinary and only real thinking, which it proposes to comprehend, our philosophical *thinking* signifies nothing, and has no content whatever ; it is only the thinking, which is *thought* in it, which signifies and has content. Our philosophical thinking is merely the instrument wherewith we construct our work. When the work is finished, the instrument is thrown aside as useless.

We compose before the eyes of our spectators the model of a body from the models of its several parts. You interrupt us in the midst of our labors, ·and cry out: "Look at that skeleton! Is that a body?" No, my good people, it is not a body, nor is it intended to be one; it is merely to be a skeleton! It is simply because our teaching can be made comprehensible to others alone by thus joining part to part, that we have undertaken the work. If you wait a little, we shall clothe this skeleton with veins, muscles, and skin.

Then, when we are done, you cry again: "Why don't you let your body move, speak, and its blood circulate? Why don't you let it live?" You are again in the wrong. We have never pretended to possess this power. Only *nature* gives life, not *art.* This we know very well, and believe our system favorably distinguished from other philosophies by knowing it. If we shape any part otherwise than it is in nature, or if we add or leave out any part, then you have a right to complain. It is to this you must see, if you desire understandingly to applaud or reprove.

The living body, which we artistically reconstruct, is *common, real consciousness.* The gradual composition of its parts are our *deductions*, which can only proceed step by step. Before the whole system is completed, all our work is but a part of it. Of course, the parts to which the last part is joined must already be completed, or there would .be no method in our art; but it is not necessary that they should always be repeated, that we should put them into every book we write. We very properly presuppose a knowledge of those first parts from our former writings, for we can not say every thing at once. You have only to wait for what may *follow* after this our last part ; unless, indeed, you know how to discover it yourself.

But even *when* we shall have completed our whole work, and thus shall have advanced it to a complete representation of all *real and common thinking,* (we have done this in many regions of consciousness— in law, morality, etc. ;* but not yet in the region of religion,) it will still be, *in the manner in which it occurs in our philosophy,* not itself a real thinking, but simply a *description* and *representation* of real thinking.

All reality arises for us only through *not-philosophizing,* that is, when either men have never elevated themselves to philosophical abstraction; or when men have again suffered themselves to descend from its height to the mechanism of life, and *vice versa, this reality vanishes necessarily* as soon as men rise to pure speculation, because then they have torn themselves loose from that mechanism of thinking which reality is based upon. Now, *life* is object ; and speculation is only the means. It is not even means to *cultivate* life, for speculation lies in an altogether different world, and life can only be

* Fichte had already completed a science of rights and science of morality ; a science of religion [Philosophy of Religion] he purposely abstained from for years.—*Translator's Note.*

influenced by what arises from out of life. Speculation is only means to know life.

That wherein we are bound up, or which we ourselves are, can not be known. To know it, we must
go beyond it, take up a stand-point outside of it.
This going beyond real life, this outside stand-point
is speculation. Only in so far as these two stand-
points are possible, it is possible for man to know
himself. You may live, and perhaps live very
rationally, without speculating, for you can live
without knowing life ; but you can not know life
without speculating.

In short : the duplicity which extends throughout the whole system of reason, and which is
grounded in the original duplicity of subject and
object, is here seized in its highest form. *Life*
is the *totality* of the *objective rational being ;* and
speculation is the *totality* of the *subjective rational*
being. One is not possible without the other.
Life, as an active surrendering to a mechanism, is
not possible without the *activity and freedom* (otherwise speculation) which *surrenders itself ;* though
the latter may not arise to the clear consciousness
of every individual ; and *speculation* is not possible
without the *life from which* it abstracts. Both life
and speculation are determinable only through each
other. *Life* is most properly *not-philosophizing ;*
and *philosophizing* is most properly *not-life.* This
is a complete antithesis, and a point of union is
here quite as impossible as it is to point out the X,
which is the ground of the subject-object of the

Ego. The only union is in the consciousnes of the true philosopher, that both stand-points do exist for him.

No proposition, therefore, of a philosophy which knows itself, is, in that form, a *proposition for real life.* It is either a step in the system, to proceed from it to other propositions ; or, if it is the final proposition of speculation concerning some particular branch of knowledge, it is a proposition to which perception and sensation must first be added, as comprehended in it, in order to be fit for use in real life. Even the completed system of philosophy can not give you sensation, nor replace it. Sensation is the only true inner principle of life. Kant already has stated this often enough, and it is the innermost soul of his philosophy. Jacobi, quite independent of Kant, nay, believing himself at variance with Kant in this, has also stated it often enough. So has Mendelssohn. I also have said it often enough, and as energetically as possible, ever since the first statements of my system were made public.

My opponents can not, therefore, but have heard it ; but they can not get accustomed to it. They may have gotten hold of it as a historical proposition, but not as a rule of their judgments ; for in all their judgments they seem to have forgotten it. *They* are the students of a philosophy which gets hold of new truths by reasonings ; and hence, whenever they hear a philosophical proposition, they at once look to see what new truth may have been reasoned out by it.

What, then, is the use of philosophy, and what need is there of all the subtle preparations of that science, when it is confessed that philosophy can say nothing new for life, nay, can not even cultivate and develop life; that philosophy is only a science of knowledge, not a school for wisdom?

It might be sufficient to say, it is at least a possible branch of mental culture which should be developed, even though it had no other use. Being possible, it should also be realized, for man should realize all the possibilities of reason.

But the chief use of philosophy, as has been frequently stated, is negative and critical. What is usually called world-wisdom labors not under the difficulty of containing too little, but too much. The just mentioned reasoned out truths of former metaphysics have been carried into that general culture and mode of thinking; whereas they ought to have been separated therefrom. Transcendental philosophers propose to separate all those reasoned out truths from general culture, and to bring back that culture to its truly human, and hence, necessary and ineradicable basis. This was also all KANT proposed to do.

But indirectly, that is, in so far as its knowledge unites with the knowledge of life, it has also a positive use. Philosophy is *pedagogical* in the widest significance of this word, for the immediate practical life. Because this science has to teach

us to comprehend the whole man, it shows from
the highest grounds how men should be cultured,
in order to make permanent in them moral and
religious sentiments, and gradually to universalize
these sentiments.

For theoretical observation, for the knowledge of
the sensuous world, that is to say, for natural sciences, philosophy is *regulative*, showing what we
must inquire of nature, and how we have to question her. But its influence on the sentiments of
mankind in general consists chiefly in this, that it
brings power, courage, and self-confidence in man,
by showing him that he and his whole fate depend
solely upon himself, or by placing him on his own
feet.

And thus a philosophy of religion is by no means
the doctrine of religion, still less is it to replace
religious sentiment ; it is simply the theory of religion, and its object here is also both critical and
pedagogical. It proposes to abolish incomprehensible, useless,and confusing doctrines about God,which
by those very qualities afford a target for irreligi-
ousness. These it abolishes by showing that they
are nothing, and that none of them fit the human
mind. It likewise shows how in the human heart
religiousness is generated and developed, and thus
how mankind can be educated to be religious ; not
by means of philosophy, which does not influence
life, but only teaches a knowledge of it, but by awak-
ening the true supersensual motive-powers of life.

The tendency of a philosophical system of religion can, therefore, not be correctly apprehended until it is completed, until it is an exhaustive picture of the whole sphere of human reason. Only then can it begin to be pedagogical.

I have begun a philosophy of religion* in the above meaning of the word, and in no other. But I have not completed that philosophy, having only laid down its basis. To thus complete it will now be my earnest labor, and I hope soon to be able to satisfy the public concerning it.

I said above: Transcendental philosophy proposes to systematically represent the real general knowledge, but it admits as valid only knowledge founded upon *perception*—rejecting all knowledge produced by argumentation. The reality of its knowledge that philosophy, therefore, always derives from perception ; but in so far as it must comprehend the necessity and show the deductions of this knowledge, it does not appeal to facts ; for, if it did, it would cease to be transcendental philosophy.

Hence, that philosophy can never come into dispute with common, natural consciousness, since it does not touch that consciousness at all, but moves in an utterly different world. It is only at variance with a new philosophy which pretends to think out new facts ; and hence, whatsoever transcendental philosophy may contradict, belongs, since it is not to be found in a system of universal reason, to that new philosophy.

* Alluding to the article : " Concerning the Ground of our Faith in a Divine World-Government."

Now, my philosophy of religion is at variance with that new philosophy, partly concerning the origin of religion, which the former holds to be in a sentiment, the latter to be produced by argument ; partly concerning the extent and content of religion, which the latter holds to consist of knowledges and doctrines, whilst I hold no such thing.

A great portion of our *theology* is such very philosophy, and a great portion of our religious educational books (catechisms, hymn-books, etc.) is *theology*. Hence, I am in conflict with these books, as far as they are theology—not so far as they are religion ; in other words, so far as their *theoretical* content is concerned ; the deduction whereof those books happily rarely attempt. My philosophy of religion can, therefore, also enter into no conflict with the religious feelings of man in common life, occupying, as it does, an utterly different sphere. Still, the *pedagogical* results of my philosophy might lead to such a conflict ; but in that case they must first appear, and as yet they have not been established by me.

It is, therefore, absolutely irrational to judge of my system as a system of world-wisdom, and to attack it with world-wisdom. And yet most of my opponents have done this.

Amongst this may be classified all that has been said concerning a Fichteian God, a Jacobian God, a Spinoza God, etc. Fichte, Jacobi, and Spinoza are something different from their philosophy. The philosopher has no God at all, and can have none ;

he can only have a conception of the conception or of the idea of God. God and religion are only in life ; but the philosopher as such is not the whole complete man, but is man in a condition of abstraction ; and it is impossible that any one should be *only* philosopher. Whatsoever is posited through reason is absolutely the same for all rational beings. Religion and belief in God is thus posited through reason, and hence is posited in the same manner for all. rational beings. In this respect there are absolutely no many religions, no many Gods ; but there is simply *one* God. Only that in the conception of God, which all must admit and agree to, is the true ; but that in their conception of God, (not the conception of the conception of God,) respecting which they disagree, is necessarily false. All are wrong in regard to those points, for the very reason that the points can be disputed. That which can thus be controverted has been derived through argumentation by a false philosophy, or has been memorized from a catechism based on a false philosophy. True religiousness says nothing about it.

Amongst this may also be classified the attempt to oppose my philosophy to Christianity, and to refute the one by the other. True, it has heretofore always been customary for the philosopher to make Christianity harmonize with his philosophy, and for the Christian to make his faith agree with his philosophical thinking ; but this only proves that the men who undertook to do this knew neither philosophy nor Christianity. Our philosophy does not dream of such a thing. Christianity is wisdom of life, is popular philosophy in the true and highest sense of the word ; and can not be any thing else without losing its rank and sinking down into the sphere of argumentation, and thereby admitting the validity of demonstration, and hence exposing itself to the dispute of philosophical systems. With Christianity as such original wisdom of life, our philosophy can not enter into a conflict ; for our philosophy is only theory of that wisdom. Only the results of our philosophy might come into conflict with the results of Christianity ; but let me ask, where are these results, and, I might add, where is true Christianity ? Has it not in all cases, where it reaches us, passed through the crucible of that argumentative understanding ?

Again, it is charged that, according to my system, God is not to be the Creator and Governor of the world, that my system discards a divine Providence ! Why, you dear, good unphilosophers ! For you the whole distinction, the whole opposition whereby one philosophical system asserts this and another denies it, does not at all exist. If you are really good and religious, continue to take it in the sense in which it is true. I was not addressing you at all, but was speaking to philosophers, who may be assumed to know that distinction, and who yet take those dogmas in the sense in which they are not true. I only wanted to contradict them ; and they, at least, ought to have understood me. Wait yet awhile, and I shall get to the other side, and show the purely religious significance of these doctrines. And then I shall show that you are correct, and that I never was quarreling with *you.*

In short : my philosophy of religion can only be judged, disputed, or confirmed from a transcendental point of view. Let that reader who does not even yet know what the transcendental point of view is be convinced, at least, that he ought not to take part in the dispute.

Most assuredly is religion a proper concern for all men, and every one may properly speak and argue about it. It is the destination of man to come to an agreement on this, the final object of reason. But a philosophy of religion is not religion, and is not written for all men, and for the criticisms of all men. Religion itself is living and powerful ; the theory of religion is dead in itself. Religion fills us with feelings and sentiments ; the theory of religion only speaks of them ; it neither destroys them nor seeks to create new ones.

The true seat of the misunderstanding of my philosophy, and of its controversy with opposite doctrines, which are more or less conscious of this opposition, is concerning the relation of cognition to actual life. The opposite systems make cognition the principle of life ; and believe that by a free, arbitrary thinking they can generate certain knowledges and conceptions, and implant them in men by argumentation, by which conceptions they believe feelings may be produced, desires excited, and thus the activity of man determined. Hence, they hold cognition to be the higher, and life the lower, utterly dependent upon cognition. But my philosophy holds precisely the reverse. It makes life, the system of feelings and of desire, the highest, and allows to cognition only a looking on of their working. This system of feelings is throughout determined in consciousness, and involves an *immediate* cognition, not derived from conclusions or from a free argumentation. Only this immediate cognition has reality, and is, therefore, alone the moving principle of life, being itself generated in life. Hence, when the reality of a cognition is to be proven through philosophy or through argumentation, a *feeling* must first be shown up—I shall call it feeling for the present, until I more definitely account for the use of this word—with which this cognition immediately connects. Free argumentation can only penetrate and sift the contents of this feeling, separate and connect the manifold of it, and thus facilitate the use of it, and bring it under the power of consciousness ; but argumentation can not increase that content, can not extend or change its sphere. Our cognition is given us at once, for all eternity ; and hence we can in all eternity only develop it as it *is*. Only the immediate is true ; the mediated is only true in so far as it is grounded in the immediate ; beyond it lies the sphere of chimeras and dreams.

Now, one of the latest defenders of that opposite system, Mr. Eberhard, asks me : " Are not moral *feelings* dependent upon the culture of reason ?"

As if there were but *one* answer to his question, and as if I could not but admit it! It would need more space than I can spare now to show up all the errors which are involved in that simple and plausibly sounding sentence. But let me ask : What does it mean to make *feelings* dependent upon the culture of reason ? It means that you want to produce the above *immediate* through argumentation, to force upon others and yourself through syllogisms what neither you nor the others originally feel or possess. Well, try and make yourself and others weep and laugh through syllogisms as much as you please.

I, therefore, reply to his question, and adopting *his* meaning of the word "reason," by no means ! That reason of which you speak is theoretical reason, is the power of cognition ! But this reason says only that and how something *be ;* but says nothing of an activity, and of a *shall,* which determines that activity. (Nothing of a conscience which tells you : You *shall* do this or that !—TRANSLATOR.)

Mr. E. proceeds : " Why are moral feelings coarse in the uncultured man, and in the cultured and educated man correct, fine, and extensive ? Is it not because the former is empty of conceptions, and the latter rich in correct, clear, and effective conceptions ?"

Tell me, what does this mean—*coarse**** feelings ? Mr. E. will please pardon me. But according to

* Original : *Rau,* (raw.)

my conceptions of feeling, the adjective *coarse* can not be applied to feeling in any manner ; and until I have the connection explained, I can not well discuss this part of the subject.

" They are *correct* in the cultured man !" Here I can at least suppose what Mr. E. means. The *judgment* concerning an object of morality may be correct or incorrect, but by no means the moral feeling itself, which as a feeling is an absolute simple, and expresses no relation whatever. But what, then, is the criterion of the correctness of a judgment ? Perhaps a logical criterion, derived from former premises ? It may be that Mr. E. so conceives it. But what, then, is the original premise ? Also a logical one ? I have not time here to point out all the absurdities.

His feeling is, moreover, " fine." Now, in popular language, one may well say of a man : His moral tact is fine, that is, he has acquired a facility of quickly and correctly judging moral matters ; but it can never be used as signifying : The original and true moral feeling (which, being absolute, can not be increased nor diminished, and which only says, this shall be, or this shall not be !) may be raised to a higher degree of perfection. But this facility of judgment, is it acquired from life or from idle speculation, and is its criterion a theoretical principle, discovered through argumentation ? I suppose Mr. E. will say yes ; but I do not say yes, from reasons which every one will find in my Science of Morality.

Feeling is, moreover, to be extensive. Now, moral feeling extends to all men *equally*, and is directed upon all objects of free activity. The man of theoretical culture—for we only speak of such a culture, and not of practical culture through the cultivation of virtue—differs in this respect from the uncultured man only in the extent of his sphere of action, but not *as such*, not in intensity of moral feeling or strength of moral will, unless, indeed, Mr. E. should prove that theoretical culture can produce and increase moral will. It is true this would be the result of his premises, but we hesitate to hold him responsible for such an assertion, until he confesses it expressly.

Mr. E. proceeds : " Why have the horrors of superstition disfigured the *doctrine* of morality ?" If he really means what he says, his question implies : Why do wrong conclusions follow from wrong premises ? But if he means to say : Why have those horrors disfigured *morality ?* then I ask him again : Why has superstition darkened and sullied the conception of God, which sullied conception could not but influence moral *judgment,* not morality itself ? And I answer : Undoubtedly by virtue of a false theoretical argument concerning that conception of God !

Hence, if a weak-minded, superstitious, religious fanatic should assist in burning a heretic, and appeal to his moral feelings for justification, ought we not to restore those moral feelings, or those original conceptions, and free them from the wrong

direction given to them by false argumentation?
Moral feeling (conscience) is correct, and can never
be otherwise than correct, if not led astray by argumentation. Or does Mr. E. seriously mean to
say that there is a variety of moral feelings for different individuals, and that amongst these there is,
for instance, *one* which incites to the burning of
heretics?

Now, what is that feeling upon which our faith
in a Divinity is grounded and shown up as real?

Let me first make a distinction of the word feeling. Feeling is either *sensuous*—feeling of a bitter,
red, hard, cold, etc.—or it is *intellectual.* Mr. E.,
and all the philosophers of his school, seem utterly
to ignore the latter class, and to be unaware that
without the latter class consciousness can not be
made comprehensible.

Now, in these pages I am not speaking of sensuous, but of intellectual feeling. It is the immediate feeling of the certainty and necessity of a
thinking. Truth is certainty. Now, how do the
philosophers of the opposite school believe, to know
that they are certain in a particular case? By the
general, theoretical insight that their thinking
agrees with the laws of logic? But this theoretical insight is itself only a certainty of a higher degree; how can they be certain that they do not err
in their certainty of that agreeing? By another still
higher theoretical insight? But whence do they
get that? And so on *ad infinitum.* It is just as
impossible to obtain certainty in this manner, as it

is impossible to explain the *feeling* of certainty.
Moreover, is that certainty an objective or a subjective condition? And how can I perceive such
a condition except through an absolutely primary
immediate feeling?

But what is this feeling? It is clear that this
feeling only *accompanies* my thinking, and does not
enter without a thinking and without a particular
content of that thinking. How could it have, indeed, such a content or a truth in itself?

It is, therefore, evident that, if the feeling of certainty is inseparable from a thinking and from the
content thereof, and if this thinking contains in
itself the condition of all mediated certainty or
rationality, all men must agree as to this feeling.
It is to be presupposed in every human being,
though you might, perhaps, only make a person
conscious of it, and not make him acknowledge it
theoretically; as, indeed, is impossible, seeing that
it is an immediate.

This feeling is, therefore, not only intellectual
feeling in general, but it is the first and most original intellectual feeling and ground of all certainty,
of all reality, and of all objectivity.

It accompanies the thinking, that in the realization of the absolute object proposed for us by our
moral nature, namely, absolute self-determination
of reason, there is a steady progress possible; and
that the condition of this progress is, the absolute
fulfillment of our duty in every position of life,
solely for duty's sake. (The absolute obedience to

the voice of conscience, or to the voice of absolute
reason, or to the voice of God.—TRANSLATOR.)
And this feeling of certainty accompanies such
thinking *necessarily*, being itself an integral part of
that object proposed for us; it is, moreover, inseparable from the consciousness that we must propose that object to ourselves; in fact, it is in truth
only the immediate expression of this consciousness.

Let us analyze further what this may involve:

I think: it is possible that reason does constantly
approach and get nearer its ultimate object. This
might, perhaps, be regarded as an arbitrary thinking, a mere problematical positing, which has no
other advantage than its own possibility. But as
such it must not be viewed. This thinking shows
itself up to be, in a certain connection, as a necessary thinking, without which consciousness would
not be possible; and hence, that which results from
this thinking by logical necessity, that is, by mediation, is equally necessary.

Now, if I posit in my acting an object, then I
also posit that object as realized in some future
time. This is a necessary, logical sequence. But,
viewing the matter simply in its logical sequence, I
might as well turn that sentence around and reverse its relation. This has often been done in the
following statement: it shall and can not propose to
myself the final object of morality, unless I am
already convinced that it can be realized in some
future time. But then, again, I might say, I can

not be convinced that it is capable of being realized unless I first simply propose it to myself. But why shall I propose it to myself at all?

In short, in the mere logical relation each is certain only under condition, and not in itself. Each link refers us to the other, but the orginal certainty of that consciousness is not explained.

This certainty can, therefore, only live in the immediateness of a feeling, and in this feeling these two links are originally one in this manner: I *shall* absolutely posit that moral object for myself, and *shall* consider it as possible of realization; I shall consider it possible of realization, and hence posit it. Neither is, in truth, the sequence of the other, but both are one. It is one thought, not two thoughts; and it is true and certain, not by virtue of a thinking which draws that conclusion, but by virtue of a necessity which I only feel.

Since, therefore, certainty is only immediate and feelable, it can not be demonstrated to any one, but can certainly be presupposed in every one, since those who have it, and who, moreover, reflect concerning the connection of human knowledge, must recognize that every other knowledge is only grounded upon it, and that every one, who knows any thing with certainty, has started from that knowledge, although, perhaps, unconsciously.

Remark this: you do not require any one to *produce* this knowledge, but simply to *find* it in himself. Every mediated certainty presupposes an original certainty. In the consciousness of every

31

one, who is convinced of any thing at all, that certainty exists also ; and every one can arise to that certainty from any conditioned and mediated knowledge.

I may here allude to another misunderstanding of my system. It is charged that, in my system, faith in God exists only for the moral, not for the immoral man. This is very correct when it means that faith is true only for man, *in so far as* he is moral ; but not when it is interpreted that ·faith exists only for those men who are moral.

For where, then, is the personified, absolute immorality ? It is an impossibility. Man can only be, and be self-conscious, in so far as he stands on the field of reason. Without any morality man is but an animal, but a product of organization, even in his theoretical knowledge.

This, then, is our result : *Absolute certainty and conviction* (not mere meaning, opinioning, and wishing) *of the possibility*—not to determine one's self, that is, one's will by the conception of duty, for this we recognize as possible by doing it, but—*to promote the object of reason by thus determining our will through the conviction of duty, even* BEYOND OUR WILL, *is the immediate of religion, and is grounded in the soul of man in the manner we have shown.*

Here I must insert a remark concerning the use of language which I can no longer postpone without making myself ambiguous, and exposing myself again to old objections.

The word *being* signifies always immediately an

object of thinking, a thought. Now, either to this
word is also applied the predicate of an existence,
a *permanent* and *lasting*, in sensuous perception
outside of thinking, and in that case it signifies real
being, and when applied to an object means, that
object *is*—or to that word is applied no other predicate of being, but its thinking—and, in that case,
the significance of such being is purely logical;
and the word *is* only signifies the logical *copula* in
which the manifold of predicates is fixed by thinking in a unity of the logical subject. In that case,
you can not say of an object "it *is*," but it is to be
thought as this or that. There are further distinc-
tions to be made here, of which I shall speak afterward.

There are other words related to the expression
" being," which have also these two significations :
The word " principle," for instance, which I have
used, signifies, in a system of real being, a first,
from which I can calculate a second and third, even
without sensuous perception and with categorical
certainty, thereby anticipating experience. But in
this sense of the word the intelligible principle,
freedom, is never principle of a real cognition, is
never ground of an explanation and anticipation,
that is, you can not foresee *what* will become actual
through freedom. We only know through perception what is actual ; and for the very reason that
we do not recognize the product of freedom as a
link of a comprehensible chain of causes and effects—it being an absolute first, and partially cog-

nizable only in perception—do we say, freedom is a principle. Not principle in the actual sense, as ground of an immediate and necessary factical determinedness, but in the logical sense, as principle of possibilities.

It is the same with the word *law.* In the sensuous world law signifies *that* determination of power from which, as principle, the consequences can be deduced in the manner just stated. But when applied to the *finite* beings—who are *free* in the empirical sense of the word, that is, who are thought as simply determinable, and not determined—the word *law* means a *shall*, a categorical imperative, that is, a determinedness of freedom through freedom, and, therefore, no mechanical, no immediate determinedness. But when applied to the infinite, or to reason, κατ' ἐξοχήν—to which the empirical freedom just now mentioned can not be ascribed, as itself the result of finity—the word law signifies simply the necessity to always expect from that reason a determined content, determined (not *materialiter*, for in so far it is absolutely unknown to us, and, *à priori*, not to be deduced, but) *formaliter*, or determined through its object, the ultimate object of reason—*to expect from it always an infinite, inexhaustible content of freedom for all rational individuals ;** although no existing deter-

---

* Or, in other words, the necessity to expect from infinite reason that it should ever manifest itself in the conscience of all individuals, and thus render them free, moral beings, or at least furnish them the content of that freedom.—TRANSLATOR'S NOTE.

minedness can be shown up from which it might mechanically result, since we are here not in the sphere of the objective, but at the absolute ideal source of spirit. The word *law* has, therefore, here also no *actual* significance from which external and necessary results might be derived, but only logical significance, as gathering together that infinite content of freedom of the individuals into *one* conception.

It is the same with the word *world*. In its actual significance it means a finished whole of existing objects, in a reciprocal determination of their being, each of which being what it is, because all others are what they are, and *vice versa;* a whole, wherein, with a perfect knowledge of the laws of the world, we could determine the nature of each particular from that of all others. When applied to rational beings, that word signifies also, it is true, a totality, an influence of all upon each one, and of each one upon all; but not an influence which can be determined in advance, as it can be in nature, because in the world of rational beings this influence has its ground in being. Hence, the word *world* has here also only a *logical*, not an *actual*, significance.

The expression, *order* of a supersensuous world, has also been used; nay, I have often used it myself. But this expression is misapprehended, when it is understood as if the supersensuous world *were* before it had order, and as if order were thus but an accidence of that world. On the contrary, that world only becomes a world by being ordered.

Hence, whenever the purely intelligible is spoken of, all these and similar conceptions, that is, all conceptions which are derived from being and only determine it further, are used only in their *logical*, not in their *actual* significance.

I state this to put an end to a reproof frequently made, that I make use of the same words which I condemn in others ; but I must use them to make myself understood, and I must take them from language in their accepted significance. But I use them in another sense than my opponent uses them, as ought to be evident from the deduction of the conceptions which they designate.

In stating our final result, we have stated the manner in which only the philosopher views religion ; not exactly as a transcendental philosopher, but generally as an abstract thinker, precisely as he seizes also the conceptions of duty, morality, etc., only in their abstraction. The command of duty can never appear in its generality to man in actual life, but only in concrete determinations of the will. In so far as a man truly and always determines his will by that command of duty, (conscience,) he is a moral man, and acts morally.

In the same way religion never appears to man in actual life in general, but only in so far as in each special case, when he determines his will by conscience, he is firmly convinced (and this conviction is a result of that determination) that what he so wills and does is also outside of his individual will, absolute object of universal reason ; that it

will occur and must occur simply because it is involved in that absolute object of reason, and that
his individual will, in determining itself by the
command of duty, is but the tool of that absolute
object. Only in having this conviction is man religious. Hence the man who, in all the conditions
of his life, acts and thinks in so acting, "I thereby promote that which shall be, that is, the absolute object of reason," is a perfectly virtuous and religious man, even though he might stop at that
simple thought and never combine the manifold of
what *shall be* into the unity of absolute reason.

But even the ordinary acting of life compels
men to unite the similar of their experience, and
thus to shape general rules out of general conceptions. As soon as this is done in any region of
knowledge, it is done in all its regions, and hence
certainly in the region of religion and morality, if
morality and religion are dear to men.

But it is not necessary that they should rise
to the highest abstraction, to a conception which
unites all others of the same kind, and from the
unity of which all others may be derived ; for this
would require a systematic, philosophical thinking.
As a general rule, men are content to reduce the
manifold to *several* forms and fundamental conceptions.

The basis of religious faith was the conviction
of an order or a law, by virtue of which from obedience to the command of duty must certainly result the absolute object of reason, and hence the

actual attainment and realization of which each individual in his moral acts can but *strive* to attain.

Let us analyze what is contained in this conviction : Firstly, that which exclusively and absolutely depends upon my own will, namely, to determine it by the voice of duty.   Secondly, the religious faith that in thus determining my will something is achieved which lies beyond the province
of my individual moral will.

The second is connected with the first by religious faith.   The *moral* sentiment is completed in
the first, but we shall soon see that it can only
arrive at a rational and confident assertion in the
second ; and that thus morality can only be confi-
dently realized in religion.   It is therefore an un-
just reproach to say that our theory utterly cancels
religion and leaves it but its name, replacing it by
morality.

Indeed, I can not *will*, except, by the law of my
finity, (I must always will a determined, limited
somewhat,) that is, except I divide my in itself infinite will into a series of finite will-determinations.
Hence, in the demand that I should will as duty
commands, is also involved the demand that I
should will a determined somewhat.   That this determining of the will through the voice of conscience
(not through argumentation as regarding the possible result of my will) can never deceive is known
through *faith*, is known immediately, not mediately, through argumentation.   Here, therefore, is

the first connecting link between pure morality and religion.

From that determination of the will an act results, and from this act, again, other consequences result in the world of rational beings ; for I see only this world, the sensuous world being simply a means for me—consequences which I can neither foresee nor calculate. In fact, these consequences are no longer in my control, and yet I have faith that they are good and conformable to the absolute object of reason. And this faith I hold with the same *original* certainty which impelled me to the first act ; nay, I could even not act unless this faith always accompanied me. Now, this is religion. I believe in a principle by virtue of which every determination of the will through duty assuredly effects the promotion of the object of reason in the universal connection of things. But this principle is utterly incomprehensible in regard to the mode and manner of its working ; and yet it is absolutely posited with the same originality of faith which pertains to the voice of conscience. Both are not one, but both are absolutely inseparable.

Let us proceed with our analysis. The determination of the will is always only the present, and contains what depends upon us alone. But for its own possibility it is at the same time accompanied by the presupposition of a something past, and by the postulate, that a future something, modified by it, will be its result.

It is accompanied by a *presupposition.* Not the fact that I have a duty by which to determine my will, for that is the result of pure reason ; but the fact that I have this *determined* duty as *mine* is the result of my position in the whole world of reason. Did I not exist or were I another, which, of course, is an absurdity, or were I existing in another community of rational beings, then such a determined duty would not enter at all as mine. But, occupying the position I do, I am bound to act according to the voice of my conscience ; and this I can not do without presupposing at the same time that this very position of mine is taken into the account of the ultimate object of reason, and is the result of the causality of that absolute principle. Hence, the faith in my conscience involves also the faith that the world of reason, which must be presupposed for the acts of all individuals, is equally produced and ordered by that principle. Expressing this popularly, or illustrating it by the analogies of our finite consciousness, it means : the world of reason is created, maintained, and governed by that absolute principle. It is accompanied by a *postulate,* that is, by the postulate of a future something, which is the continued causality of that determination of our will to promote the final object of reason, and hence the maintenance and equable development of all rational beings in the identity of their self-consciousness ; everlasting progress of all toward the ultimate object of reason. All rational beings must, therefore, be maintained in their eternal existence, and their fates directed toward blessedness, that is, toward their liberation through pure morality.

It is clear that we here think only acts, events, a flow of action, but no being, no dead permanency; a creating, maintaining, governing, but by no means a creator, maintainer, governor. The faith we have spoken of does not enter upon these theoretical questions. It rests upon its own basis with firm conviction, and there is not the least ground for going beyond it.

The confession of faith now reads as follows: I, and all rational beings, and our relations to each other, in so far as we do distinguish ourselves, are created by a free and intelligent principle, which maintains them and leads them toward an ultimate object; and whatsoever does not depend upon *our* action to realize that object is done without our interference by that world-governing principle itself.

Still, the principle of which those many predicates are asserted is to be but one. I can not, by the laws of my thinking, proceed from one of these predicates to the other, without presupposing a permanent substrate to which these predicates belong, or without *generating* that substrate by this my very thinking. I do not, however, look upon this substrate *as my production*, for the simple reason that I produce it *necessarily* by virtue of the laws of my thinking. Now, this thinking of the one principle which unites the manifoldness and the distinction of the predicates is itself the perma-

nent ; and hence, we have in the one act two determinations which always accompany each other *as*
opposites, but each of which is only through the
other, and which only in this opposition form the
act of thinking ; namely, one thinking which is always the same, that of the unity of the principle ;
and one flowing and changeable thinking, that
which proceeds from the one predicate of the principle to its other predicates. *These predicates* have
arisen in me *immediately* together with my moral
resolve, and with the original certainty which accompanies that resolve. But the *oneness* of the
principle arises in me only when, by abstracting
from that moral requirement which contents itself
with the certainty of the predicates, I proceed to
reflect upon the separation of those predicates from
their moral relation.

The *oneness* I get merely by *mediation ;* the *predicates* themselves I have *immediately.*

The only fitting parallel to that immediateness
and mediating thinking is furnished by the thinking of our soul, (mind, or what you will call it.)
My feeling, desires, thinking, willing, etc., I know
of immediately by accomplishing those acts. They
come into my consciousness by no act of mediation, but only by my positing them, by my being
in them ; they are the immediate κατ' ἐξοχήν. So
long as I remain in this consciousness, as I am
wholly practical, wholly life and deed, I only know
my feeling, desiring, willing, etc., as they occur one
after the other, but I do not expressly know *myself*

as the unity and as the principle of these various determinations. It is only when I elevate myself above the *reality* of these distinctive acts, and, abstracting from their difference, gather them together in me only in their commonness, that the consciousness of the unity arises in me as the principle of these manifold determinations ; and this product of our abstracting and comprehending thinking is what we call our *soul, mind,* etc.

Now, if I am but ripe for that abstraction, that is, if I take it from out myself, and do not accept it traditionally, then that one principle can only be thought as a for itself existing and working principle, but not as a mere quality or predicate, inherent to some substance or another. It will, therefore, have to be described not as spirituality pertaining to some substance, which, being not spirit itself, could thus only be thought as matter, but as *pure spirit;* not as a substantiated *world-soul,* but as a pure, for itself existing being ; not as a creating, maintaining, and governing, but as *creator, maintainer,* and *governor.* And this very properly and in accordance with the laws of our thinking, if we are once resolved to rise from the immediateness of life and activity to the field of theoretical abstraction.

Let it not be forgotten both conceptions have arisen only through thinking and through an abstract, not through a necessary or concrete, thinking. They are, therefore, not related to perception, but are only *logical subject.* They are by no means *real subject*, or substance.

Only the predicates of both conceptions occur in perception, and hence contain a necessary, *real* thinking, that is, in sensuous perception various predicates occur in a sensuous, objective connection ; and in this respect it may be said that the subject or substrate of these sensuous predicates belongs to the realm of real thinking. But this can not be said with reference to those supersensuous subjects, the soul or the creative spiritual principle.

What, then, may these conceptions involve ? Evidently nothing but the predicates of the perception, from which they have arisen by an abstracting thinking. Thy soul is nothing but thy thinking, feeling, etc. God is nothing but the creating, governing, etc.

You may draw conclusions from the conception of the real substance, but never from that of the logical subject. Through the former our knowledge may be expanded, not through the latter. If something is real substance, it comes under the conditions of sensuous perception ; is somewhere and at some time, is accompanied by sensuous predicates. But none of these determinations can be applied to these conceptions.

Even the conception of pure spirit can not assist in such further conclusions. Even the determinations, borrowed from our soul, do not suit that conception. We ascribe them to our soul, not through

mediating thinking, but through immediate consciousness. But concerning God immediate (moral) consciousness says only what has been stated.
And to draw conclusions from this beyond it, we
have no ground, and there is no possibility to do it.

What I have here stated is transcendental philosophy, not life-philosophy. From it the regula-
tives for the construction of a life-wisdom must first
be deduced. Only that which proceeds from life
has a retroactive effect on life—mode of thinking,
of acting, etc. Life gives birth only to the immediate faith I have mentioned ; but not to the logical subject, and its erroneous further determinations.

That immediate faith is, therefore, to be pre-
eminently cultivated, and held as the main thing.
The logical part will come of itself, and is correct,
proper, and not dangerous *only in so far as it thus
forms itself of itself.* That faith, however, is not to
be cultivated by argumentation, but by practice in
life and moral development.

Only through the culture of this immediate faith
do men arise to religious faith, though they may
not know it ; for it alone is the true and universally valid origin of the religious faith. This, of
course, is only proved by the investigations of a
thorough transcendental philosophy.

The pedagogical rules for a religious education
of the people are, therefore, as follows :

Religious culture can not be begun by teaching religion ; for religion without morality is utterly incomprehensible ; and, since people try at least to comprehend it, leads to superstition. (It can only begin in a culture of the heart, and ingrafting in it pure virtue and morality.)

Through virtuous sentiments religion creates itself ; and all the teacher needs to do is to call attention to this faith of religion, which accompanies all moral consciousness, and neither needs proof, nor is capable of proof, because it announces itself as the most original part of our being. Religious culture, indeed, must not be regarded as something which is to be placed into a man—for whatever thereof you place into him is surely false—but as something, which is already in him, and needs only to be developed, of which he is only to be reminded.

Hence, there is to be no *teaching* of religion at all, but merely a developing of that original, religious consciousness.

But least of all should such teaching begin with pretended doctrines of the *existence* of God. We are only immediately aware of his relations to us, and you must begin with these. The " existence " will then come of itself, and will be *truly* believed only when it has thus developed itself.

Nor is the being of God to be determined, characterized, and its specific mode of existence to be pointed out ; for this our thinking can not do, as we have abundantly shown. [We are only to speak of his acts, and to vivify, strengthen, and keep in consciousness always the faith in them.) *The conception of God can not be determined by categories of existence, but only by predicates of an activity.*

32*